THE DESTINY OF
A CONTINENT

THE DESTINY OF
A CONTINENT

BY MANUEL UGARTE

EDITED, WITH AN INTRODUCTION AND BIBLIOGRAPHY BY
J. FRED RIPPEY

TRANSLATED FROM THE SPANISH BY
CATHERINE A. PHILLIPS

AMS PRESS
NEW YORK

Reprinted from the edition of 1925, New York
First AMS EDITION published 1970
Manufactured in the United States of America

Library of Congress Catalog Card Number: 71-111476
SBN: 404-06700-X

AMS PRESS, INC.
New York, N. Y. 10003

CONTENTS

INTRODUCTION

Manuel Ugarte, author of *The Destiny of a Continent,* is one of Latin America's most brilliant thinkers and writers. The son of Floro Ugarte and Sabina Rivero, he was born in Buenos Aires in 1878 and educated at the Colegio Nacional of his native Argentine. When barely twenty he left for Paris to complete his literary training and to seek his fame. He won almost immediate recognition among the *élite* of the French capital. In 1900–1901 he visited the United States and Mexico and became convinced that Latin America was in danger of being absorbed and dominated by the United States. He returned to France, where for the next decade he divided his time between pure literature and propaganda designed to arouse Europe and his compatriots of America against the Yankee Peril. He carried on his propaganda through numerous journals of France, Spain, and Italy, and, in 1910, he brought together his ideas on the subject in a volume published at Valencia under the title of *The Future of Latin America.* Soon afterwards he deserted his writing-table and mounted the platform with the view of more effectively warning his native land against the menaces which threatened both from within and from without. His first lecture was delivered in Barcelona on May 25, 1910. In October, 1911, he spoke at the Sorbonne, where he announced his intention of carrying his message throughout Latin America. During the next two years he addressed audiences in every capital of the Latin-American nations and again visited the United States, giving a lecture at Columbia University. At the invitation of President Carranza, he made his third journey to Mexico in 1917. Returning to Buenos Aires, he remained in his native republic until after the close of the World War, when an invitation from El Centro de Cultura Hispano-Americana, of Madrid, brought him once more to Spain. From Spain he proceeded to France, and the preface of the volume here presented in translation was written at Nice in July, 1923.

Such in brief is the career of the Argentinian *littérateur* and publicist. The work we now introduce is at once an account of his tour of propaganda and a statement of his convictions with reference to the policies and the future of Latin America. For this reason alone it will doubtless be read with interest by the English-speaking peoples. To readers of the United States it should be doubly interesting as a revelation of a Latin-American state of mind little realised by the average layman and fully appreciated only by the few who are specialists in the relations of the American nations. And, lest it may be assumed that Ugarte's attitude is eccentric and exceptional, we must hasten to present a brief survey of Hispanic-American apprehensions regarding what our neighbours to the south are accustomed to denounce as "North American imperialism."

This fear of aggression from the United States is as old as the Spanish-American nations themselves. The following quotation from a letter written by a renowned Cuban economist to the Spanish Cortes in 1811 shows how early it appeared: "We see rising up . . . in the northern portion of this world a colossus which has been constructed by all castes and languages and which threatens to swallow up, if not all our America, at least the northern portion of it . . . This precious isle is exposed to the terrible risks of proximity to the Negro King Enrique Cristobal and to the United States." [1]

Naturally those nations nearest to the United States were the first to suffer anxiety. Less than twelve years after the Cuban uttered his foreboding, an agent of the Mexican government wrote from New York saying he was convinced that the American people would be the "sworn enemies" of his country. "The haughtiness of these republicans," he continued, "will not allow them to look upon us as equals but merely as inferiors, and in my judgment their vanity goes so far as to believe that their capital will be that of all the Americas." [2]

The annexation of Texas, the war with Mexico, and the raids of the North American filibusters during the fifties of last century extended these apprehensions to the utmost limits of Hispanic America. Two illustrations will suffice at this point. Near the close of 1851 a

[1] Quoted in Carlos M. Trelles, *Estudio de la bibliografía cubana sobre la doctrina de Monroe*, p. 219.

[2] Quoted in W. R. Manning, *Early Diplomatic Relations between the United States and Mexico*, p. 279.

navy officer of the United States dined at the home of a prominent citizen of La Paz, Bolivia. The lady of the house, an educated and intelligent woman, expressed great fondness for the North Americans, but remarked that they were too warlike, and condemned the seizure of Mexican territory in 1846–1848. The officer attempted to satisfy her on this score, whereupon she inquired the meaning of all the articles which she saw published in the La Paz newspapers regarding Cuba, and then, turning suddenly and fixing her eyes upon him, asked: "What are you doing here, Señor Gibbon? Do you want Bolivia also?" Another explanation followed, and the hostess concluded the subject with the remark that she believed the North Americans would "some day govern the whole of South America." [3] Again, passing to the second illustration, the Latin-American congress which met at Lima in 1856 was largely motivated by uneasiness aroused on account of William Walker's filibustering operations in Central America.[4]

The secession of the South, the war to save the Union, and problems of reconstruction proved sufficient to absorb the energies of the United States for nearly two decades. During this period Hispanic America was relieved of much anxiety. Then came the attempt (1877–1879) to coerce President Díaz of Mexico, and the efforts of this executive to rally the Latin-American states to his support. This was followed by the energetic efforts of James G. Blaine to play the *rôle* of mediator on the American Continent, Secretary of State Frelinghuysen's contention that European nations should not be permitted to arbitrate disputes in Latin America, and the assertion in many quarters of the United States of a desire to dominate the canal zones. Next came the unpleasant incident with Chile, known as the "Baltimore Affair," and the vigorous action of Admiral Benham to prevent the restoration of monarchy in Brazil. Latin Americans became conscious once more of an energetic, an intrusive, and possibly a dangerous neighbour. Naturally criticisms of the United States appeared in some quarters.

Space will permit the notice of only two examples of the anti-Yankee literature produced at this time. Both of these were written in the same year, 1893, both were books which attempted a general

3 Herndon and Gibbon, *Exploration of the Amazon*, II, 115–116.
4 Alvarez, *The Monroe Doctrine*, p. 16.

survey of the Latin-American policy of the United States, and both severely censured the Yankees for their imperialism, their presumptions of hegemony, and their materialism. They were *The Monroe Doctrine*,[5] by José María Céspedes, and *The Yankee Illusion*,[6] by Eduardo Prado. It should be added, also, that Prado was a Brazilian monarchist who hoped to advance the monarchist cause by a denunciation of the greatest American republic and that Céspedes wrote, as he himself admits, with the view of discouraging his Cuban compatriots who longed for annexation to the United States.

The interposition of the United States in the Anglo-Venezuelan boundary dispute occasioned discussions south of the Rio Grande which revealed that the Monroe Doctrine had been the source of no little uneasiness. In general, the stand taken by the United States at this time (1895–1896) appeared to bring relief to Latin Americans. They were very careful, however, to divest the famous doctrine of all its tutorial implications before expressing their approval of it; and after the arbitration decision sustained the claims of Great Britain, there were not lacking hints to the effect that Venezuela had been the victim of a frame-up between the two powerful Anglo-Saxon nations.[7]

The Spanish-American War witnessed a strong current of pro-Spanish sentiment and a disposition to denounce the aggressiveness and brutality of the United States.[8] "The inevitable defeat of Spain," as one Spanish-American writer puts it, "awakened a profound moral echo among our peoples . . . We saw in the triumph of 'Yankeeland'—as we wrote with a certain innocent bitterness to which we strove to communicate a deeply sarcastic air—the victory

[5] *La Doctrina de Monroe*, Habana, Miranda y Cía., 1893.

[6] *A Iluçao Americana*, Paris, A. Colin, 1895. A Spanish translation was recently brought out by Carlos Pereyra under the title *La Ilusión Yanqui, Editorial-America*, Madrid, n. d.

[7] Cf. Rippy, "Some Contemporary Mexican Reactions to Cleveland's Venezuelan Message", in *Political Science Quarterly*, XXXIX (June, 1924), p. 280 ff.; Robertson, "Hispanic American Appreciations of the Monroe Doctrine," in *Hispanic American Historical Review*, III (February, 1920), p. 1 ff.

[8] Rippy, "Literary Yankeephobia in Hispanic America," in *The Journal of International Relations*, XII (January, 1922), p. 351; *Literary Digest*, XVI (May 21 and June 25, 1898), pp. 625, 772.

of the strong over the weak, of the lusty barbarian over the delicate and exquisite being." [9]

The victory of the United States was followed by a growing aggressiveness in both the economic and the political sphere. President Roosevelt's conduct with reference to the Panama Canal Zone and his brandishing of the Big Stick in the West Indies and Central America, Taft's "Dollar Diplomacy," and Lodge's Magdalena Bay Resolution aggravated the uneasy suspicion of Latin America until it broke forth in a veritable epidemic of Yankeephobia which swept the entire region from Mexico City to Santiago and Buenos Aires. Publicists, literary men, ministers, political orators, educators— almost everybody was affected by the disease. No important visitor from the United States failed to mark its manifestations. The director of the Pan American Union, a Yale professor, several prominent statesmen—among them Secretary Root and Ambassador Sherrill—all felt alarmed at the growing aloofness and hostility.

At the same time, foreign observers noted the symptoms and, some of them at least, rejoiced. Indeed, it must be pointed out that Europeans had been partially responsible for the Latin-American state of mind. Moved largely by political and economic jealousy of the United States, they had been crying "wolf!" for a hundred years. During the opening decades of the nineteenth century the Spanish Minister uttered warnings from Washington and British diplomatic agents sought to arouse suspicion in Mexico and at the Panama Congress (1826).[10] Their propaganda became more vigor-

---

[9] Jesús Semprum, "Norte y Sur," in *Cultura Venezolana*, December, 1918. English translation in *Inter-America*, II (August, 1919), p. 327.

[10] According to Carlos Pereyra, Luis de Onis, the Minister of Spain in Washington, wrote the Viceroy of New Spain on April 10, 1812, to the following effect: "This Government [namely, the United States] has proposed nothing less than to fix its limits at the mouth of the Rio Norte, or Bravo, following its course to the 30th degree and, from there, tracing a direct line to the Pacific, taking in accordance therewith the provinces of Texas, Nuevo Santander, Coahuila, New Mexico, and part of the provinces of Nuevo Vizcaya and of Sonora." In 1820 this same Minister published an alarming memorial in which he alleged that the American people and their leaders were confident that their dominion was "destined to extend . . . over all the regions of the new world." (Pereyra, *El Mito de Monroe*, p. 269; Manning, *op. cit.*, p. 279.)

ous toward the middle of the century when Spain and England were assisted by France. Since 1890 it has increased in volume and violence; Germany has joined England, France, and Spain, and Latin America has been flooded with their literature and their agents—or, perhaps it would be more correct to say that Germans, Englishmen, Frenchmen, and Spaniards have carried on this anti-Yankee propaganda, for it has been largely of an unofficial nature. The efforts of Frenchmen and Spaniards, thanks to racial and cultural affinities, have been most influential. They speak a language easily understood in Hispanic America, and many a young Latin has returned from his studies in Spain or France a confirmed Yankeephobe. The careful reader of Ugarte's work here presented can hardly fail to perceive this influence in the psychosis of Ugarte himself.[11]

President Wilson made the correction of this Latin-American attitude one of the first concerns of his administration. He observed that the aloofness and distrust of our southern neighbours had been occasioned by what they were pleased to call "Yankee Imperialism and Yankee Presumptions of Hegemony." He promised their representatives that his government would not seek to acquire another foot of territory by conquest; that it would not give countenance to economic imperialism, whether of Americans or of Europeans; that it was determined to apply the principles of democracy to international affairs by championing the rights of small nations. He even went so far as to offer to sign a mutual and reciprocal guaranty of the territorial integrity and the national independence of the American states. This was the soul of honesty. These little countries had feared our economic power and our imperialism. We had assured them of our gentleness and our perfect self-restraint, but our words and our actions frequently appeared inconsistent. Our willingness to sign a pledge was the acid test of our self-abnegation. Wilson likewise evinced a disposition to counsel with the Latin Americans on matters relating to the western hemisphere, thus partially abandoning our pretensions to continental hegemony. By this policy he gradually regained the confidence of the Hispanic-

[11] Cf. Rippy, "Pan-Hispanic Propaganda in Hispanic America," in *Political Science Quarterly*, XXXVII (September, 1922), p. 389 ff.; F. I. Carter, French Opinion of the American Policy of the United States. (M. A. thesis, June, 1925, prepared under my direction at the University of Chicago.)

American states and people. There were a few, Manuel Ugarte
among them, who did not appreciate his Mexican policy and failed
to understand the European danger which appears to have determined his action in the Caribbean.[12] But in general he was trusted
and praised.

The apparent acceptance of Wilson's leadership by the people of
the United States led the Latins of America also to revise their opinion of their Anglo-Saxon neighbours. For a time they almost ceased
to consider the Yankees as "rude and obtuse Calibans, swollen with
brutal appetites, the enemies of all idealisms, furiously enamored
of the dollar, insatiable gulpers of whiskey and sausages—swift,
overwhelming, fierce, clownish." [13] While they proclaimed Wilson
to be "the loftiest summit in the scenery of this dramatic hour of
the world," another "sweet Gallilean," a "modern redeemer of
humanity," they began to look upon the American people as mighty
champions of the ideals of justice and of liberty and beheld in the
"erstwhile champion of the Big Stick a heroic paladin." [14]

With the passing of Wilson, Hispanic Americans once more began
to relapse into a state of Yankeephobia. The pertinacity with which
the United States Senate insisted upon the incorporation of the
Monroe Doctrine into the League Covenant alarmed them. Article X of this covenant guaranteed the territorial integrity and the
national independence of all the signatory powers, great and small.
This was the only feature of the Monroe Doctrine which they had
ever approved, and they maintained that such a guaranty constituted
the very essence of the doctrine. The League of Nations was merely
seeking to extend this principle to the whole world. Why should
the Anglo-American Senate demand express mention of Monroe's
manifesto in the league constitution? Latin Americans feared that
it was because the interest of the United States in its southern
neighbours did not end with this guaranty. They took up their old

[12] Cf. Shippee, *Recent American History*, pp. 390–391. It is hardly con-
ceivable that Wilson would have deviated from his principles except under
the threat of an European danger.

[13] Semprum, *op. et loc. cit.*

[14] Cf. *ibid. See also,* for a collection of friendly sentiment towards Wilson,
C. D. Eaves, The Hispanic-American Policy of Woodrow Wilson (M. A.
thesis, University of Chicago Library.)

suspicion that the Monroe Doctrine was designed to protect them from Europe only that they might in due time be absorbed by the United States. To many of them the attitude of the Senate called up spectres of hegemony, spheres of influence—all of those terrifying policies which had soaked the world in blood.

The refusal of the United States to join the League of Nations appeared to point in the same direction. The Anglo-Americans were refusing to co-operate in the establishment of an international order and were preparing to seize the lion's share of spoils in the colossal nationalist scramble bound to follow if the league which they had declined to enter failed to function.[15]

This is the way many Hispanic Americans felt. And European propaganda, with its accusations of Yankee greed and Yankee economic pressure, with its warnings against the North American Peril, sought to confirm them in their suspicions. But some of them refused to be easily or hastily convinced. Perhaps the recent attitude of their neighbours represented merely a temporary lapse, a transient confusion occasioned by complicated domestic politics. These neighbours had once found their way out of the jungle of selfish materialism. Perhaps they would do so again.

Secretary of State Hughes, the outstanding figure in the new administration, seemed occasionally to catch the lost gleam. At Cleveland, Ohio, on November 4, 1922, he had declared: "We do not covet any territory on God's broad earth. We are not seeking a sphere of special economic influence, and endeavouring to control others for our aggrandizement." A month later, while speaking to the delegation of the little states of Central America, he had assured them that the United States "had no ambitions to gratify at" their "expense, no policy which" ran "counter to" their "national aspira-

---

[15] Expressions too numerous to permit citation here bear out this change in attitude. See, for instance, Pinheiro (a Brazilian economist and statistician), in *The Pan-American Magazine*, XXX (January, 1920), pp. 127–130; R. E. Lara, in *Juventud* (Santiago, Chile), November-December, 1920; Enrique Molina, *Por los dos Americas* (Santiago, Casa Editorial "Minerva," 1920), pp. 148–151; Alfredo Colmo, "Panamericanismo y Compañía," in *Nosotros*, June, 1921; Enrique Pérez, in *Cuba Contemporanea*, July, 1921; F. P. Porta, in *ibid.*, January, 1922; Ingeneiros, in *Nosotros*, October, 1922.

tions, and no purpose save to promote the interests of peace and to assist" them to solve their problems to their "own proper advantage." During the Christmas holidays he expressed a friendly attitude towards the World Court.[16]

All these appeared to be favourable signs. Another Pan-American congress was soon to assemble. Here would be presented an opportunity to test out the new Anglo-American policy. A spirit of fairness demanded that in the meantime the Hispanic Americans should suspend judgment.

This congress met at Santiago, Chile, on March 25, 1923. The Latins sought immediately to discover the purpose and disposition of their neighbours. Were the Yankees really sincere in their professions of concern for the territorial and national integrity of Latin America and in their denials of imperialistic designs? If so, perhaps they would not object to a definition of the Monroe Doctrine, a pledge not to encroach upon their neighbours, and such a reorganization of the Pan-American Union as would prevent it from appearing similar to the British Colonial Office. An attempt on the part of the Hispanic Americans to secure commitments on these issues was the leading feature of the assembly. The delegates of the United States were forced to take an unequivocal stand, and in almost every instance the policy of the United States proved a partial or a total disappointment to the Iberians of America. A resolution providing for minor changes in the organization of the Union was agreed upon, but the Washington delegates refused to consider the definition or the Pan-Americanization of the Monroe Doctrine and replied to a proposal of an American League of Nations providing a pledge of territorial integrity and national independence, with a *noli me tangere*.[17]

Many Hispanic Americans were thus confirmed in their former

16 Cf. Graham Stuart, "The Pan-American Policy of the Harding Administration," in *Southwestern Political Science Quarterly*, IV (June, 1923), p. 63 ff.; New York *Times*, December 30, 1922.

17 For a discussion of this Congress, see Samuel Guy Inman "Pan-American Conferences and their Results," in *The Southwestern Political Science Quarterly*, IV, pp. 239-266, 341 ff.; J. Warshaw, "The Fifth Pan-American Congress," in *ibid.*, III, p. 323 ff.

attitude. They were convinced that Wilson had been a voice crying in the wilderness, an idealist in the midst of crass materialists, an internationalist lost amidst the narrowest and most selfish provincials. Once more they took up the refrain of bitter denunciation, swelling the chorus of the Latin-American irreconcilables, chanting the refrain of Latin-American solidarity, Pan-Hispanism, Pan-Latinism, of European and even of Asiatic alliances.

It is in the light of these facts that Ugarte's *Destiny of a Continent* should be read. It is not the raving of a maniac or the mere frothing of a lone radical. Ugarte is a radical and an idealist, but, as the previous paragraphs have shown, many of his compatriots—more even than Ugarte in his moments of discouragement may realise—share his convictions and his aspirations. In my opinion, many of his statements are one-sided and inaccurate. A few of them may be corrected by unimpeachable sources now available. The documents bearing upon others are still sealed to the investigator. From our present viewpoint, however, these blemishes in Ugarte's work are not of great significance. Americans of the United States should be concerned first and foremost to know what our Latin neighbours are thinking of the policies of our government and of our masters of finance and captains of industry. If the notions of these neighbours are erroneous, they should of course be corrected, but we can do little until we·know what these notions are.

This is not the place to pass judgment on our Latin-American policy, nor do I feel qualified to act as judge; but I cannot avoid suggesting here the possibility that the views of Ugarte and of all those Latin Americans who fear and distrust us are not without a measure of justification. With regard to the fact of our expansion, we must note the advance of our flag across the Floridas to the Gulf and across the Mississippi to the Rio Grande and the Pacific Coast. This is familiar history. We must also note the less familiar fact that the "North Americans," as the Latins of the South call us, are now virtually in control, officially or unofficially, of the political and economic life of fourteen of the twenty Hispanic-American republics. Only Brazil, Argentina, Chile, Uruguay, Paraguay, and Venezuela are outside of our sphere of influence. And how shall we describe the character of our suzerainty? Ugarte and many individuals among

the little peoples whom we have brought under our control, political
or economic, feel that our rule is rarely benevolent, frequently
haughty and intrusive, and sometimes oppressive. Are they mistaken?
Broadly speaking and in the long run has not the general tendency of
the United States and its citizens to annex, penetrate, control, and absorb their neighbours to the south been accompanied also by a tendency to exploit and oppress? The people of the United States are
not in a position to answer this question. The widespread conviction
that all our acts and policies are gentle and generous is more a matter
of blind faith than of accumulated evidence. We are uninformed
regarding our relations with many of the Latin peoples of America.
We have given the subject little consideration. The Hispanic Americans have great newspapers, such, for instance, as the Argentine *La
Prensa* and *La Nación*, the Brazilian *Jornal do Commercio*, the
Chilean *Mercurio*, the Uruguayan *El Plate* and *Diario de la Plata*,
the Mexican *Imparcial* and *Universal*, the Central American *Diario
del Salvador*, the Cuban *La Lucha*, etc.; but what North American
libraries place these in their public reading-rooms? Our southern
neighbours likewise have many great periodicals, such as *Nosotros* and
Revista Argentina de Ciencias Políticas, of Buenos Aires; *Revista
Chilena* and *Revista de Political Internacional* of Santiago; *Revisto
do Brazil*, of São Paulo; *Cultura Venezolana*, of Caracas; and *Mercurio Peruano*, of Lima; but who of us reads them? What citizens of
the United States need at present is an understanding of the viewpoint
of men like Ugarte. Some day we who profess the democratic creed,
we who brought our nation into existence by the exercise of the right
of revolution, may be startled by the realisation that, in respect to
Latin America, we have placed order above democracy and liberty
and, renouncing our former faith, have pledged ourselves never to
recognize a régime brought into existence by the right of revolution.
"As a Spanish American, I revolt against this policy," says Ugarte.
"I fling all I possess into the sea, and I make my life one unquench-
able protest against the possible annihilation of our nationalities."
Will the citizens of the metropolis hear the appeal which comes up
from the provinces? Appended is a brief bibliography for those who
desire to pursue the subject beyond the volume here presented.

Professor Carlos Castillo has kindly advised me regarding the translation of obscure passages. Doctor Bertha Ann Reuter has given generous aid in reading the proof. It is a pleasure to acknowledge their assistance, but they must be absolved from all blame for the defects of the work here presented.

J. FRED RIPPY, PH.D.

University of Chicago,
April 20, 1925.

AUTHOR'S PREFACE

There is an overwhelming impulse which has driven strong bodies in all ages to impose their interference or tutelage upon the weak. Alexander, Cæsar, Napoleon, and, in recent ages, those peoples who stand at the head of enormous colonial dominions, no matter what pretexts they have advanced,—authority, culture, liberty, or civilization,—have really aimed at one thing only: universal subjection to a man, a group, or a race; or else to some historic mysticism which considers itself destined to spread the fire of its own life.

Imperialism begins at that point where the combination of homo geneous elements ends, and a sphere of military, political, or commercial oppression by extraneous bodies begins. It cannot be said that Prussia was imperialist in bringing about the unity of Germany. It is not fitting to reproach Piedmont with it for hastening the unification of Italy. It would be equally unjust to accuse the United States of imperialism if they were to-morrow to bring pressure upon the island of Jamaica, which in entering the planetary system of Washington would remain in a suitable *milieu* as regards language, religion, and traditions. Bolívar's policy was not imperialism, nor would be that of a Latin-American nation which should undertake the reconstruction of the primitive family of nations within the limits set to it by history. But the policy of England in Asia is imperialist,—the subjugation of those races which were the first to shed any light on the darkness of the world. So is that of the United States in Panama, and that of every country which imposes itself in an orbit different from its own. Whether it be a question of coercion and military conquest, or of infiltration and indirect penetration; whether the intervention be solely by means of diplomacy or commerce, or whether the appeal be to arms, imperialism always exists when a people turns aside from its course to invade, directly or indirectly, lands, interests, or consciences which have no antecedents or bonds of similarity drawing them to it.

The moment that the states of Latin America were born to independent life a fundamental problem presented itself: namely, that of ascertaining in what form and by what means they might succeed in unfolding their free evolution, in view of the fantastic growth of the emancipated English colonies. This preoccupation is growing more urgent at the present moment. If the great powers of Europe have come to tremble for their safety in the *sauve qui peut* of the nations arising from the recent cataclysm, how can the future be regarded without anxiety by our republics, which have hitherto only been safeguarded in appearance by abstract right, but in reality by the remoteness of the various conquering offensives or the balance held between them?

Nobody admires more than I do the greatness of the United States, and few can have a clearer idea of the necessity of entering into relations with them in the future developments of our life. But this has got to be carried out on a footing of equality. In spite of the reputation of a Yankee-hater which has been ascribed to me,—a legend as false as many others,—I have never been an enemy of this great nation. For anyone who reflects, hatreds cannot exist in international politics. I have estimated tendencies solely from the point of view of what is harmful or favourable to our safety. If I have protested against the pressure which weighs upon Mexico, Cuba, Nicaragua, the Philippines, Panama, Porto Rico, etc., it has been in the name of a general necessity. If I have spoken of resistance it was with a view to the exigencies of the future—and this apart from all animosity, and on the firm ground of patriotism. I believe that we are bound to oppose a united policy to the interferences of the North. In France, in Germany, and in England, there are thinkers who favour various solutions [of European problems] and show themselves partisans of a *rapprochement* with one country or another, or of a policy of aloofness, in accordance with their honourable interpretation of the interests of their group. Nobody attributes to them any ill-will or prejudice in consequence. A diplomatic conception involves world orientations which move in orbits higher than instinct, amity, and sentiment.

Far from any acrimony, then, there is not in these pages the slightest desire to proceed against anything or anybody. Whoever reads carefully will perceive beneath their serene movement all that I have gladly left unsaid.

If some chapters have the character of reminiscences, that is because anecdote serves to convey an appreciation of typical conditions. But the writer does not fall into the error of supposing that the ray of sunlight falling upon them comes from himself. The very poverty of the style proclaims that the work has grown up unpretentiously, with no literary aim, and in sincere communion with the younger generation and the people, like a cry arising from the popular consciousness. Not for an instant did the overweening idea of modifying the international situation present itself to my mind, still less the fanciful intention of putting myself at the head of a political tendency opposed to that of the governments. The author confines himself to relating what he has thought and seen, to expressing his disquiet, to explaining a conviction which has proved itself, in all conscience, since he has been defending it for more than twenty years.

Perhaps it is useful that action should be consecrated by suffering. We should distrust ourselves if we had not cultivated fortitude in bearing adversity. We should have doubts of our collective aim if we had not confidence in its justice. From those who have attacked us we beg a fair hearing for our ideas. This slight exploration of past facts, present realities, and future possibilities draws its inspiration from an ideal which, though embarrassed, thwarted, and annulled in its realization and results by divisions, errors, and appetites, still endures in the heart of our peoples, and derives its origin at once from the insistent force of reality and the logic of history. The further we go from the country in which we were born, the nearer we are drawn to it. May this book be received by our younger generation in an atmosphere of lofty patriotism. The author has written it in all sincerity.

MANUEL UGARTE.

Nice, July, 1923.

THE DESTINY OF
A CONTINENT

CHAPTER I

THE WOLF AND THE SHEEP [1]

My first visit to New York—Symptoms of the problem—The errors of a race—The sentiment of patriotism—A few traits of the North American character—Strange power of penetration—Mexico under Porfirio Diaz—A campaign launched from Europe—A trip round Latin America.

To arrive at the origin of my conviction of the danger to the Spanish and Portuguese-speaking peoples of the New World which is represented by North American imperialism, I should have to go back to the year 1900, when, barely twenty years old, I made my first voyage to New York.

In the depths of my memory, I can see the Dutch boat at anchor in the vast harbour, bristling with masts and blackened with smoke. The ships' sirens were howling like a pack of hounds round a gigantic figure of Liberty, signalling out to sea with her symbolic arm. The sky-scrapers, towering disproportionately above other buildings of ordinary dimensions, the pavements crowded with hurrying pedestrians, the railways running overhead along the avenues, the shop windows in which the most varied wares were drowning in oceans of light—all that strikes the eye of a new arrival in a first hasty, nervous glance—made me enter my hotel full of joy and panic at finding myself among the people with the most exuberant life and the most extraordinary vigour that I have ever seen.

I had come straight from France, after passing two years in Paris, and my voyage, which had not been made with any concrete object or preconceived idea, was merely that of a curious tourist, a wandering poet in search of new lands and unknown landscapes. After publishing various books in Paris, I had felt a curiosity to know the life and customs of that portentous country which was beginning to astonish the world; and a few articles published in small reviews

[1] Editorial notes are marked with the asterisk, dagger, etc.

reflected the first feelings of wonderment which I felt at the time. As a traveller, I had two points of departure or comparison: Buenos Aires, where I was born, and Paris, where I had just started my career as a writer. I will add that my culture was exclusively literary, entirely divorced from sociology or international politics. I knew nothing of imperialism, I had never stopped to think what might have been the cause and consequences of the Spanish-American War, and I was far from suspecting the grave, silent drama which is being played out in this New World, cleft in two by origin and speech. So there is no need to attribute to me any preconceived antipathy, prejudice, or hostility. The North American people was nothing to me at that time but a great example of superior life, and I had nothing but praise for the unprecedented forces which had been developed in little more than a century. Comparisons painful to our Spanish-American patriotism, conclusions disquieting for the future, the proofs of what imperialism boded for the rest of the continent—it was actually on United States territory that all this began to rise up before my eyes.

I imagined in my simplicity that the ambition of this great nation was limited to rising within its frontiers to the highest pinnacle of wealth. The idea had never occurred to me that this national splendour might turn out to be a danger in continental politics to my country or to the nations which are sisters of my country by blood. In confessing this, I confess that I had never stopped to meditate upon the course of imperialism in history. But one day, while reading a book on the politics of the country, I came across a phrase quoted from Senator Preston in 1838: "The star-spangled banner shall float over the whole of Latin America as far as Tierra del Fuego, the sole limit recognized by the ambition of our race." *

The surprise was so great that I was staggered. This was impossible. If, I said to myself, a responsible person had really taken it into his head to pronounce these words, our countries of the South would at once have risen in unanimous protest. When, after my first shock of incredulity, I went back to the source, I was able simultaneously to verify two bitter facts: one, that the statement was

* Senator William C. Preston of South Carolina was a staunch advocate of the annexation of Texas, but I cannot find the statement attributed to him here in any of his available speeches.

true; and the other, that Latin-American politicians, enervated by their wretched internal quarrels, by their puerile frontier disputes— by that narrowness of vision, in fine, which had led to the decadence and eclipse of our position in the New World—had passed it over in silence.

From this moment onwards, setting aside my preoccupation with poetry, I read with particular interest everything concerning this matter. Was it possible to lull oneself with the delights of literature, when the future, and the very existence, of our family of nations were called in question? It was thus that I learnt that the territory occupied by the United States before the Declaration of Independence, was bounded on the west by a line running from Quebec to the Mississippi, * and that the old English colonies were thirteen in number, with a population of four million men, in an area of a million square kilometres. I next became aware of the significance of the second Continental Congress of Philadelphia in 1775; of the campaign against the Indians; of the acquisition of Louisiana, which was bought from France in 1803; of the occupation of Florida, which was ceded by Spain in 1819; and of the bewildering advance of the western frontier towards the Pacific, annexing lands and cities which bear Spanish names.

These elementary notions, which—owing to the incomplete and desultory instruction of South American schools—I had never had within my reach while I was studying for my baccalaureate, increased my curiosity and my disquiet. I read in a newspaper an article threatening Mexico and making a menacing allusion to four dates, the significance of which I proceeded to inquire into. In a historical text-book I discovered that in 1826 Henry Clay, the American Secretary of State, prevented Bolívar from extending the revolutionary movement for independence into Cuba.† In a study of the separation from the mother country of the Viceroyalty of New Spain, I found in the separatist movement of certain colonies traces of an intervention of the United States foreshadowing the policy which was afterwards more clearly defined in the Antilles. Later

* The boundary according to the treaty of 1783 was the Mississippi from its mouth to its source, thence northward to the Lake of Woods.
† Cf. Manning, *Early Diplomatic Relations between the United States and Mexico*, p. 89 ff.

on, I learnt of the demands of General Wilkinson, the interested defender of the establishments of Ohio, and I began, though without understanding as yet its full scope, to receive a revelation of that subtle policy which tended to hamper the action of Spain by taking advantage of the conflict between Ferdinand VII and Bonaparte.*

The important book by the Mexican writer and diplomatist Don Isidro Fabela † had not yet been published, and no general history of imperialism on the American continent was in existence.

Thus, as the result of haphazard and summary reading, directed by chance and the untutored impulses of my early youth, my mind began to receive fragmentary and disjointed impressions of certain fundamental truths, based on incontrovertible facts known to all enlightened men throughout the world. It was only to us Spanish Americans, sunk as we were, and as we still are, in an inexplicable lethargy, that they appeared to be unknown; though it was we whom they most particularly concerned.

Then query after query sprang up in succession. How was it that no protest was raised throughout all Spanish-speaking America when the Mexican territories of Texas, California, and New Mexico were annexed to the United States? Why was there no revolt of consciences on the North American Continent when those who had fomented the separatist movement in Cuba in the name of liberty, invoking lofty principles of justice, and arguing from the right of peoples to self-determination, imposed the Platt Amendment, and exacted the concession of strategic naval stations on the coasts of the island? Can the existence at Washington of a department for the Spanish-American republics, organized like a Ministry for the Colonies, be reconciled with the full autonomy of our countries? Does not the Monroe doctrine imply a protectorate? Etc.

Peculiar significance was given to my queries by the map. Within a century, the thirteen English colonies, which had a population of four million men and occupied an area of a million square kilometres, had been transformed into an enormous nation consisting of forty-five States, with a population of a hundred million inhabi-

* General James Wilkinson was a notorious schemer whose projects were probably in no way countenanced by the United States government.

† *Los Estados Unidos contra la Libertad*—a violent denunciation of our imperialism, published recently in Barcelona.

tants and an area of ten million square kilometres in the aggregate,
in which our names—Sante Fé, San Francisco, Los Angeles—fix the
attention like a voice coming from the depths of the ages to upbraid
the carelessness and indifference of a race.

Superimposed upon the coloured lines of the geographical map,
there was something which struck the eye: the miserable drama of
a continent, discovered under the flag of Spain—the first to flutter
on the seas of the New World—won for civilisation by the brains
and the blood of heroic explorers speaking the Castilian tongue,
fertilized by our religion, annexed for a moment at the height of
our glory—then without a rival in the world—and afterwards
assailed by alien influences which gained a footing upon it, and
with resistless force expanded their might, conquering the first comers
and making them withdraw, not only from possession of the soil, but
from the sphere of moral influence; and this not only in the present,
but for the future.

A lack of dexterity in diplomatic contests, an absence of foresight and order, an indiscipline accompanied by paralysis, perhaps
a natural fatigue after the long adventures of the centuries—in a
word, lack of character and will—had cracked and dissolved the
immense empire, isolating the ancient Spanish metropolis on the
summits of memory, and abandoning in mid-ocean, at the mercy
of the storms, twenty republics that had lost all idea of steering a
course. For the great patriots of the days of independence, who had
always inclined towards federation, had been succeeded by weak
or ambitious bosses (*caudillos*) or governors, who, after a generation
of multiplying subdivisions in order to set up vested interests and
hierarchies, found themselves enmeshed in past mistakes, struggling
in the *sauve qui peut* of a mere multitude without solidarity.

Nothing remained of the grandiose dream of the great men who
had headed the insurrection of the old colonies save a distant memory,
and a palpable failure. Bolívar in the North and San Martín in
the South had initiated vast combinations which tended to convert
the old viceroyalties into a coherent union, a vigorous nation, which,
thanks to its extent and population, might have aspired during this
century to balance the weight of the United States. But petty
rivalries, local narrowness, violent ambitions, base envy, all these
meaner instincts, had frustrated the action of these heroes by mul-

tiplying artificial dismemberments, and transforming Latin America into a powerless nursery of small republics, some of which had fewer inhabitants than a city ward in New York.

Here, then, were these twenty-six million square kilometres, ranging down from the tropics to the icy south, with every kind of crops, with riches passing the bounds of probability. And in this enormous area there lived eighty million men, some of them of indigenous races, the heirs of the greatest civilisations which America had known before the conquest, others of Spanish or mingled origin, but all united, with the addition of numerous immigrants, into a single mass speaking the same language, sharing the same religion, living under the same customs, and feeling themselves bound together by the same interests. Instead, however, of forming a single nation, as the Anglo-Saxon colonies which had separated from England had done, they were divided into twenty different countries, at times mutually hostile. And these subdivisions, which only served to confirm their collective helplessness and weakness, appeared to have neither rhyme nor reason.

A study of the map revealed that they had not even respected the old divisions of the viceroyalties—the only ones which might to a certain extent have justified a fragmentary organisation of that body of peoples which at one and the same time had demanded or achieved independence. Out of anxiety to multiply public offices, in order to satisfy the greed of those who, in many cases, had no other object than domination and the satisfaction of personal aims, the frontiers had been traced in obedience to caprice, for the most part without even seeking a precarious justification either in local traditions, geographical accidents, or particular economic interests. Countries had frequently been born of a military rising or a conflict of vanity between two men. And what might have been a great and noble force, intervening effectively in world discussions, and defending the interests and ideals of a really solid group created by history, was reduced to a dismal, clamorous collection of feeble units, fighting among themselves and exhausting each other in absurd revolutions, without possessing sufficient material or moral force to win as a united whole the respect of the great nations.

Thus I proceeded to learn the history of our own Spanish America, in the fullness of its consequences and with its ultimate philosophy, side by side with the history of imperialism. What I had learnt at school had been a local and mutilated interpretation of the vast movement which had separated the ancient colonies from Spain a century ago—a local chronicle in which anecdote predominated and no higher conception, no analytical judgment, no clear perception of the significance of this phenomenon for America and for the world, succeeded in emerging from the names and dates. And with a knowledge of our common history came the bitter grief of understanding that our ills were far more the work of our own incapacity to struggle, of our lack of knowledge of the laws of sociology, of our narrow vision and self-absorption, of our dispersion and forgetfulness of higher interests, than of the greed of outsiders.

From first to last the United States, in the process of expansion, were only obeying a necessity of their own safety, like the Romans in their palmy days, like the Spaniards under Charles V, like the French at the time of Napoleon, like all peoples overflowing with vigour. But we, by our failure to grasp the menace, and by not taking joint measures to hinder it, gave proofs of an inferiority, which in the eyes of determinists and authoritarians almost justified the attack on us.

If, when the Anglo-Saxon colonies of the North separated from England, each of them had aspired to constitute itself a nation independent of the rest; if they had bled themselves white in a hundred civil struggles; if each of these groups had had an independent diplomacy, would the United States have arrived at the privileged position which they now occupy? Is it possible to write a history of the state of Connecticut apart from the history of the United States, offering to youth a higher ideal than that of cohesion and restraint? If rigid customs-barriers existed between the different states of the North American Union, would it be possible to conceive the stupendous commercial development of which we are seeing the proof to-day? From the very origins of their independence, when they stipulated that the troops accompanying Lafayette should go home to their own country after helping to win American independence, instead of attempting to reconquer Canada, which France had just lost; since the time when they managed to frustrate the Congress of Panama; even in the midst of the disorder produced by the War of Secession, the United States have been developing a central idea of solidarity, autonomy, and greatness within the bounds of a policy of clear-sightedness and self-defence. On the other hand, those of our Spanish-American republics, which have at times accepted the support of nations outside their own family group in order to make war on adjacent and sister states; which have gone so far as to request this outside aid in their internal struggles; which have handed over the exploitation of their treasures to enterprises of economic penetration; which believe naïvely in the good faith of international politics, and have harnessed themselves to the chariot of a fallacious Pan-Americanism: are they not committing national suicide? Are they not worthy descendants of our admirable, romantic Spain, which, blinded by the spume of its sterile internal debates, failed to see that in alienating Florida in 1819, it was setting its signature to the inevitable loss of the Antilles, and that at no distant date?

Thus did the present writer argue as he walked the streets of New York, in the glare and glory of the portentous metropolis. Certain words of Bolívar's which he had just read were ringing in his ears: "Our native land before everything. With its elements it has formed our being. Our life is naught but the inheritance of our poor land. There are to be found the witnesses of our birth, the creators of our education. There lie the sepulchres of our fathers, and demand of us security and rest. Everything recalls to us a duty, everything awakes in us soft sentiments and tender memories. There was the scene of our innocence, of our first loves, of our first sensations, and of all that has made us what we are."

This lyrical paragraph was in harmony with my youthful enthusiasm. "Yes," I added to myself as I walked down Broadway amidst the indescribable din of that vast beehive, "my native land before everything. No comfort, no progress, no riches, no civilisation are worth so much as the warm and modest corner where we were born. If great railways, houses thirty stories high, and a giddy whirl of life have to be purchased at the price of our autonomy, I would rather that the backward patriarchal life of our distant villages should last for ever." And side by side with the monstrous Babel at the mouth of the Hudson, there rose up in my imagination, not the shadow of my native Buenos Aires, which was already, too, at that time a great city in the European sense, but the memory of remote half-savage settlements which I had had occasion to visit in Latin America. Amid the dizzy vortex of the business quarter, where the very stones seemed to quiver with human activity, I called these villages to mind with particular satisfaction. That world might be absurd, it might be uncomfortable, it might be barbarous; but it was mine.

In proportion as my admiration for the United States increased, in proportion as I sounded the power and greatness of this people, which eclipsed, without a doubt, all the material progress of which I had dreamed in Europe, my fears were confirmed and aggravated. The North American flag waved on towers, balconies, and shop-fronts, it appeared on posters, on books, on tramways; it was enthroned on the stage of theatres, in the pages of magazines, and even on the wares of chemists, in a delirium of triumphant nationalism, as if a nest of giant eagles had been disclosed, ready to carry into effect the forecasts of Mr. Stead in his book, *The Americanization of the World in the 20th Century.**

How powerful the United States were! My Spain with its tumultuous and teeming populace, with its great, surging multitudes pouring at nightfall into the narrow streets, amidst the cries of the hawkers and the noisy chattering groups of people; my dear, leisurely Paris with its gay boulevards covered with tables, from which a hum goes up as one wanders in the grey twilight; my gaily coloured Italy, rich in the suggestion of the sunny south, made up of languors and of high lights, of hatred and of love; all the old Latin world, after its ages of triumph, was left so much in eclipse, that in the interminable avenues, cut across in every direction by panting locomotives vomiting smoke toward the windows and deafening the passing throng with the crash of their wheels, in the streets blocked with automobiles and pedestrians, across which a way was opened from time to time by the feverish ringing of a bell, amidst the infernal career of the fire-engines, I felt as if I had left the orbit of my destiny to explore unknown ages, in vague and distant epochs which were yet to come.

My disillusion increased along with my wonderment.

Oh, the land of democracy, of puritanism and liberty! The United States were great, powerful, prosperous, astonishingly progressive,

*New York, H. Markley, [1901].

supreme masters of energy and creative life, healthy and comfortable. But they were developing in an atmosphere essentially practical and proud, and principles were almost always sacrificed in the end to interest or social superstitions. It was enough to see the position of the Negro in this equalitarian republic to understand the insincerity of the premises which were proclaimed. Excluded from the universities, hotels, cafés, theatres, and tramways, he only seemed to be in his right place when in the name of lynch law he was dragged through the streets by the crowd.* And the fact remains that although there exists in the United States an *élite* of superior quality capable of understanding all questions, the rough, imperious masses, like all the great groups which have exercised domination throughout the centuries, aim at nothing but ultimate victory. With the exception of the group of intellectuals, the mentality of the country, from the point of view of general ideas, smacks of the rough-and-ready morality of the cow-boy, violent and vain of his muscles, who civilized the Far West by exterminating simultaneously the virgin forest and the aboriginal races in the same high-handed act of pride and domination. They feel themselves to be superior, and in the ultimate logic of history, they are so in reality, because they have triumphed. It matters little that, in response to the jests about our revolutions, our mixed races, our southern tastes, and our literary point of view, we force ourselves to wear a smile on arriving in New York, to satirise Yankee tendencies, to fit attractive names to bad actions, imitating the simple cunning of the character in the French novel who called rabbit fish, so as to fast during Lent without ceasing to eat meat. It remains an incontrovertible fact that the United States, in sacrificing principles so as to safeguard their interests, believe that they are actually accomplishing a duty, since in so doing they are preparing to dominate the world, a task for which they believe themselves to be singled out. A supreme contempt for everything foreign, especially for all that proclaims its Latin origin, and a lively self-satisfaction, rather parvenu in aspect, but solidly based on palpable success, gives the North American character a certain rough and brutal tendency to outdo other races, a certain diabolical exclusiveness which crushes and humiliates the new-comer. More

---

* Such treatment of the Negro is confined largely to the southern States, and Ugarte's statement is somewhat exaggerated even for this section.

than once I was forced to answer stiffly, or to break off a conversation, in order not to listen to insulting opinions upon Latin America. To the popular mind we were savages, ridiculous phenomena, degenerates. In cultivated circles a deprecating attitude was avoided as far as possible, but nobody concealed his Olympian disdain for the "little republics of adventurers" which swarmed to the south of the North American Union. The great newspapers were outspoken about the necessity of making the "strong hand" felt in these "dens" and putting an end to the tumults and disorders which interrupted Uncle Sam's sacred business. Politicians poured forth the most amazing declarations in the Senate, as if the White House really exercised jurisdiction as far as Cape Horn, and as if it had not the vaguest notion of the autonomy of our republics. And the atmosphere was so charged that during a great electoral meeting, in which the prestige of the new democracy triumphed in all its splendour, I heard the applause which greeted statements foreshadowing the historic phrase which later aroused so much comment: "We have begun to take possession of the Continent."

We have begun to take possession of the Continent! A well-known politician could make this statement in a public assembly, and the whole of Latin America was silent! What lethargy, what blindness, what mental derangement held our people paralysed in the runaway car which was bearing us all to the abyss? Those who govern Spanish America, obsessed by the little circle in which they live, hemmed in by minor interests, with no broad vision of the Continent and of the world, have an ingenuous conception of diplomacy. They do not pay attention to facts, but to words. But why did they take no notice of these words? *

Thus for a century Latin America has become more and more anæmic, and English America more and more robust, thanks to the simplicity of the former and the supreme cleverness of the latter. The United States have proved themselves creators in every sphere, and have had the knowledge and skill to transform laws and procedure, principles and systems, ranging from education to journalism, and from agriculture to building construction.

* Perhaps Señor Ugarte took the jingoists of 1900–1901 too seriously. By no means all of us were jingoists. Yet, have we not followed the jingoists from afar?

A wise development of initiative and a tendency to experiment have given this nation the capacity necessary for revolutionising and perfecting knowledge, surpassing all that existed in the civilisations which they at first imitated. It would be idle to suppose that this progress has had no counterpart in diplomacy. Their material superiority has not been an isolated mechanical fact, but the result of a greater mental capacity, which reveals itself in every department. There are ideas fifty stories high which correspond to the fifty-story buildings.

From New York, by way of Chicago, Omaha, and Salt Lake, I arrived at San Francisco, where, we may say in passing, there are numbers of "Mr. Pérezes" and "Mr. Gonzálezes," who, having shaved off their origin with their beards, talk with peculiar disdain of their former brothers in the South.

The prodigious force of attraction and assimilation of the United States is based, above all, on the possibilities ("opportunities" as they are called there) of prosperity and action offered to individuals by this land. The abundance of business enterprises, good government, new methods, the manifold flexibility of life, and marvellous prosperity, open a field for every kind of initiative. Once a measure of success was achieved, it would be motive enough to hold the new-comer by gratitude and pride, even if he did not soar high; since the contagion of pride in the atmosphere would entirely dominate him. Some Spanish Americans who, driven by political discord, emigrate from small republics and succeed in carving out for themselves a fairly good position in the populous cities of the North, even become denationalised; and their blindness goes to such lengths in some cases that they are even able to sympathise with the attacks which are made on their own country. It is an ordinary occurrence, in another sphere, for very young students who have gone from us to follow a course in the universities of the Union, to have their heads turned by their new surroundings, or the material conveniences which they offer, and to return to their native land contemptuous and arrogant, proclaiming in English the necessity for submission,—unconscious auxiliaries of the very force which is to devour them. In this pliancy lies perhaps the worst symptom of our decay and vulnerability. We may admire the progress and greatness which in a century of its life have raised this land to the most exalted heights. We may champion the policy of cultivating excellent commercial and diplomatic relations between the Spanish-American nations and the United States. We may wish to see all improvements in education, order, comfort and prosperity acclimatised in Spanish America. But this must be effected without yielding a jot of the autonomy of our nations, treating as country with country, as power with power, without abdication or submission, safeguarding our distinctive languages, our pride, our flag, our present and our future.

Latin America, prosperous and in the full tide of progress in some republics, delayed in its evolution in others, has everything to learn from the United States, and requires the economic and technical assistance of this great people. But is it necessary for her, in order to attain this, to renounce her own peculiar possibilities of development, her own clearly defined personality, her ineradicable traditions, her faculty of self-determination?

In this frame of mind, I continued along the coast as far as Los Angeles and San Diego. From the latter of these cities I arrived by railway at the frontier of Mexico, desirous of knowing this country which had suffered such injustice at the hands of the United States, and which, lying next their frontier, in the extreme north of the Spanish-American portion of the Continent, represents something in the nature of a common rampart and historic breakwater which has withstood the floods for a century past and defends the whole South.

At the period during which this first journey took place, about which I am only speaking by way of introduction, General Don Porfirio Díaz was just rising to the head of the republic, surrounded by a group of men peculiarly inclined to temporise with the danger and so to play the enemy's game.

It was in this republic at that time that were being carried to the extreme, those methods of mildness, good nature, and obsequious deference which most of the southern countries are still employing without realising that the greater the concessions, the greater grow the demands,—the process being to accustom a people to one act of submission, which inevitably entails another. This process is the high-road leading to one of two abysses: either to a total obliteration of nationality, gradually brought about by successive abdications, or else, in the end, to a desperate resistance, when it will be forced to face under worse conditions the very conflict which it originally desired to avoid.

From the very frontier the irreconcilable opposition between the two communities presents itself vividly and obviously. The Anglo-Saxon, hard, haughty, and utilitarian, infatuated with his success and his muscular strength, improvises towns, dominates nature, imposes everywhere the impress of his activity and ambition; and, like the Romans in their palmy days, has as his auxiliaries and servants the subject races,—Indians, Chinese, Africans,—who gather up the crumbs of the feast in return for discharging subaltern tasks. As opposed to him, the Mexican, of pure Spanish or half-breed descent, continues in his easy-going customs and accepts the fruits of the earth, true to those contemplative, dreamy tendencies which lead him to be disinterested, open-handed and a *caballero*. Standing on his dignity with his equals, affable with his inferiors, he lives amidst surroundings rather patriarchal in character, in which the Indian is not classed according to race, but, like other men, according to his personal distinction and culture.

From the very bridge over the river Bravo, which separates the two territories, we at once find traces of a persistent, ceaseless infiltration in every branch of activity,—business enterprises, hotels, transport,—as if the shadow of the United States were ominously projected over the neighbouring territories. The railway which took me to the Capital, via Chihuahua, Zacatecas, Aguas Calientes, and Guanajuato belonged at that time to a North American company, and the overseers and employés of every kind spoke English almost exclusively, to the serious inconvenience of travellers, who could not make themselves understood in their own country.

There has been a certain change in this respect since then, owing to the Mexican revolution of 1913, which from the international point of view represents a reaction. We shall deal with this matter in due time in another chapter.

General Díaz's policy, as we have already said, consisted of bowing the knee to the United States. This policy began with the Northern railways and ended in the concession over Magdalena Bay, after affecting all the most important activities in the country. It was the moment when the United States were carrying out their "peaceful penetration," and the "scientific party" in Mexico were employing the tactics of "skilful concessions"; till the time came when the Mexican government, opportunist and conciliatory though it might be, could make no further concessions. The famous interview between General Díaz and President Taft at El Paso [October 16, 1909] had for its result a tacit rupture. A negative reply to the demand for strengthening North American jurisdiction in Lower California; the protection extended to the President of Nicaragua, Don José Santos Zelaya, who escaped from reprisal in a Mexican gunboat; and an alleged secret treaty with Japan were the reasons put forward officially. Perhaps other reasons came in, too. The fact remains that from this moment the old Mexican autocrat began his tardy resistance to imperialism. And by a singular coincidence, from this day onwards the first revolution, headed by Don Francisco Madero, had become a possibility.*

When in 1901 I arrived for the first time at the capital of Mexico, it was a prosperous city of more than half a million inhabitants, in which one breathed an atmosphere of culture and well-being. I remember the reckless luxury, the frequent holidays, the progress of urban development, and the characteristic and picturesque note struck by the imposing progress of the President along the Calle de Plateros in a great coach followed by a regiment of that "rural guard," so typical and elegant, which performed the functions of the *Gendarmerie* in France and the Civil Guard in Spain, a select corps who with their gaudy Mexican *charro* costumes and their spirited horses with characteristic national trappings, produced a strange and bizarre impression.

The first thing which one noticed on arriving was the lack of internal liberty. The only political party was the one which had the upper hand. Not a single opposition paper showed its head. Not a political meeting was held, except to belaud the government, that irremoveable institution which went on without a hitch from one phase to another with all the serene continuity of a monarchy. The central power was skilful enough to attract some by means of sine-

*One would like to have the docmuents on this matter. Somewhere in the government archives or in the private files of the participants they may be found and when found they may confirm Ugarte's view—and they may not.

cures, and to intimidate others by the threats of consequences, thus establishing an artificial appearance of unanimity. None the less, one could detect, as a counterpoise to this submission, a latent and frustrated sentiment of rebellion which was bound to give rise to future anarchy.

From the point of view of prosperity, the country was apparently in an excellent condition. Great public works, powerful business enterprises, railways under construction, monumental buildings, surprised the traveller who had heard the neighbouring country spoken of so contemptuously in the United States. But beneath all this appearance of financial development and national prosperity, one could detect the wires of gold which, coming from abroad, set in motion the whole mechanism of the country. In reality the country was economically in the power of the United States.

During my stay in Mexico I got to know and associate with the young intellectuals of the country, who formed a group connected with a publication unprecedented in Latin America, which has not been continued. I refer to the *Revista Moderna*, edited by Don Jesús Valenzuela, a man of distinguished ability who died a short time afterwards, leaving behind him more stories than work accomplished. There I got to know Luís G. Urbina, later Secretary of the Mexican Embassy in Spain; Ciro Ceballos, director of the National Library; Amado Nervo, who died on the way to take up his office as Minister to the Argentine; Juan Sánchez Azcona, Minister to Spain; Jesús Urueta; the artist Julio Ruelas, who died in Paris; Alfonso Cravioto, Rubén Campos, and many others who have occupied or occupy high official positions. Never had Latin America seen such a galaxy of brilliant minds as that which was coming into prominence at that time in what they used proudly to call the Aztec capital.

Besides the above-mentioned, I remember the painter Ramos Martínez, who gained remarkable success in Paris; José Juan Tablada, who represented his country later in Colombia; the sculptors Guerra and Nava, who were also destined to win approval in Europe; Bernardo Conto, who died very young, and Don Justo Sierra, who by his reputation, age, and political position was the spiritual father of the group.

I found no. opportunity of making the acquaintance of the politicians who were then guiding the helm of State. I heard a financier, a general, and a diplomatist referred to as able and clear-sighted men; but it is fairly certain that internal politics, the maintenance of government, the preservation of the places which they' had obtained,—our invariable official shams,—entirely occupied their attention. Neglect and lack of ideals have been the distinctive features of our government. And since at that time not many of the tangible causes of disquiet existed which are now perturbing people's minds, the oblivion must have been deeper and the dream more complete.

Among the people, on the other hand, and especially among the younger men, there was a feeling of keen resentment and marked hostility against the gringo.[2] In hotels, cafés, and theatres could be noticed an obvious antagonism which was arising, as great collective sentiments do arise, without logic or reflection, from confused memories and instinctive perceptions. The contemptuous and arrogant bearing of North American tourists played its part in bringing this about; but great tendencies do not arise from separate and casual incidents. Something more serious was growing up from year to year, in the profound verbal tradition of the people, who do not read newspapers or take part in city gossip: a feeling amounting to an inextinguishable grudge against the inequitable war and spoliation of 1845 and 1846; a feeling expressive of the indelible wrath of a valiant community, disarmed and at the mercy of injustice; a feeling which seemed to revive in people's hearts the cry of the last cadet of Chapultepec as he threw himself into the abyss before the triumphant invasion, without losing his grip of the flag. The people knew that half the territory of their native land had been torn from them by the neighbouring country; they felt the growing influence that this same country was beginning to exert over the territory which remained to them; and they foresaw the new aggressions which were bound to take place in the future. A voice from the past and a voice from the future murmured in the ear of the pelao,*

[2] This term is applied in Mexico exclusively to North Americans, and not to all foreigners, as in the Argentine.

* South American term for a poor Indian, literally one stripped (pelado-peeled) of possessions.

lost on the plains, and of the youth just about to enter the university, that the foreign invader was always in the cities, if not in the form of soldiers, in the form of loans, diplomatic intrigues, influences occasionally exerted over their own governments. And the eternal presence of this shadow over the land, bled and mutilated by the enemy, kept up a latent irritation and anger, in spite of the precepts of the newspapers and official demonstrations. There was no necessity to work it up. This state of mind was not the fruit of a propaganda by agitators. Nobody made public speeches on the subject. But dumbly and passively, among men isolated from one another, the same opinion was simultaneously arising, directed against the intruders, who, after despoiling them of their land, were supplanting them in wealth; against the *gringo*, who was abusing his superiority in strength and cunning to exploit them on every occasion, to overreach them at every turn, to humiliate them at every moment with a refinement of cruelty, always preserving an innocent appearance, while casting the blame and ignominy upon their victims.

The more humble the rank in society, the more clearly did this sentiment appear, as if lack of culture, economic interests, and social obligations stimulated sincerity and the free expression of a general sentiment. The younger the men, the greater was the force with which this tendency exhibited itself; as if, as time went by, and the days of sacrifice and suffering became more distant, the rancour caused by injustice became more and more confirmed in the younger generations.

The implication of this sudden annexation of a territory of two million square kilometres, stretching from the gulf of Mexico to the Pacific coast, have not yet been grasped. From the names of the first explorers—Camillo, Alarcón, Coronado, Cabeza de Vaca—to the names of the towns—Los Ángeles, San Francisco, Santa Barbara, everything points to a purely Spanish origin. They had belonged to Mexico since the epoch of independence, geographically, as well as by language and by race; and there was not the shadow of a dispute which might have justified setting up a claim. At a given moment, notwithstanding, the invasion was let loose, the armies reached the capital, and Mexico had to sign whatever was exacted from her. Not a voice was raised amongst all humanity to condemn this attack.* The nations remained unmoved. The noble humanitarians who, though they were not French, wept over the fate of Alsace Lorraine, and, who, though not Poles, were moved by the sufferings of Poland, had no word of sympathy for the victim. The attack was carried out in darkness, and oblivion fell upon it so soon, that when it is called to mind to-day, there are some who almost doubt that it happened.

Such has been the destiny of our race up to the present. Justice, right, solidarity, clemency, the generous sentiments on which the great nations plume themselves, have not existed for Latin America. Hence she has drawn down on her head every sort of aggression—violations of territory, persecution of her citizens, mutilation of her lands, interference in her internal affairs, coercion, spoliation, expeditions landed on her coasts on some unjustifiable pretext—while the world has remained unmoved, and not a voice has been raised in pity. Thus it seems to have become understood that the integrity of our lands, the liberty of our fellow-men, the possession of our wealth, all that constitutes our life and our heritage, are bound to be at the mercy of any troops in quest of an adventure; of any government desiring to foment disturbances in order to depose a president who is not sufficiently docile; of any naval squadron which may take it into its head to force its visit upon us. For us, when any difficulty arises with a powerful country (and when I say powerful countries I do not only refer to the United States, but to certain European nations as well) there exists neither arbitration, nor international law, nor human consideration. They may all do what they please, without responsibility either to contemporary opinion or to history. Since the old Spanish colonies had frittered away their strength, the imperialist governments had seen across the sea nothing but weakness. Hence the settlement of the English in the Falkland Islands and so-called British Honduras; hence the initial success of the Archduke Maximilian's expedition; hence the origins of Panama; hence the seizure of Texas, Arizona, California, and New Mexico. We are placed on a level with certain peoples of the Far East or Central Africa in that vast proletariat of weak

* This is a very broad statement. The war was condemned in certain sections of the United States, and likewise in France and in England.

nations which are oppressed, bled, decimated, and annihilated in the name of progress and civilisation; and the attacks which are made on us will never arouse a clamour of protest, because the lips of the world are sealed by complicity or fear.

This situation is particularly conspicuous in the case of Mexico. The opinion of the world,—skilfully prepared by a misleading campaign of publicity discrediting this country, and true to its attitude of harsh indifference, which is only affected when the three or four dictator nations which have a share in world dominion find it profitable,—has brazenly encouraged the outrages of which she has been a victim for a century past. The only occasion on which Europe made any attempt to check the imperialist advance was not intended to benefit the suffering country, but to bleed it again for the benefit of Europe by means of the Austro-French expedition of 1864. In order not to succumb, Mexico would have had to defend herself single-handed against the stratagems of others and her own inexperience, suppressing civil war, laughing at the traps laid for her, and, after the disaster, holding in check the very force which had overwhelmed her, without support from anybody or anything; not even from Latin America, not even from the sister republics of the South, which not only from racial solidarity, but also from their analogous situation, should have made her conflicts their own, at least in the sphere of diplomatic representations.

But in Latin America we are so far from having a clear idea of our interests and destiny. In vain do we realise that the injustice which depresses our *morale* is a result of our own disunion. Divergencies are multiplied to beat us in detail, and we continue to let ourselves be made fools of with the same simple-mindedness as the Gauls before Cæsar or the Indians before Hernán Cortés, without arriving at a sense of the logical and natural demarcation which gives us our separate character, and our position on the Continent and in the world.

Such was the course of my reflections as I set sail once more for France, after passing a few weeks in that land where so many proofs remain of the colonial grandeur of Spain, where so many monuments are left of the splendour of the Aztecs; where two pasts were united, and promised a splendid future. My twenty-year-old enthusiasm estimated the magnitude of the task which the younger generations seemed predestined to accomplish: to work towards the ideal of a Continent morally united, so as to recreate, at least by diplomatic means, the homogeneous community dreamt of by the pioneers of independence; to retrieve by means of this union the honour and security of our territories, and to make each republic stronger and more prosperous, within a higher organisation which should be the supreme guaranty of their regional autonomy.

Possessed by this ideal, and profiting by the publicity assured in our Latin America to a voice coming from Europe, on my return to Paris I undertook a journalistic campaign lasting for many years, and making use of every medium: *El País*, of Buenos Aires, the editor of which was then Dr. Carlos Pellegrini, afterwards President of the Argentine: *La Época* [3] of Madrid, a Conservative and Government paper, which had a decisive influence in the political clubs; *La Revue Mondiale*, of Paris, edited by M. Jean Finot. I spoke of the illusory Pan-American congresses; of the commercial offensive which was winning for the United States all the markets of Latin America, to the detriment of other nations; of the Latin mentality of the republics of the South; of the reaction of French thought on our countries, and how far it might contribute towards rousing the great communities of the Old Continent from their slumbers, and leading them to action capable of countering the advance of imperialism. Finally, in the *Paris Journal*,[4] which, at that time, under the editorship of M. Gérault Richard, was the best written and most generally read newspaper, I completed the exposition of the problem in a dozen leading articles.

In France, nobody shrank from the truth. The press made constant references to the subject, and distinguished controversialists like Paul Adam declared in the clearest terms, "The Yankees are awaiting a propitious moment for intervention. The menace exists. A little longer, and Brother Jonathan's cruisers will land the troops of the Union on these lands steeped in Latin blood. The fate of these republics is to be conquered by the forces of the North." The great writer said this in one of his brilliant articles in *Le Journal*, under the heading of "An Amicable Intervention!" M. Charles Boss, for his art, spoke insistently in *Le Rappel*, as follows: "We in Europe,

3 Numbers of October 27, 1906, February 8, 1907, etc.
4 Numbers of February 13, October 5, 1911, etc.

because we are impotent to oppose it, are going to look on at the subjugation of the Latin republics of the South and their transformation
into regions subject to the protectorate of Washington." Many
noble minds like M. Jean Herbette [5] confirmed this conviction, born
of impartial observation. None the less, in some of our republics
the reality of the situation was still called in question. Strange
blindness! All realised that the attack was pending, and protested
against it; the only one which neither saw nor protested was the
victim. And this attitude was all the more paradoxical because in
the United States themselves courageous voices were uplifted against
imperialism, and more than one prominent North American called
in question the attitude of his country with regard to the Spanish
American republics. Moved by the desire, if not to make others
share my conviction, at least to impel them to discuss these matters,
I next wrote *The Future of Latin America* (*El Porvenir de la América
Latina*), the first edition of which appeared in 1910.[6] It is not
for me to say how this volume was received, which Rubén Darío in
one of his articles stated to be "sensational," [7] nor what was written
about it in Spain and America. But though Max Nordau said in
La Nación, of Buenos Aires, that "the programme set forth in this
book is grandiose" and Enrique Ferri wrote "I also have laid down
the lines of this problem in a lecture and come to exactly the same
conclusions"; while Francisco García Calderón declared that I had
"endowed America, sunk in anarchy, with a directing idea"; some
newspapers in certain Spanish-American republics reproached the
work with being inaccurate and alarmist. It was useless for the
New York *Evening Mail* [8] to declare that the book was "excellent,
logical and complete"; or for the New York *Times* [9] to devote an
unusual amount of attention to it in a long six-column analysis with
head-lines. When the latter paper asked "an Argentine diplomatist
resident in New York" for his opinion on the matter, he answered

[5] "The Latins of the New World understand the danger, as is shown
by the eloquent work of M. Manuel Ugarte: *The Future of Latin America.*
Europe will perhaps repent of not having been clear-sighted enough."
                                          Le Siecle, of Paris, March 1, 1911.
[6] Editorial Prometeo, Valencia.
[7] *Mundial*, February, 1912.
[8] *The Evening Mail*, February 17, 1911.
[9] New York *Times*, March 5, 1911.

that "the author was very young, and accordingly his way of thinking was not the same as that of older Argentinos of mature critical judgment." In answer to which the writer of the article shrewdly argued: "All this may be admitted: but the fact that moderate minds think like this does not imply that the youth of South America allows itself to be more influenced by them than by Ugarte, who enjoys great popularity in those countries."

The error which gave rise to these discrepant judgments in Latin America arose from that narrow local conception which had done us so much damage. Each republic considered itself,—and still considers itself,—totally detached from the fate of the rest. Instead of being furious and agitated about matters which, though beyond its own frontiers, yet lay none the less within the logical bounds of its destiny, whether geographical, diplomatic or economic, it regarded the dangers which might be incurred by the other republics as foreign to its interests. Some went so far as to reproach me with taking too much interest in "foreign countries." They forgot the words of José Enrique Rodó: "For Spanish-Americans the fatherland means Spanish America. The sentiment of patriotism includes that no less natural and indestructible sentiment of attachment to one's province, region, or territory; and the provinces, regions, and territories of that great fatherland of ours are the nations into which she is politically divided. For my part I have always understood it in this way. The political unity which should consecrate and make incarnate this moral unity,—Bolívar's dream,—is still a dream, the realisation of which will perhaps not be seen by the generations now living. What matter? Italy, before it had been turned into a political expression by the sword of Garibaldi and the apostolate of Mazzini, was not merely the geographical expression of Metternich. It was the idea, the genius of the fatherland; it was the fatherland itself, consecrated by all the sacred ceremonies of tradition, right and glory. Italy existed, one and individual, less corporate, but no less real; less tangible, but no less vibrant and intense, than when she assumed an outline and a colour on the map of the nations." *

The ever more clearly recognised necessity of contributing towards

* See Isaac Goldberg, *Studies in Spanish-American Literature* (New York, Brentano's, 1920), p. 230.

the salvation of Latin America's future by means of a propaganda which should arouse in men's minds superior impulses and noble idealisms, capable of laying the first foundations, if not of a unity like that of Italy or Germany, at least of a co-ordination of international policy, thus led the peaceful writer to desert his table and mount the platform, in order to come into direct contact with the public.

My first lecture on this subject was delivered in Spanish. The municipality of Barcelona was celebrating on May 25, 1910, the centenary of the Argentine Republic, and it was in the historic *Salon de Ciento* that I expounded the "Causes and Consequences of the American Revolution."[10] I recall this fact because it represents the starting point of the campaign which I afterwards undertook throughout the whole of South America.

I have always thought that Spain should represent for us what England does for the United States: our antecedents, our honourable origin, the strong root from whence flows the life-giving sap of the tree. In order to sustain the impetus and connection of our history in a state of political disintegration and during a stage of unassimilated cosmopolitanism, it is fitting that we should not lose sight of this glorious starting-point, this backbone of our memories.

In this historic past lies the central point of our common history in Latin America. Moreover, to speak of the independence of one of the Spanish-American republics as if we were dealing with a local and isolated fact, is to give proof of a limited outlook. Every province in each republic might with equal justice aspire to possess an independent history, multiplying subdivisions *ad infinitum*. In movements of this order we must go down to the fundamental causes of similar phenomena and reactions, embracing wide horizons, seeing each phenomenon in its full bearing, comprehending, in fine, not merely the isolated facts, but the rhythmic flow of a vast current. The leaves fall and flutter in the air, but it is the wind which bears them away.

In this lecture I maintained that, as the insurrection of the different colonies took place about the same date, it was only possible to talk of the independence of any given republic of the Continent within the

[10] *Mi campaña hispano-americana* (speeches and addresses). Editorial Cervantes, Barcelona, 1922.

general concert of Spanish-American independencies. I added that, little as I wished to depreciate their nobility, heroism and glory, the different separatist movements of 1810, in which the political or commercial interests and expectations of England and the United States played, however indirectly, some part, were premature in some territories. This is proved by the fact that, even in the more prosperous regions, after seeking for foreign monarchs to govern us, we accepted the direction of ideological systems of government, always calling upon others for what it was not yet possible to draw from our own resources.

When we look at the world in general, we see that the political independence of people is the consequence or corollary of racial differences, commercial capacities, or underlying theoretical conceptions. Possibly these factors had not yet reached definitive development in every part of South America. For in their weak infancy, on leaving the mother's breast, certain new republics had to be spoon-fed by other nations, thus in reality giving the lie to the very aims at which the movement of insurrection had originally aimed.

None the less, the real malady of South America a century ago, was not so much that it was not mature enough for an autonomous existence, as that it lacked knowledge of international politics. When, after the abortive ending of Bolívar and San Martín's epic enterprise, they split up into eighteen republics, they failed to foresee the historical impossibility of many of these tiny countries, or the precarious position in which some of them would find themselves, in trying to develop within their sphere from such precarious elements, or the strategems to which they were bound to fall victim amidst the vicissitudes of life.

Hence, when we consider facts from a higher, broader and more philosophical point of view, and not from the point of view of petty vanities, we can affirm that the results of separatism have not been equally satisfactory in every quarter of Latin America. Further, though we consider that we have certain legitimate and local reasons to be proud of it, yet, considered as a whole, it can be interpreted, like all great historical liquidations, as a balance of profit and loss. It involved considerable losses for the Spanish language and civilisation (Texas, Arizona, California, New Mexico,

Porto Rico, Santo Domingo, etc.). Certain territories merely changed the direct sovereignty of the mother country for the indirect sovereignty of a foreign nation. But in general, the aggregate of these countries fell under an Anglo-Saxon protectorate; for such is the essence of the much-talked-of Monroe Doctrine, on the one hand, and the powerful influence of England on the other.

I have had occasion to declare that writing for the public does not mean printing what the public wants to read, but saying what sincerity dictates, or what the supreme interest of our country suggests. And it is my country, in its direct and concrete form—namely the Argentine—and in its virtual extension—namely Latin America—that I have undertaken to defend, facing every sort of obloquy. On October 14, 1911, I gave a lecture at the Sorbonne.[11]

In envisaging the American problem from the point of view of the Latin world, my object was to increase the scope of my patient propaganda, by arousing an interest in countries of like genius, and making an appeal to their material and moral sympathies.

France has considerable interests in Latin America, not only from the economic but from the intellectual point of view. The diffusion of her ideas and spirit in these new lands has created her a sort of moral empire, which she has always regarded lightly, but which she will ultimately have to consider with a growing interest. The ideals of the Revolution, her tendencies in philosophy, literature, and art in general, and, in addition to this, her ways of life, her tastes and human aims—all that is the expression of a national soul; all this has left such a deep imprint and such an indelible trace in the Spanish-American republics that it may almost be said that France lives in our life, and that the annihilation of our autonomous existence and characteristics would mean an enormous diminution of her image as reflected in the world. In calling her to our aid we are

[11] This lecture was organised by the *France-Amérique* Committee and the *Groupement des Universités*, with M. Paul Appell, then Dean of the Faculty of Science, now Rector of the Sorbonne, in the chair. At the end of his speech introducing me he said: "This writer is also a man of action, of an independent character, who maintains his position apart from the direct policy of any particular country, and follows a vaster and more elevated ideal: that of realising a union in independence of the Latin republics of America, for the purpose of developing a common future of civilisation and progress."

in reality doing no more than prompting her to defend a part of her spiritual patriotism.

At that time we were far from foreseeing the war which was to break out three years later, and it was a moment when France saw with dislike the bewildering advance of North American infiltration in lands which, without being false to their origin, responded to her cultural leading and followed her inspiration. Her hard ordeal meant that this great nation could not attend to anything but her own defence. But during those years, I used to say, France was perhaps the European nation which most freely censured imperialist action in Latin America, and my campaign was received with particular goodwill. My assiduous contributions to Parisian reviews and newspapers, the dozen volumes which I had published, and above all, the coincidence of interests which connected our nationalist claims with French tendencies and aspirations, contributed towards giving this lecture an effect unusual in a capital which is as a rule deaf to the affairs of America.[12]

A fortnight later I started off on that continental tour of which I shall speak in the following chapters. I wished to establish a contact with each of the republics whose cause I had defended *en bloc;* to get to know them directly, to observe their true situation at close quarters, and complete my general impression of the Latin-American territories by travelling right through them, from the Antilles and Mexico to Cape Horn.

The different regions are unfortunately so isolated from one another, our information about them is so deficient, that an Argentine can talk with more propriety about Korea than Guatemala, and a Paraguayan knows more about Alaska than Cuba. My object was to break with the traditional apathy; to live, for however short a time, in each of these countries, so as to be able to correct or ratify, by observations made on the spot, my conception of the nature of our great fatherland. With this primary object was combined a desire to establish personal relations with governing circles, with business men, writers, publicists, those controlling the government and opinion, and, finally, with the young men, the pulse of whose

[12] The whole press, from the *Temps* and the *Figaro* to purely political organs, such as *L'Action, L'Aurore* and the *Petite République,* published long reports and favourable comments.

sympathies I could feel from a distance, in the comforting echoes which reached me.

Latin America to which I had devoted my efforts since my early youth, whose political interests I had defended at every turn, whose youthful literature I had brought together as a whole in one volume, with whose leading minds I was in correspondence, whose every throb reached my writing-table in Paris from all the republics alike, was, with the exception of the Argentine, where I was born, and Mexico, where the common problem had been revealed to me, none the less still a region whose geography was unknown to me. Beyond the notions which I had acquired from references in books and the information of every sort which had been sent me, I vaguely guessed at new lines and details, complementary ramifications, general impressions, colour and atmosphere—all that eludes writing or photography and can only be understood and grasped by seeing them directly.

What I was most interested to discover was the state of men's minds in these vast territories, and their attitude towards independent life; proceeding to what might be called a sounding of their collective soul in the difficult times which bade fair to come upon the New World. A Spanish-American setting out like this to visit the Continent, with no mandate from any government, without the support of any institution, struggling for an ideal with no arms but his patriotism and disinterestedness, was naturally bound to be in some men's eyes an unwelcome visitor and a tiresome witness. I guessed what bitter hostility and hard struggles were awaiting me, just as I foresaw the enthusiasm which my action was sure to arouse in the younger generation. It was deliberately, and with a full realisation of what I was doing, that I undertook this difficult journey. On the basis of the knowledge which this first tour enabled me to acquire, I have since accumulated notes, collected during a constant study of American questions, and observations which I have made during later journeys. What I hope will be reflected in this book is a general view of the situation, at a time when the lines of a new world-policy are beginning to define themselves, and we Spanish Americans are asking ourselves, "What is to be the position of our republics in the turmoil of the future?"

CHAPTER II

THE SHIPWRECK OF THE ANTILLES

A vision of Havana—Cuba and the Panama Canal—The Plätt Amendment—Methods of Exerting Pressure—The Opinion of President Gómez—A Hypothesis—Santiago de Cuba—The Island of Santo Domingo—Ironies of History—The Mirage of Words.

En route for Havana during the lost hours of my sea-voyage, on a still ocean, which seemed like an image of imperialist policy— so innocent in appearance, but yesterday it had engulfed an ocean liner!—the whole continent rose before my imagination, with all its history, all its uncertain future, from the time when Columbus's caravels discovered it till the era of intensified expansion; passing through the colonial stage, the process of separatism, and an independence which was in some respects fleeting and insecure.

The words of Sáenz Peña, at that time President of the Argentine Republic, returned to my memory: "The Latin race is undoubtedly passing through a period of obscurity and depression, which contrasts with its past historic greatness; but the eclipse is transitory, and the race which held the sovereignty of the world, diffusing its mighty breath across the immensity of the seas and into regions undiscovered and unknown, must one day recover the heritage of its energies and initiative, its enterprise and its glory. It can do this by setting in motion the springs of that will, which are attributes of the soul which Edmond Demolins desires to change for another, without recalling that it has inspired heroism, glory, and greatness; explorations, inventions, arts and sciences, which are not the patrimony of the Anglo-Saxon, and form the rich treasure of the Latin race. The Latin-American League is a conception which can be seen to be fruitful and advantageous in view of future eventualities. It was perhaps dangerous for our formless republics in those doubtful days when it was conceived by Bolívar. But it will not be so in the future, and should not be so to-day, now that the sovereignty

31

of nations is defined on a basis of mutual respect. Within these organisms a unity of destiny and of thought is a political necessity, and so is the solidarity of principles which ought to defend the nations of this Continent, now that a special law of nations aspires to preside over their evolution."

I landed very early in the morning. The narrow streets, crowded with vehicles going from the harbour to the central parts of the city, gave me the impression of a prosperous centre of trade. Commerce, activity, life, and wealth struck the new-comer's eyes, impressing him with the fact of a victory. But it was also easy to recognise the preponderant influence, if only by reading the shop signs. In the Hotel de Inglaterra, organised on the North American plan, the impression was confirmed. The Yankee commercial traveller and the foreign tongue carried all before them. The dollar was the official currency. For a moment I believed myself in New York. The barber, the shoeblack, the chauffeur, might have been transplanted straight from Broadway. I cast my eye over a newspaper almost wholly occupied with football [baseball], and read: "A batting realling [*sic* for rally] of the Blues in the ninth inning. . . . The picture shows Baker's run home just as Mathewson forces Merkle to make an out. . . ." All this with huge headlines and pictures three columns wide. In the hall, opposite the elevator, a group of Cubans were arguing in English. Yet, in spite of this, the city, a classic Spanish colonial capital, with its two-story houses painted in bright colours, and its grated windows, was a living witness that another life existed, which had not yet made its morning appearance in this early activity, monopolised by tradespeople and hurrying travellers, but pulsed in retirement behind its closed doors, sunk in its national memories and hopes; another life which, whether through conservatism or faithfulness to its old traditions, held aloof from the giddy whirl which appeared to be carrying all before it.

Under a brilliant sun, I went along the Paseo Martí towards the sea, through the still cool city, between two rows of sumptuous private residences, an evident sign of the brilliant life of the great Cuban families. A little way along, I noticed on the sidewalk a placard with the inscription: "This park was laid out under the administration of the American General X" (here followed the name). I was not yet acquainted with the fondness of the coloniser for putting up monuments to himself. In the course of my travels I afterwards discovered the self-excuses of Panama and the improbable allegorical group at Puerto Cabello ("To the North American soldiers who contributed towards the independence of the country"), usurping a place which might be claimed by Macgregor's Englishmen.*

A hired automobile enabled me to drive down the fine promenade along the edge of the sea, the picturesque avenues of the Vedado, the central streets full of luxurious shops, and the banking quarter. As the chances of my drives gave occasion, illustrated by the commentaries of the chauffeur, I tried to form a superficial idea of the whole, observing, as I passed, the salient features: the enormous building of the Club of Commercial Employés with its 32,000 members; the flourishing Clubs of the Spanish residents (Asturians, Galicians, Catalans, etc.);[1] the premises of the great newspapers, with their modern installation; the office of the Secretary for Public Health, installed in Manhattan House; the lavish mural advertisements; the excellent pavements; a Hospital still bearing the name of "Royal Hospital of San Lázaro, 1861"; the abundance of book-shops, the invasion of luxury; the University, housed in a picturesque situation in the suburbs of the city. . . . So much for things. . . . As regards the people with whom I exchanged a few hurried words in passing, I found some discouraged, others full of energetic decision. A French merchant said to me: "Everything is finished here. Formerly four French boats a month used to arrive; now there is hardly one. The North Americans allow no competition and will end by being the sole masters." On the other hand, a young intellectual declared to me, "This people has shed too much blood in order to gain its independence, for there to be any fear that it will ever resign itself to losing it again. Try to penetrate the depths of the Cuban soul."

As I returned to my hotel at ten in the morning, when the city

* Perhaps reference is made to Sir Gregor Macgregor whose filibuster operations in the West Indies and on the Florida Coast during the second decade of the nineteenth century occasioned anxiety both in Spain and the United States.

[1] Of the 38,296 immigrants who entered Cuba in 1912, 30,660 were Spaniards.

was beginning to take on its true and varied aspect, I realised that there were great forces pitted against each other, and that the problem of Cuba was so complex that it eluded the tourist's first impressions. Nothing is easier than to make definite assertions when the writer only aims at surprising or interesting the reader. But when the book he is attempting to write is not a matter of vanity or imagination, but a sincere and patriotic work, divorced from all speculative intentions, the subject becomes less manageable. No considerations of prudence or popularity will hinder me from telling the whole truth in the course of these pages, painful as what I shall outline may prove to be for the local pride of any region or for the Spanish-American ideal. But I have also to be on my guard against letting myself be blinded by appearances, against paying tribute to prejudice, or seeing things solely from the point of view of a thesis, forcing the facts, as some do, to fit in with a predetermined conclusion.

In the matter which we are examining, this danger is more apparent than in any other. So much has been said about the subordination of the island, the annihilation of its nationality, and even about the betrayal of Cuba in relation to that family of nations to which it belongs ethnically and morally, that on one's arrival he feels the pressure of what he has read weighing upon his mind, the comments and the atmosphere created from without with regard to an international situation unique in history, and therefore worthy of more careful study and extended examination.

The "manifest destiny" of peoples frequently serves to encourage slackness, but it is undeniable that given historical or geographical conditions exercise a strong pressure which may bring a community to an *impasse*, from which it is difficult to find an escape.

Cuba is the central point between the Panama Canal and Florida. "It was with the Canal in view," says the Cuban writer Carrera y Justíz in his book *Orientaciones necesarias,** "that, as early as 1826, Henry Clay, the famous American Secretary of State, suggested the neutralisation of Cuba, thus preventing Bolívar from invading this island with an army. It was mainly with the Canal in view that the Monroe Doctrine was affirmed in a wider sense, which influences world-politics to-day and sways the destiny of Amer-

* Habana, La Moderna poesia, 1911.

ica. With the Canal in view Colombia was mutilated, and lost its proud future of political greatness. It was with the Canal in view that the new state of Panama suddenly appeared—that beautiful American Andorra. It was the Canal, more than any other cause, that brought about the Spanish-American War, in order that no European nation should have any influence on this means of communication between the two oceans. It was the Canal that brought Cuba the Platt Amendment and° the permanent treaty with the United States and the foreign naval stations on our territory. And the Republic of Panama has, in the same way and for the same reasons, similar amendments or treaties or naval stations. If the mere prospect of the Canal gave rise to all this, if all this was the ominous prologue to an event of such weight in the political and social history of the world, only consider what immense consequences will ensue, both immediate and remote, once the longed-for communication between the two oceans is open for the use of the whole world. Consider what a great effect they are bound to exercise on Cuba, partly on account of its exceptional geographical position opposite the Isthmus which is going to be cut, partly because our island is more or less on the highway between New York, the great American metropolis, and Panama, the future centre of a world movement."

The Nicaraguan publicist Don Alejandro Bermúdez, adds in his book *Cuba y Panama:* "Cuba paid a heavy price for the Panama Canal, and she will continue to pay it," and then quotes a note addressed by the American Secretary of State William L. Mercy [*sic* for Marcy] to the Minister James Buchanan, in which Cuba is spoken of as a region falling within the sphere of the United States in virtue of its geographical situation.[2]

It is clear that this view of strategic dependence and of the inevitable results of proximity might lead, little by little, to the conquest of a world. Every new position which is acquired involves rights over others, or opens up ever-widening zones of influence,

[2] In the year 1852 [1854], the United States ministers in England, France, and Spain, who had met at Ostend, proposed to purchase Cuba declaring that if Spain did not accept, the United States "would consider themselves justified, by every consideration, human or divine, in taking it from Spain by force."*

* But the action of these diplomats was disapproved by the administration.

and there is no logical reason for coming to a halt in these wandering enterprises. But we unfortunately know that in international
questions right is in fact no more than a word which serves to
designate the economic or military power of an expansionist community. It is "the right of commerce," "the right of order," "the
right of public health," "the right of civilisation," according as
economic, pacific, prophylactic or cultural pretexts for conquest are
invoked. In dealing with weak peoples, the right of protecting one's
own land is the only "barbarism," and it is "just" that countries,
flags, traditions, and languages which hinder the expansion of the
conquering groups, should disappear even if these be ethically inferior. The progress of the world has followed this rule from the
very beginning, and all those who have not understood it in this
way have been "insurgents" or "rebels" for defending their own
territory. International bullying has been by means of a fantastic
jurisprudence which manages to give the name of "higher right"
to the worst injustices. It is obvious that the political inexperience of the peoples sacrificed also helps towards this end. How
is it otherwise to be explained that the sale of Florida by Spain
should afterwards have given the right to despoil this nation of
Cuba?

Spain, to the grief of her detractors, has always displayed in her
colonial policy a consistent greatness, a strong idealism, a legendary
heroism. But from the administrative and commercial point of
view, she has committed blunder upon blunder, not only in the
17th and 18th centuries, when she was narrow and rigid, but also,
and above all, when, in a clumsy attempt at reaction against past
errors, she desired to be open-minded and tolerant, as during the last
years of her domination in Cuba. To allow the commercial interests of North America to become supreme on the coast of the
Antilles was tantamount to an abdication of sovereignty, allowing
the situation to arise to which Dr. Evelio Rodríguez Lendián refers
in studying the effects of the McKinley Bill. "We realised," he
said, "that we were not economically dependent upon Spain, but
upon the United States, that our powerful neighbour was *de facto*
our trade metropolis; that it needed only a word from this neighbour,
a simple modification of the tariff, for the prosperity and well-being
which Cuba enjoyed to disappear completely, and for the country

THE SHIPWRECK OF THE ANTILLES   37

to sink into ruin and misery; that, in fine, our future depended entirely upon the will of the United States." *

Thus Cuban separatism and Spanish resistance were two noble impulses condemned by circumstances to prove sterile, two manifestations of our character as eternal dreamers. For both of them were based upon generalisations and political theorising, which left out of account the two determining points of the problem, namely, geographical position and economic sovereignty over the island. Even if Spain had succeeded in permanently suppressing revolution, she would retain to-day nothing but a nominal dominion over a territory, and a dependency in which to find posts for her surplus officials. Even if the Cubans had achieved true independence, with no Platt Amendment, they would only have succeeded in postponing the definition by treaty or constitutional provisions of a dependence which existed *de facto*. The lack of foresight on both sides, kindred in race and error, brought about the actual situation. It might perhaps have been avoided at the time, if one side had conceded that wide autonomy which was claimed by the moderate elements in Cuba, and if the other side had adopted those special measures which should ensure the economic possession of the island by the natives, that is to say, true liberty. "The United States are our best customers" was the cry raised at that time by those who were fascinated by momentary profit. But did the United States really consume all that they imported from Cuba? There is reason to believe that they were so supremely clever as to supplant the metropolis, and even the islanders themselves, in the administration of the local wealth; and that in the majority of cases they were merely middlemen, who controlled the export market and regulated the price of products, the best part of the profits remaining in their hands.

The circumstances in which the Cuban revolution took place certainly do not diminish the nobility of the plan of those generous patriots, like José Martí, Máximo Gómez, Antonio Maceo, Bartolomé Masó, the Sanguily brothers, or Antonio Zambrana, who believed in the good faith of the United States. The resolutions adopted by Congress before going to war with Spain proclaimed

* Cf. Lendián's *Los Estados Unidos, Cuba y el Canal de Panama.* Habana, Imp. Avisador Comercial, 1909.

their disinterestedness, and defended the Americans "emphatically" (as they say in New York) against having "the least intention to exercise sovereignty, jurisdiction, or control over Cuba." They constantly insisted on the point that "the Cuban people was, and of right ought to be free and independent." But all good diplomacy has always done the opposite of what it says. And the romantic impulse of the Cuban revolution, which stirred the youth of the Continent, and impelled those of us who were still boys to make demonstrations in the streets, in those heroic days when Estrada Palma and Gonzalo de Quesada were wandering in exile, inflaming men's hearts with their speeches; the triumphal sacrifice of the *guerrilleros* who watered the jungle with their blood, struggling with those of their own kin in the name of an impossible national ideal; the thrilling epic of an indomitable people pressing towards a hope, breaking away from their own fathers under the fascination and bedazzlement of a great piece of international Quixotism; all that had soared into the air, lighting up the horizons and the pathways of the sea, fell lamentably to earth, like the burnt papers and broken sticks of those gigantic fireworks which had nurtured for years the childlike credulity of a race. With a debilitated Spain, where politicians who had been unable to foresee the disaster continued to carry on their eternal struggles for primacy; with a weak Cuban nation, eaten up by the ambition of factions and bosses; with a Continent thunder-struck, all that stood fast as iron, final and categorical, were Articles 3, 4, 6, and 7 of the so-called Platt Amendment:

"*Article III.* The Government of Cuba consents that the United States may exercise the right to intervene for the preservation of Cuban Independence, the maintenance of a government adequate for the protection of life, property, and individual liberty, and for discharging the obligations with respect to Cuba imposed by the Treaty of Paris on the United States, now to be assumed and undertaken by the Government of Cuba.

"*Article IV.* The acts of the United States in Cuba during its military occupancy thereof are ratified and validated, and all lawful rights acquired thereunder shall be maintained and protected.

"*Article VI.* The Island of Pines shall be *omitted* from the boundaries of Cuba specified in the Constitution, the title thereto being left to future adjustment by treaty.

"Article VII. To enable the U. S. to maintain the Independence of Cuba, and to *protect* the people thereof, as well as for its own defence, the Government of Cuba will sell or lease to the U. S. lands necessary for coaling or naval stations, at certain specified points, to be agreed upon with the President of the United States." *

One thing which gives the measure of the portentous illusion under which some politicians live in the greater number of the Spanish-American republics—an illusion skilfully kept up by the news-agencies of the North—is the frequency with which there flutters through the air, like a dark-hued bird, the statement that "the United States gave her liberty to Cuba and then retired." They do not know that the new methods of economical exploitation, backed by political pressure, make a permanent occupation of small countries almost useless in modern days. It is actually a convenience for the conquering countries to refuse a direct mandate, seeing that a series of subtle provisions or propitious circumstances reserve to them the higher *rôle* of economic dictators, arbiters in internal quarrels, and supreme protectors in international matters.

The situation of Cuba was defined by Mr. Sidney Brooks in *Harper's Weekly,* in an article which was translated and reproduced *in extenso,* without any protest, by *La Discusión* of Havana, thus acquiring a sort of *imprimatur* as a truth recognised by the Cubans themselves.

"When the Republic of Cuba actually stepped upon the international stage," says the writer of the article, "it was seen at once to be neither free nor independent. It was so surrounded with conditions and restrictions, as to be almost as much a vassal as an autonomous state." †

It is sufficient to recall the purchase of arms from Germany by Cuba before the War, which was frustrated by a simple representation from the United States; or the well-known affair of the North American company which obtained the concession for the paving

---

* This is a quotation from the original as given in Malloy's *Treaties,* not an English translation of Ugarte's Spanish version.

† *Harper's Weekly,* LV (Nov. 4, 1911), p. 13.

and sewers of Havana owing to the intervention of the Government of the United States. This concession obliged the Government of Cuba to accept without any objection, and maintaining all its own responsibilities, such modifications as the company desired to introduce in the contract already signed, modifications which in the words of a Cuban politician, "involved both prejudice to the said works, and a lesser guaranty of their efficiency."

After the separation, the Cuban found himself in a peculiar position. Though the blood that he had shed was still fresh and his grievances against the mother country from which he had just separated were still lively, he none the less preserved indelible characteristics, that fundamentally alienated him from the new power which dominated him. Thanks to an illusion of independence he had fallen under another sovereignty, and after emancipating himself from Spain, he realised that she remained mingled with his very being. Between the past and the present the life breath was snuffed out of a new nationality, which had not had time to grow strong nor knew as yet what to rely upon,—a chimera shattered between the conflicting egoisms of men. The shadow of Spain still hung over everything. The shadow of the United States was already reflected on every hand. Where did Cuba stand? [3]

It was this perplexity which was expressed by a Cuban deputy in an article the wit of which barely hides its melancholy:

"The servant handed me a post-card.

" 'From the United States?' I asked.

" 'No, Señor, from the city.'

" 'Ah, yes,' . . . And, in fact, the address said 'Ciudad (City),' in spite of the fact that the card bore a stamp with these words, Postal Card, Two Cents; and the headings: United States of America; Write only the address on this side. I was just about

---

[3] In reality Cuban national sentiment, which was growing strong before independence, has declined ever since. The deputy, Don Ezquiel García Ensenat, said in the Chamber of Representatives, in so many words: "The son of Spanish parents born in Cuba was always a Cuban; and this truth does not destroy the other truth, that the son of an Anglo-Saxon is always an Anglo-Saxon. Here the North American preserves all his customs, his character, his prejudices, and above all his national feeling; having gone so far, after the military occupation of our land, as to import his very food, and carry away his very dead."

to get indignant when I bethought me that we had no grounds for complaint, since we had gained something, for we had had for some time past other post-cards which, in addition to the portrait—of whom? Of Martí? Of Cespedes? Of Maceo? No! Of *Jefferson* —had the stamp defaced with such charming inscriptions as *Havana, Carrier's Dept.*

"The card required an immediate answer. I dressed hurriedly. I wrote a note. I stuck a stamp on it with a picture of three palm-trees or a steamboat, I don't know which, though I certainly remember that it was not the arms of the Republic. And I ran to a neighbouring letter-box. But I stopped and hesitated before the official apparatus, for on it was printed, in conspicuous characters: *Pull Down Letters, U. S. Mail,* and I suspected that it might belong to one of the new American Companies—perhaps to a *Pull Down Co. Ltd.* . . .

"We went to the elevated railway, and as I had pointed out to my companion that there was a shield with the arms of Spain on the Chamber, another on the Customs House, another large marble one on the Treasury, and that on every gate of the quays shone the castles and lions, or the arms of Havana with a royal crown, he said to me, as we got out of the car:

" 'Look! This street is called Calle del General Enna, in honour of the fact that he had a row with Narciso López. It comes out in front of the President's palace, which in its turn displays on the principal entrance the arms of Spain, carved in marble, with no signs of the arms of Cuba, even below them.'

"I interrupted him with a request that he would come with me to the post, so as to go on with our conversation. I walked up to a counter. On the wall was a big almanac, on which was to be read *Tuesday* 17*th May;* and underneath the copper plate on which was engraved *Packages* was a temporary placard badly translating it as *Buzón.* The word *Registry* was over three slides, and *Certificados* only over one. Above others were *Money Orders, Stamps, General Delivery,* etc., and each of the nine hundred pigeon-holes had as an ornament a bronze American eagle. Nine hundred eagles!"

I knew these details beforehand, and many others which I omit, so as to avoid multiplying quotations; and when I observed the balance and interplay of the actual life of the island at close quarters, what astonished me—let me say it once for all—was the vigorous current of Cubanism, ever increasing and widening, irrespective of realities; as if a moral force, so strong that nothing can make an impression upon it, were actually able to hold in check the material forces in opposition to it.

Though the country is economically conquered and internationally immobilised, the spirit of Martí none the less protests and rebels in the enthusiasms of its people; in the ideals of its youth, in that general throb of life which, far removed from ambition or venality, interprets the collective instincts in its pure essence. It is true that among the landowners, merchants, and politicians, individuals are not wanting who will make a compact with the invader, and more or less indirectly encourage infiltration, giving as their vague excuse—since all they require is a pretext to put forward—the non-existence of any danger, or the impossibility of averting it. It is true that the necessity for keeping afloat and prospering in an atmosphere saturated with intrusive Anglo-Saxonism obliges some persons to conceal their ideas and act as the servants of this triumphant force. It is true that there are some so blinded by snobbery as to regard the loss of their nationality as a step upwards. The honourable, vigorous masses of the urban and rural population maintain a distrustful and hostile attitude in face of the hustling foreigner, who breaks the even flow of their customs, annihilates their nascent history, and monopolises their national wealth.

All that is needed is an authoritative summons or a timely call, for the forests to be filled as of yore with *guerrilleros*, ready once more to give their lives for an impossible independence. But who would distribute arms to them now? The very statue of Maceo, set up on the sea-front as a challenge to the prejudice against the coloured race, is symbolic of their state of mind. The illusions have vanished which made possible the idea of the original intervention, with its apparently generous motives. There remains a deep-lying uneasiness due to the chaffing of their *amour propre*. This feeling of hostility, added to the constant restraint which everyone finds himself forced to exercise so as not to furnish pretexts for intervention—so much so that all the activities of life are subordinated to this idea—has created among the lower classes and the younger generation an atmosphere of discontent, which is aggravated by such conditions as that prevailing on the Isle of Pines, where the land has passed almost entirely into the hands of North American owners, and Cuba exercises an illusory jurisdiction, subject, however, to that "future adjustment of ownership" provided for by the Platt Amendment. But at this point we are faced with a most curious contradiction. Although popular sentiment is unfavourable to the United States, an insurrection will never be possible in Cuba; and not only does this apply as against foreign influence, but even as against the local organs of government set up under its auspices. War is made by means of arms, money and transport rather than ideals. To whom would Cuba sell her produce? Who would equip her with stores? What cables, what telegraph lines, what wireless masts would help her to communicate with the world? The attraction exercised by North America is a misfortune which could only be shaken off on that remote day, on which the United States might be conquered, as a consequence of a new conflagration, and in the midst of a world-wide disaster. But in this *débâcle* would not Cuba perish also?

Every imperial power employs the same methods of penetration. Pressure exerted upon the politicians, whose political ambitions are forwarded or not according to the varying intensity of their goodwill to the dominant race; pressure upon the financial magnates, making them dependent upon interests foreign to those of their country, and sometimes harmful to her; pressure upon the upper classes of society, which are fascinated by means of the elegancies of New York, and so induced to treat slightingly the life of their own native land; pressure, in the last place, upon the foreign colonies, and especially the Spanish, which by its number and possessions might constitute a nucleus of resistance, by means of flattering their interests and interweaving them with those of the invader. Thus every movement, every act, and every instant of the popular life in certain circles is influenced, so that admiration having been aroused in some, cupidity in others, and discouragement in yet others, and the way having been barred to all that does not contain some germ of the North American spirit of interests, the very flag of Cuba, floating in the blue sky, ends by casting on the pavement the shadow of a Yankee eagle.*

The unfortunate experiences of a writer with the proprietor of a newspaper drew attention to how far this tendency may go. Just after a visit to the United States, the owner of *El Diario Español* wrote to its editor, Don Adelardo Novo: ". . . You have now, of course, seen the result of the elections in this country; and as I feel it in the air that they will end by swallowing poor Cuba, I think we must take to changing, from time to time, our established sys-'tem of attacking the North Americans." To this the editor of the paper replied violently: "You insist in your letter on the change which the *Diario Español* is to undergo in obsequiously welcoming the policy of expansion. This is impossible. I had already learnt by cable of the result of the elections in the United States, and could see in it no reason which should lead us to vary the policy of the paper. It would not be a very noble *rôle* for a Spanish paper to play, to associate itself with the plans of our enemies—enemies both of Cuba and of everything which smacks of the Latin spirit. To walk humbly before them would be to contribute towards the prevalence in North America of the belief that we Latins are little less than contemptible. There can be no other programme for the *Diario Español* than that of defending the interests of the race in America, constantly putting up a barrier against the expansionist plans of those eternal instigators of Central American revolutions, fomented with the express purpose of fishing in troubled waters. While there still exists in Cuba a Cuban who, from love for the traditions of his race, claims to preserve his native independence, conquered with the loss of so much blood, and turned into a fratricidal strife, the *Diario Español* should stand at his side or disappear."

It was in this atmosphere of struggle that I had to give my lecture on the American problem, which was really on the case of Cuba.

The function took place at the University with the Rector, Dr. Berriel, in the chair, and the formal presentation was made by Don

* To test the accuracy of these statements would involve long and careful investigation. It can only be pointed out here that Señor Ugarte does not distinguish between the acts of officials and those of private interests.

Evelio Rodríguez Lendián, Dean of the Faculty of Laws. There were present, to quote one of the papers, "the *élite* of the intellectual society of Havana," and no protest was made against the thesis which I put forward. The Press made favourable reference to it, especially the semi-official daily *El Trinfo* which said:

"Those same aspirations which make the greatness of Ugarte, were one of the dreams of our never enough lamented martyr José Martí, and are destined to be the labarum brandished and carried to victory by a healthy, vigorous generation, which shall make these Utopias into a religion."

Cuba was not alone responsible for the Cuban situation. Some responsibility was also borne by Latin America. Such at least was my impression when I visited the then President of the Republic. The portrait of General Gómez can be drawn in four lines. A soldier, rough and frank, with keen eyes, looking more like a *caudillo* than a statesman, who listens much and speaks but little, and suggests more than he says; he expresses himself with some eloquence, but at times reveals what he wants more by gestures than by words; a dour energy, a rudimentary diplomacy, and a touch of the subtle shrewdness of the *guerrillero* complete the chief outlines of this well-marked personality, with its characteristic and fundamentally Cuban traits. After the short introduction by Don Baldomero Fonseca, the Argentine Minister (I had not yet been laid under an interdict by the Government of my country), the President suddenly said to me, as if he were continuing a conversation:

"You reproach us with not having put up a good defence of our legacy of Spanish civilisation. But what have you all done to encourage us, to support us, to make us feel that we were not alone?"

This reproach stirred the very depths of the South American soul. "It is not we who broke the link"—Cuba seemed to call to us through the mouths of its representatives—; "it was you who broke it, in allowing it to be cut." I afterwards heard Don Orestes Ferrara, President of the Chamber of Deputies, say something to the same effect, when he gave me a dinner at which were present, among others, Don Carlos Fonts Sterling, Don Carlos Armenteros, Don Fernándo Ortíz, Don Ezequiel García, Don Mario García Kohly,

Don José A. González Lanuza, Don Ricardo Dolz, Don Jesús Castellanos, and Don Manuel María Coronado, editor of *La Discusión*.

My first relations with the Minister for Foreign Affairs, an office then held by the old patriot Don Manuel Sanguily, were at a luncheon given me by Don Modesto Morales Díaz, editor of *El Triunfo*. There was also present Don Ramón A. Catalá, President of the Press Association and editor of *El Figaro*. The Chancellor was a nervous, talkative man who improvised questions and answers, carrying on a dialogue with himself, and did not let fall a single word on the racial conflict which divides the New World. But when the subject was mentioned, a gleam like that of a *machete* in the backwoods lit up his eyes.

Among the intellectuals whose acquaintance I made, I will mention at random, with the omissions inevitable owing to the lapse of time, Don Sergio Cuevas Zequeira, Don Wilfredo Fernández, editor of *El Comercio*, Don Eliseo Giberga, Massaguer the caricaturist, the brothers Carbonell, Don Juan M. Dihigo, Secretary of the University, Marco-Antonio Dolz, Enrique Fernández Miuyares, Federico Urbach, Carlos de Velasco, Lola Rodríguez de Tió and Enrique Fontanílls.

I can confidently say that I did not hear a voice raised in favour of abdication or the abandonment of the ideals of independence. If the metaphor were not too daring, I would say that men's souls were on tiptoe and stretching upwards to receive the light of independence which still entered through the bars of Cuban liberty.

It is very easy to condemn the attitude of others from afar, and to trace austere rules of conduct from the comfortable seat of the on-looker, free from all the influences of the *milieu*. But it is quite another thing to live in the country, to be subject to those forces of attraction, those commitments and influences implied by permanent residence in one place. It would be easier for the crew of a ship to wish to hold aloof from its course and navigation, or for the inhabitants of this planet to seek to escape from its orbit and wander in others, than to keep oneself isolated, immune, and alien to the currents which sometimes, in the course of the centuries, overwhelm the destiny of a nation.

The economic and moral forces which direct Cuba, wrested from their course by the lasting effect of deeds apparently harmless in their origin, and prisoners of the consequences of irreparable errors, are, by the fateful effect of realities and the attractive force of interests, committed to attitudes and movements which are reflected with more or less intensity in the corporate life of the nation. But, I thought, what is true in the case of a small and isolated country, would not be so, supposing that this country was closely bound up with others of the same origin, and attempted, with the moral support of a continent, to recover control over its movements; seeking out new markets for its produce, creating mutual interests, and incurring risks which would be counterbalanced by the advantages of union.

Public men who are responsible for the destiny of a community, if they hold their direct ambitions subordinate to the higher good of the community in the future, have to consider various hypotheses, and place themselves in imagination in every possible situation, foreseeing the contingencies which may present themselves as each of them arises. Hence it often occurs that there exist within the same nation persons of equal authority and sincerity who advocate opposite solutions, though inspired by an equal anxiety for the public weal. It is therefore desirable to launch out right and left in imagination into the unrealised, sending out great exploring raids, and ask ourselves what would happen if, after direct consultation with her sister republics of the South, Cuba were one day to raise a loan in France, to buy locomotives in Germany, and to engage Japanese officers to organise her army; and if, on the inevitable protest of the ministers of North America, instead of bowing to it as usual, Cuba were to answer that, as a tribute to the good faith of the United States, she desired to prove before the world that the promises of twenty years ago had been fulfilled, that she was free to exercise her own choice, and that, far from weakening the bonds which unite her with the Anglo-Saxon Republic, this would draw them closer. The possibility of bombardment and the landing of troops may be debated. All-powerful as a nation may be, it dare not incur universal reprobation by committing *ex abrupto* a crying injustice, especially if Latin America as a whole were to make its moral solidarity felt. There can be no doubt that action would at first be indirect. Would the United States close their tariff walls against Cuban products? Since some of these are indispensable to life in North America, the commercial reprisals would probably be of a mixed character, only striking those commodities which would not involve retaliation, and leaving the rest alone. Would they foment a revolution by the aid of a few ambitious individuals? Cuban patriotism alone can give the answer to this question. For my own part I am of the opinion, that a Government capable of these steps would be so popular that not a word would be heard in contradiction of it. Would they intrigue to bring about difficulties with Europe? To resort to this expedient would be to forget that the economic emancipation of Cuba would indirectly benefit Europe, to which new markets would be thrown open which are now closed to her. Imperialist policy would be bound to hesitate, until it could invent an avowable cause of conflict, which, by a preliminary preparation of public opinion, would enable her to make her action formidably felt. But there can be no doubt that this action would end by disarranging all programmes. Moreover, there is nobody either in Cuba, in South America, or in the whole world, capable of making such an attempt at the present moment. It might perhaps have been done, but since it was not done in time, perhaps it never can be. And this is the bitter conclusion which presents itself at every turn when we analyse our situation.

The young men of Havana, just after my visit, summoned assemblies and meetings,[4] and founded Latin-American centres of defence under the presidency of Roger de Lauria, Sergio la Villa, Guerra Núñez, Martínez Alonso, and many other enthusiastic spirits of the younger generation. The *milieu*, circumstances, and dis-

[4] "The first public act of the Latin-American Association in Cuba—a body which owed its origin to the inspiration of the Argentine writer Manuel Ugarte, who is going from country to country preaching Latin-American solidarity as the only possible remedy against Anglo-Saxon hegemony in the New World, which, without this check, might become a melancholy reality—was a truly fine one. We must congratulate those who with the enthusiasm of youth and conviction have taken upon their shoulders the hard work of maintaining an active propaganda which cannot be of the slightest tangible and immediate benefit to those who accomplish it, unless it be the moral well-being produced in the good citizen by the fulfilment of his duty to his country." (From a leader in *El Triunfo*, of Havana, February 26, 1912.)

couragements checked the first impulse; but their spirited attempt remains as a precedent.

When I went into the interior of the island and came into contact with its amazing natural riches, the impression was increased. The plains, of a marvellous verdure, from which rise tall palm-trees, extend their rolling undulations beneath a delirious sky, strewn with white clouds. In the motionless, heated atmosphere, above the grass and the mud of the uneven roads, cut up by the deep ruts of the wagons, which go slowly on their way at the measured pace of the oxen, flutter swarms of butterflies, which give the rural landscape a curiously idyllic suggestion. One realises what fighting must have been like in the broken surfaces of these lands, with their exuberant vegetation, in which men and armies disappear as if by diabolical agency, in an orgy of ambushes and surprise attacks. From time to time there appears between the trees the straw hat of a rustic. One knows that he is on horseback by the rhythmical movement which appears to rock him among the leaves, as if an invisible wave caused him to rise and fall, or as if the palpitating tropical soil were carrying him on its breast, heaving with sultriness and fatigue. The telegraph wires, and the very railway by which we are travel- ling, seem a profanation in the midst of this tameless nature. Great, solemn birds cleave the still space, and as the clouds float close to the top of the hills, they seem at times to gather suddenly in the sky and descend on top of the trees. Maize fields, coconut groves, coffee plantations, and plantain trees succeed one another in a whirl of riches. And the little wooden houses, with porches in front of them, before which the horses doze, hitched to a post by the halter; the melancholy, straying oxen which pause and gaze fixedly at the passing trains; the lonely horizon beneath the glow- ing streaks of the twilight, give one a romantic sensation of liberty, poise, and woodland serenity, which makes one remember with con- tempt the well-regulated life of Europe. Happiness is not to be found in London or Paris; it is not to be found in Havana itself, where modern comfort and formulas are gradually sweeping away the last vestiges of its pleasant ancestral life. Perhaps true, simple happiness is to be found in these fertile, fragrant plains, across which there vibrates from time to time a plaintive song; where white-robed women seem to be waiting at their doors, as if for their illusions to take bodily form, and where nature retains her mystery, her rustic charm, and her strong, invigorating sap. . . .

Some of the little stations bear the names of foreign landowners and in certain places the signs have been violently torn down by mute inglorious patriots. On arriving at Camaguey, in the patriarchal hotel fringed by water-jars and tropical plants, where they offer me novel fruits,—custard-apples, *chirimoyas*, *mamés*, and pine-apples,—and from whence I can see graceful feminine silhouettes, wrapped in pale-coloured draperies, passing along the streets, followed by a chaperon, and flirting their fans, I feel myself to be really in the heart of Cuba. "Mixtures of blood, far from decreasing the worth of peoples, merely augment it," says Jean Finot in his work on race prejudice. And perhaps it is the result of a mixture of Indian, Spaniard, and African that one notices as one enters the animated, turbulent streets, full of vociferous groups, discussing the episodes of the latest cock-fight. When we observe nature we see that one form of defence for creatures of small size is to become "non-comestible." The creature which is refractory to, or unassimilable by, those who would sacrifice it has in this fact its sole guaranty of survival.

Naturally, all things are relative. Methods are perfected in the course of the centuries. The imperialism of the earliest ages annexed the inhabitants in the guise of slaves. Afterwards it annexed the land without its inhabitants. Now the procedure is being established of annexing only its wealth, without either land or inhabitants, thus reducing to a minimum the expenditure of the forces of domination. A nation which holds in its hands the control of the wealth and commerce of another country is in reality master both of it and of its inhabitants, not only in things appertaining to the economic order, but even in matters of internal and external policy, since the whole framework of a country in modern times rests upon finance, which regulates its varied activities.

At Guantánamo, La Caimanera, and, above all, in the property belonging to North Americans, with its wireless installation, its coal-boats, its warehouses, and its cruisers anchored in the bay, one feels the presence of a new Rome, keeping silent guard around its Mediterranean.

I arrived at Santiago de Cuba by the *Cuba Railroad Company* one evening when a demonstration of the coloured population was being held in honour of the deputy Don Evaristo Estenoz. A crowd on foot and on horseback was descending from the station to the centre of the city, surrounding the open carriage of the *caudillo*. Perspiring men, women with babies in their arms, and a crowd of inarticulate *negrillos* were clamouring round the leader. It was a rebellion of slavedom, which, though abolished by law, is in fact maintained by prejudices slow to die.

Santiago de Cuba is a beautiful city, prosperous and gay, with the characteristic aspect of tropical towns. Light, flowers, beautiful women, abundant gesticulation, grated windows, and, together with these customs arising from their own ideals, the commerce, exchange, and life of to-day. I thought I noticed a more ferocious nationalism in this city. Provincial capitals, preserved from the cosmopolitanism concentrated in the capitals, almost always maintain more vigorously their distinctive character. Havana is in daily contact with the world. Hence the apparent superficiality which we notice in some centres. Santiago de Cuba has grown great by cultivating almost exclusively the characteristics of its colonial life, and this explains its strong Cubanism.

I found this tendency in particular at the luncheon given me by the Press Association, in the *Vista Alegre* theatre. The speeches of the President of this Association, Señor Espinosa; of Don Joaquín Navarro (*Ducazcal*) and of Señores Valencia, Aristigueta and Clarens, gave utterance to such deep and pulsing nationalism that we felt ourselves to be enfolded in the national flag and full of a sense of its destiny.

The scheme by which some persons attempted to stultify the campaign I had undertaken broke down in Santiago as it had previously broken down in Havana. It seemed to some that the cleverest way to silence the voice which I raised was to represent me as an enemy of Cuban independence and the champion of an impossible return to the Spanish colonial system, in a country which had just come through a war of secession and in which the natural passions of this struggle still survived. But good sense intervened. What I was defending was quite another thing. Who ever could have dreamed of recreating situations which had been definitely abolished, by reviving fantastic viceroyalties in the 20th century?

I was concerned solely with the spirit and the soul left by Spain in these new lands, that is to say, in reality, with our nationality itself; for, if we look at it well, this is no more than the resultant of our ethnical and cultural antecedents.

Defence of the Castilian tongue, opposition to the Anglo-American conquest, the struggle for the maintenance of our present autonomy, these are acts of true independence. This is how everybody understood it; and so fell harmless to the ground this first stone thrown at me by those who, throughout the rest of my journey, never ceased to attack me, seeking by intrigue what they could not obtain by other means.

On the last day of November, after passing a month in Cuba, I continued my voyage in a little coasting boat, *en route* for the Republic of Santo Domingo, at the capital of which I arrived two days later.

This country had just gone through one of its painful upheavals, a *coup d'état*, revolution, or whatever it was—in which President Cáceres had lost his life. I had been warned of it before leaving Cuba. I was shown a leader on the timeliness of my visit published in the *Listín Diario*, then the official organ of the Government of Santo Domingo.[5] But alas, civil discords are so frequent and

---

[5] This newspaper said: "We have been informed that a group of writers in this capital was thinking of cabling to Manuel Ugarte, who is at present in Havana, suggesting that he should not carry out at present his plan of visiting this Santo Domingo of Guzmán, as the famous Argentine publicist intends. It appears that the young intellectuals who are preparing to cable to Señor Ugarte in this sense, are doing so because they would regret it if the South American *littérateur* did not have the reception he deserves, owing to the natural retirement in which the members of our society are at present living; but we believe that, though Ugarte's reception cannot, of course, be as splendid as we could wish, he would none the less be fêted as he deserves, and would have the opportunity of hearing from the lips of authoritative citizens what we think here about our future, and this fervent Latin-American idealist would observe the laudable efforts which we are making to elevate the republic.

"If this fruitful thinker comes, it will be in a few days' time, and men's minds will then be more calm; the natural quiet which is undoubtedly bound to prevail will allow us to be more assiduous with this messenger of peace

normal in some republics that to omit to visit them in the middle of these disturbances would be to give up the idea of really knowing them.

The island where Columbus landed, at the outset of that portentous series of discoveries and explorations which was to trace new shores round unknown seas, was, from the beginning, the region of the New World most ravaged by wars, revolutions, conspiracies, and military landings. But throughout all its vicissitudes and blood-stained endurance, under the original colonial régime, during the French irruption, in the midst of the second period of Spanish domination, in the struggle against the Haitian invasion, during the third war of independence, and the innumerable mutinies and insurrections of its final years of autonomous existence, we can observe, like a central connecting thread, the same stubborn spirit, uniting the filibustering of early days with the endemic spirit of opposition of later days, as if by a chain traced with links of blood around an impossible dream of liberty.

In most cases of shipwreck, it is not by fault of the boat or of the sea, but of the winds. And it has been the winds of international ambition which have brought about all this miserable slaughter. In the early days, France tried to supplant Spain in Santo Domingo, and England supported Spain in order to weaken France; in latter days, the United States completed the defeat of the Latin ideal, by asserting their domination where Spain and France had broken down.

The racial wars in the island, like the party wars in every division of it, were nothing but contributory actions or blind instruments placed at the service of the subtleties of international policy. The one reproach which may be laid at the doors of the inhabitants of Santo Domingo is the nervous ingenuousness which made them fall into the toils, dissipating their combative energies in fratricidal

and progress to our peoples than those imagine, who think it would be better to advise Ugarte not to visit the country. Let the leader of South American youth, the friend of peace, come, and may his fraternal words act as a bond to unite in duty and love those who love their country and desire for her an eternity of good fortune and great achievement." *Listín Diario.* Nov. 25, 1911.

struggles which led the way to their own subjugation. The situation was not determined by climate or atavistic tendencies only, as some allege. It was also the result of diplomacy, which brings about shipwrecks in order to pick up what remains on the shore, sometimes sacrificing sources of new life which might have borne fruit in history by paying their tribute to universal progress. Left to themselves, the inhabitants of the Antilles would have developed smoothly, in accord with their own character and the cycle of ideas implanted there by the first universities of Latin America. We repeat, the fault is not that of Santo Domingo. And if one day a balance of historical responsibility were drawn up, we should realise that the little Antilles, far from having perished by their own mistakes, have been overwhelmed by what we might call the vortex of civilisation.

My first vision of the country on landing was the Customs House under the management of North American officials. As a guaranty for the payment of the interest and sinking fund on the total debt of the country (20 million gold pesos), the Government of Santo Domingo found itself obliged in 1907 to hand over this first installment of its autonomy to the United States. To suppose that such a concession may be temporary, is to be ignorant of the tendencies of history. Santo Domingo hoped to redeem itself in fifteen years, i. e. in half the time stipulated in the contract; and with this object it made the necessary sacrifices, suppressing expenses and increasing the revenue from internal taxation. But in these cases it is to the economic and political interest of the mortgagee that the debt should not be liquidated.* Later on we shall see the same procedure in speaking of the economic situation in Nicaragua and that of the railway from Guayaquil to Quito, which are in agreement with the higher principles of financial penetration.

At the end of 1911, when I arrived at Santo Domingo, the course of action which was to develop afterwards was still in the latent stage. In the harbour rose the motionless grey turrets of the

* The Caribbean policy of the United States may have been influenced by benevolence, by fear of European intrusion, and by desire for economic opportunities. Of these possible motives Señor Ugarte can only see the last. He is no more inaccurate than those who will only see the first or the first and second.

cruisers, and among the people were circulating, like a cold breath, rumours presaging the future upheaval.

The town is gay, with brightly painted houses, *plaças* in the Andalusian style, and broad streets full of light, rapid vehicles. The old churches and colonial monuments recall the splendour of what was once "La Española," the first flower in America of the vast Spanish empire. In a crypt is an urn containing the remains of Columbus. The simple, domestic life, intensified by the natural retirement following immediately on a political crisis, and the dread of the foreign menace, was no obstacle to an open-hearted hospitality. At the Athenæum I made the acquaintance of the best minds of the country. In the school managed by Señora de Henríquez, I became acquainted with the praiseworthy educational efforts which were prospering in spite of every difficulty. And in some homes which were thrown open to me with generous courtesy, I realised that the little town has a large heart.

When I launched out on the subject of my tour in the fine hall at the Athenæum, through whose open windows could be seen the sea and the foreign war-ships, I felt an atmosphere of concentrated attention which I shall never forget. Not a murmur of applause was heard throughout the lecture, nor was that which broke out at the end tumultuous. But the fervour with which they all gripped my hand, and the tears which I saw drop from many an eye, spoke volumes. As I had dispensed with rhetorical ornament, the public dispensed with conventional applause, and the emotion which oppressed us was a silent one. The lecturer had merely said that Latin America was being stifled, and that the invaders drew their support from our own lack of discipline. But these elementary truths harmonised with men's secret thoughts, and when the problem was carried beyond the national boundaries and transferred to the territory of the Continent, the conflict took on a wider aspect; and once the idea of solidarity was before them, the hope of redemption arose in men's minds.

Argentina, Chile, and Brazil appeared in the south of the Continent as the saving force which, in combination with Latin Europe, might put the brake on events. Everybody knew that the policy of cohesion and of "selfish altruism" which was to guarantee the common security by defending the other kindred nations of the Continent, was far from meeting with general acceptance in the South. But a hope was dawning that other men and new generations would see the urgency of this course.

The thesis which I maintained during my journey was that of an *entente* of the Spanish peoples of America, in order to ensure their autonomy and oppose a solid front and a common attitude of resistance, every time one of the strong nations of the world tried to abuse its power by subjugating piecemeal territories which ought to be considered as forming one whole.

It is evident that this general attitude of foresight is bound to apply particularly to the United States, not by any express wish of ours, but as a logical result of the policy of absorption which this country is developing. But the original and underlying proposal, in its higher moral bearing, involved no particular hostility against any country. It tended towards the preservation of our nationalities as much in the economic and cultural as in the political sphere and the defense of ourselves against everything which might impair or modify the present situation.

The President of the Athenæum of Santo Domingo, Don Federico Henríquez y Carvajal, whose brother was afterwards President of the Republic in the trying days of the North American occupation, Américo Lugo, delegate for his country to the Pan-American Congress at Buenos Aires, Julio Cestero, who then occupied the position of Minister of the Republic of Santo Domingo in Cuba, and such intellectuals of the country as I met: Federico García Godoy, Logroño, Piñeyro, Pérez Alfonseca, Rafael Sánchez, Primitivo Herrera, Del Castillo Márquez, and many others of acknowledged distinction whose names elude the pen in a hasty enumeration—all felt the urgency of this continental necessity.

But the little republic was doomed to perish. When I set sail again, I felt a presentiment that I was taking leave of a country in its death throes. Five years later the events were precipitated to which I shall refer at the end of this book. A captain of the North American navy swept away all that remained of the national sovereignty, stifling all protests amidst the silence and inaction of the Continent, whose eyes were blinded by what was happening in Europe.

I did not visit the neighbouring republic of Haiti, because it was already overwhelmed by imperialism, and because it is painful to learn by experience that history has its sanguinary ironies. A country with a coloured population like Haiti, "protected" and "civilised" by a nation which isolates and persecutes the negroes in its cities, closes its universities to them, and burns them in the public squares, is one of those paradoxes which sometimes rise to the imagination of great humourists. There has never been in the whole history of humanity a people which has despised, harassed, and exterminated the negroes with more fury; no race throughout the centuries has had a greater repulsion and hatred for them. And it is precisely this community that has set up its flag definitely in Haiti in the name of "higher principles," supplanting the original rights of Catholic Spain which discovered it, of liberal and equalitarian France, and its own movement towards national independence, in so far as that was reasonable. Absurdity is one of the forms of national logic, but never has it presented itself in such a flagrant form as in this case.*

I only succeeded in unravelling the intrigue which prevented me from stopping at the island of Porto Rico a few years later, when the President of the Chamber of Representatives, Don José de Diego, remonstrated with me for my omission, and we discovered that my telegrams from Havana and Santiago de Cuba had not arrived at their destination. Of course, my intention had also been to go as far as San Juan, the capital of one of the most prosperous sections of the archipelago. The very special conditions under which this region has remained since the Spanish-American War increased this desire.

Under Spanish domination, Porto Rico enjoyed ample autonomy. It had two Chambers and an Executive Cabinet. All the mechanism of administration was in the hands of Porto Ricans. The mother country confined itself to nominating a governor-general, and the island was in reality independent. The "old-fashioned" monarchy of Spain, "old and behind the times," had implanted the most liberal régime it is possible to conceive. When, without insurrection

---

* There were about 4,000,000 negroes in the United States in 1865. There are 12,000,00 at present. Is this extermination? The writer overlooks the benevolent work of the Fiskes and Rosenwalds and the numerous efforts at racial harmony which are constantly being made.

or revolution, or unpleasantness with the mother country, by the simple imposition of a treaty following on a war, Porto Rico passed into the power of the United States, matters were radically changed. I have seen notes of the Bank of Porto Rico in English. The "modern" democracy of the "land of equality" imposed other customs. In contrast to the former régime, there was a military government, an upper chamber nominated by the President of the United States, a North American bureaucracy, and a supreme tribunal emanating from Washington.

Spain committed every possible error in America. But one day the world will understand—and so shall we ourselves, deceived though we are by interested denunciations and tendentious discourses—that her administration, calumniated by those who aspire to supplant her, was often, while it lasted, more mild than that of other colonising countries. Hostile interpretations have gained such credit that it almost seems a heresy to recall in this connection anything but "inquisitorial obscurantism." But the most superficial investigation suffices to prove that the slaughter of Indians in America was carried out equally by Anglo-Saxons and Spaniards, with the sole difference that while the Anglo-Saxons continued it up to 1900, and scarcely a hundred thousand Indians survive in the United States, the Spaniards ceased in 1800, and there are fifty millions left in Spanish America.* The proof is accessible to all that slavery was abolished in the Spanish colonies much earlier than in the English colonies, and that the negro, who even up to the present day is a prisoner in the United States, enjoys the widest liberty in those regions which were dependent on Spain. The contradiction becomes even more glaring when we compare the system formerly prevalent in Porto Rico with that which is beginning to-day.[6]

* There are more than 300,000 Indians still surviving in the United States. The original Indian population was much greater in Spanish America than in the United States. It was likewise more civilised and docile, and therefore more worth preserving as a labour supply. A large element of Indian labour also explains, in a measure, Spain's attitude toward negro slavery: the negroes were not needed.

[6] The Governor of Porto Rico, Mr. Yager, said at Washington, whither he had been summoned by President Wilson and Mr. Baker, the Secretary of War, "We shall never withdraw our flag from Porto Rico or Santo

Hitherto the magic of words has dazzled us. In the name of "liberty," "progress," and "civilisation," we have been made to do or accept whatever was favourable to foreign interests: separatism, free trade, Pan-Americanism, Monroism. And we, eternally credulous, in our anxiety to equal the great peoples, have ministered to their interests. Foreign interests have disguised themselves as general principles or noble sentiments, and we have been unable to see through them to their true intentions, when they have furnished us with the means of "balancing our finances," when they have helped us to "achieve liberty," when they have lent us their support in "overthrowing tyrants," when they have offered us aid to "obtain victory" over some neighbour nation of the same origin or when, in the name of "humanitarianism" or "peace," they have interfered with the issue of our disputes. These fine protestations merely served to enable the predominating influences to develop to greater advantage.

As one travels through the Antilles, and reviews their recent history, this painful truth strikes the eye with peculiar force. Latin America has been duped, as Spain was duped in entering into a war of sentiment. The tendencies of this body of nations have led to its ruin. But when we consider as a whole the general causes of the disaster which may prejudice the characteristic development of these peoples in the future history of the world, two complementary phenomena rise clearly and evidently before our eyes: the knowledge which others possess of our defects; and the inexperience which prevents us from foreseeing the consequences of idealism.

Domingo, for to maintain order and encourage prosperity in the Caribbean, it is essential that we should exercise political, military, and naval control there. The United States dominate at present all the lands bordering on the Caribbean Sea, and though we have no imperialist tendencies, we hold it both a duty and a necessity to keep the West Indies as a safeguard of the Monroe Doctrine."

CHAPTER III

THE ROCK OF MEXICO

Salient features of the Mexican character—President Madero's illusion—Palace intrigues—North American and Mexican opinions—Popular agitation—Internal and international politics—A pacific conference—Mr. Knox's tour—The vital force of a people.

BEFORE setting sail for Mexico, it dawned upon me what scope and proportions my tour was acquiring, by no wish of my own, but by mere force of circumstances. The telegraphic intelligence which I received in Cuba, the references in newspapers, and the resolutions carried by important bodies in the Mexican capital, revealed such great enthusiasm that I saw I should have to go much further than I had foreseen. It was not as a literary man that I was waited for in Mexico; and if some remembered my works, it was only as shedding light on my past. The masses and the younger generation were preparing to receive me as the author of a doctrine of resistance. In that mutilated country the idea found a wonderfully favourable soil. It was really an idea which was on its way to them, and only thus can we explain the avalanches let loose during the struggle to which the blindness of certain politicians gave rise.

What had begun as a thought was being translated into action. I confess that for an instant I hesitated. I should have to change from a theorist into an orator and a politician. The quiet approbation which surrounded me would be succeeded by strident controversy. Should I have the strength to carry on the campaign to the end? But personal considerations disappeared before the urgent necessity for carrying into effect a work which all the dictates of duty and promptings of instinct made it impossible to postpone. And it was with a full realisation of what I was risking and what awaited me, that I accepted this new aspect of my voyage.

At the port of Vera Cruz one already feels that impression of originality and strength which is the distinctive quality of the Mexican nation.

There is no more homogeneous group in America, nor one more peculiar in type and customs. In the very midst of modern civilisation and the brilliant diffusion of the highest forms of European life and culture there persists a proud current, which is becoming more distinct, of an indigenous character, derived from the original of Aztec civilisation.

The results were not the same in the two powerful indigenous communities which the Spanish conquest found in the New World. The fusion of the races, the mingling of Indian and Spanish, was effected in Upper Peru with the invaders, in Mexico with the invaded, as the predominating element. Setting aside political domination, during that slow process of amalgamation which was to determine the lines of future development it was the new elements which obtained the upper hand in the former case, and the old ones in the latter, carrying with them in their progress all elements that came into the country later.

It is this distinctive feature, rising above race into the spiritual sphere, which has given Mexico a more strongly-marked and deeply-rooted character. This has been accentuated by the incessant menace from abroad, and the collective will to endure as a distinct community has been confirmed by danger. Add to this a dour, haughty, imaginative disposition, intense pride, a certain happy aptitude for the arts, and a combative, indomitable character which has proved itself in the most varying circumstances. All this goes to make up that stubborn rock of Mexico against which the tide of imperialism has been beating for so long past, without succeeding in demolishing it or covering it; so that it remains like a gigantic watch-tower for the remaining peoples of our Latin America.

I spent the three days which I passed in Vera Cruz in visiting the prosperous and picturesque city, the workmen's clubs and the branches of the people's Athenæum, and in discussing the best means of reaching Mexico without getting into close touch with the political parties, so that nothing should give anyone a handle for ascribing to me any preferences or sympathies in one direction or the other. It was no easy task to achieve this in a country rent by discord and still ringing with the echoes of a recent revolution.

In spite of the temporary condition of stability the original divergencies continued to exist, while new antagonisms were springing up even among the victorious party. The telegrams which I received from the capital, and the envoys who arrived to escort me, confirmed my forebodings. It was obvious that, being legally a foreigner, I had nothing to say in the struggles, which only interested me from the point of view of the greater or lesser capacity of the country for defence against foreign pretensions. But partisan suspicion might see a hidden meaning in the most harmless act. The atmosphere was charged with politics—a situation which I afterwards found repeated in most of the Latin-American republics. To be in company with one party inevitably involved being against the others. Those who have not experienced such situations at close quarters, cannot have any idea of the nervous tension and sensitiveness with which the atmosphere is charged. Hence my vexation at finding myself in the position of accepting the escort of two deputies, delegates of Señor Madero's government, on my journey. One of them, Señor Cutberto Hidalgo, was afterwards in 1922, Minister for Foreign Affairs, under the presidency of General Obregón, about whom we shall speak in another chapter, at the end of this book. I remember that during the journey, while the train ran along the edge of precipices through that immense series of astonishing turns and declivities which leads from the coast to the central plateau, I had a premonition of what was bound to occur on my arrival at Mexico City. Crowded deputations of young men and men of the people were awaiting the arrival of the train at certain stations, especially Orizaba and Córdoba, and when they noticed the presence of the parliamentary deputies in question, they showed evident signs of displeasure. It was in these circumstances that I arrived at the capital of the republic on January 3, 1912. There was a band at the station, flags were waving, and speeches were made; but there was an atmosphere of confusion and distrust. "He is sold to the President." These were the very words of a *pelao* as I went by. A group of young intellectuals retired in silence. And when I entered my hotel, I found myself surrounded by official personages.

The stratagem consisted in isolating me, in allowing me to speak before some little assembly of faithful adherents of the Government, and then letting me leave the country without establishing contact with public opinion, which coincided so remarkably with the arguments I was maintaining.

The revolutionary disturbance which the Mexican Republic had first experienced at that time, after thirty years of uninterrupted peace, has been generally considered as simply a reaction of the democracy against the dictatorship of General Díaz. And it is obvious that, on its popular and internal side, it could only be a reaction of young blood and independent opinion against electoral dead-lock and political asphyxia. All this was a proof of national health and vitality. But from the external point of view, the matter takes on another aspect. How did this movement become possible? All the motive forces of the country were in the iron grip of the tyrant, and nobody could succeed in moving except by his grace. Madero did not enjoy any particular prestige. But peculiar circumstances were necessary to enable the insurrection to succeed in so short a time in carrying everything before it and imposing itself on such a vast country. The revolutionaries themselves were certainly ignorant of these circumstances; but even without any wish of theirs, these facts were of decisive weight in the outcome of the conflict.

The interview which took place at El Paso between the President of Mexico and Mr. Taft, President of the United States, led, as we have already said, to a rupture as its immediate consequence. The concession with regard to Magdalena Bay, a secret treaty with Japan, and the protection extended to the President of Nicaragua, set the old dictator of Mexico at odds with the growing demands of imperialism. And there is a coincidence which somebody will ultimately clear up with the aid of documents: the culmination of the Maderist insurrection coincided almost exactly with the tardy reaction against the policy of obsequiousness started by General Díaz. The revolutionaries, absorbed in the internal struggle, did not notice this fact. Political passion, exasperated by long years of enforced silence, concealed everything. But on the other side of the frontier the hope was expressed of obtaining, in the midst of these civil struggles, what had been refused by a tardy scruple of the dictator.

Whether from conviction, fear, or complaisance, Señor Madero's Government was from the outset a great friend of Pan-Americanism and the policy of Washington.*

The young men and the masses, those reservoirs of healthy energy, have a mysterious instinct which tells them what is what. It is not force which guides them; they do not even need to reason; they do not know whence the light comes; but come it does. And something of this kind must have happened to the Mexican people. It was whole-heartedly in favour of the revolution which restored to it its rights, it was vain of its triumph and applauded its leaders; but, true to its traditions, it kept watch to see how far things would go. Throughout all its different governments, in the course of its whole history, throughout the fits of conciliatory weakness or unreflecting imprudence of some of its representatives, it has always maintained an attitude of mistrust, because an obscure instinct makes it conscious of an ambush lying in wait for it in the darkness.

By studying the life of the country in detail, through the medium of the newspapers, during a slight indisposition which kept me shut up in my hotel for a few days, I began to piece together a few leading ideas about the true situation of the country. General Orozco was showing his discontent in the North; in the South Zapata's insurrection was spreading, and General Reyes, who represented the survivors of the previous régime, had just been put in prison. The most unpopular man in the city was a brother of the President's, Don Gustavo Madero, who was accused of discreditable dealings. The Press was exulting in great liberty, as if desirous of making up for so many years' silence. A North American mining company, with a capital of $2,250,000, paid in dividends that year $1,180,000. A North American obtained a concession of 600,000 acres of land in Chiapas. The enormous theatre which was under construction, and all public works, had suspended operations. The typical costume of the Rural Guard was abandoned, and replaced

* It is difficult to believe that the conservative Taft government would have backed a radical of the type of Madero. It does appear, however, that Díaz was at the last moment fearful of and hostile toward the United States. The documents necessary to determine the exact connexion of the United States with the overthrow of the dictator are not yet accesssible. It may indeed be that there was no connection.

by the khaki uniform; an exact copy of that worn by the North American Army.[1] The Trade Unions were reaching a high stage of development, and exercising a growing influence. The memory of the seizure of Texas was present in the minds of the young men.[2] A strange multiplication of parties was to be noticed. Commerce and industry showed a certain shyness. And in every rank of society, over and above the enthusiastic declamations of a people inaugurating, so to speak, a new life, was to be remarked a profound bewilderment, a confused effervescence, quite explicable after such a vast and fundamental upheaval. Amid this state of public uncertainty and nervousness, mistrust, as I have said, was the predominant sentiment. It was the most formidable enemy I had to conquer in the city. We will speak of the others afterwards.

My first visit had naturally to be made to the head of the country. My intermediary in this matter was Don Juan Sánchez Azcona, then secretary to the President, whose acquaintance I had made on my first visit. After some uncertainty, he let me know that the head of the state would receive me in the Palacio Nacional.

Señor Madero was a man of short stature, with large eyes and a dark complexion. He gesticulated freely. I can still see him standing in the middle of the spacious saloon, with one elbow on the

[1] This detail caused me, on one occasion, to make an exception to the obligatory rule of non-interference in internal affairs. In the midst of the altercations which ensued, I said one day, speaking from a balcony, "They may tear from our soldiers their historic costume, but we swear that they shall never put our souls in foreign uniforms." This comment on local affairs arose from a spontaneous enthusiasm; and though it did not arouse the slightest protest, but, on the contrary, enthusiastic applause, I quote it as a symptom of that higher sentiment which has always led me to identify myself with the fate of Mexico.

[2] It is as well to recall the course of this affair with dates. Since 1912 [sic for 1812] imperialist policy had been intriguing to gain control of this territory. Under the presidency of Adams (1827) it tried to obtain the cession of it. Under that of Jackson (1828) * negotiations were renewed with no success. In 1830 † it provoked a revolutionary insurrection. In 1835 [1836] it succeeded, with the help of a few malcontents, in setting up an illusory independent republic in this territory. And in 1844 [1845] this paradoxical republic was annexed to the United States.

* (1829–1837.)

† No revolution occurred in Texas in 1830. Late in 1826 a small rebellion took place in eastern Texas, but the United States had nothing to do with it.

back of a chair, declaiming about the benefits of the revolution. He had a touch of the *illuminé,* and a great deal of doggedness. As his rise to power had been like an adventure on the cinematograph, he retained from his sudden elevation a newly-gilt pride which showed itself in everything

When I tried to turn the conversation towards international politics, he became monosyllabic, and talked of, "Pan-Americanism—progress—civilisation." But the case of Cuba? Of Panama?—"Geographical necessities." Mexico was a nation "traditionally friendly to the United States"—"the New World"—"progress beyond that of outworn Europe." Not a single commonplace was wanting of what we call, with the aid of an expression still familiar in France, Spanish-American *défaitisme.* Sánchez Azcona tried to turn the President aside from these formulas, which have obtained a footing in public life by prescriptive right. But the chief remained inflexible. There was an indomitable energy in his character, at once ingenuous and combative.

I listened with the greatest respect to the representative of the people, and at the end of the interview, answered his lead in that innocent game of dominoes which I was afterwards to repeat with so many Presidents in the course of my journey:

—"The Argentine is progressing wonderfully."

—"Mexico is in a state of great prosperity."

These two dominoes always correspond to each other:—"It is a great country."

—"This country is no less great."

But I left the Palacio Nacional with the impression that, in spite of all conventions, that man was sincere, limited and unequal to his position though he might be. For him the only problem in his country was to overthrow the "tyrant" and implant "democracy." The realisation of all that is implied in this word appeared to him half-veiled in mist, nor was he very sure of how to achieve such a high ideal. None the less "this was his mission." And on this he took his stand, without admitting that other problems might crop up. Partly from inexperience of international politics, and partly from the ostentatious prudence of a neophyte in such complicated affairs, he held that the best tactics were verbal immobility in the face of men, and immobility of action in the face of facts. As he considered himself a great statesman, he was sure he would be able to improvise anything if the need arose. An idealist and a dreamer, he did not know that the petroleum trust and the Standard Oil Co.[3] are unfortunately more important for our Latin America to-day than the French Revolution and the Declaration of the Rights of Man. The conflict of ideals,—the live problem was still for him the same as between the Girondins and Dantonists. Life could not have gone on advancing since then. Madero's error was in supposing that the platform for his speeches and the theatre of his action lay in those books which he had read excitedly and unsystematically before launching out as a captain of *guerrilleros*. He was superstitiously attached to the principles of the *Marseillaise*. And amid the realities of a storm-swept continent, his adherence to out of date doctrines could but be crowned with martyrdom, since all those who meet their downfall in bloodshed are martyrs. And so went sliding smoothly to the grave this bookworm-demagogue, about whom the Cuban writer Marquez Sterling * has written some fine, if sometimes improbable pages. The film ended in something analogous to the tumbrels of the Convention or the adventure of Varennes. From the internal point of view his romanticism was not in vain, for it cleared the way for an awakening of the people. From the external point of view, it gave rise to an aggravated form of every danger.

My formal visit did not avert the hostility of the men who controlled the situation. Obstacles accumulated before me, while every facility was given me in appearance. Thus it was announced that the Minister of the Interior would lend the Teatro Arbeu for a lecture, at a time when, as I learned by experience, I could not find a hall for it, even by paying for it out of my own pocket. The official paper, *Nueva Era,* published a leader in which, after singing my praises, it declared that I came to defend "a union between the two Americas," this forcing me to send a preliminary letter in

[3] This is not the moment to ascertain what hopes had been placed in him by the Standard Oil Company, the rival of the Eagle (*El Aguila*), which had been favoured by General Díaz shortly before his fall.†

† For hints of the rivalry between the American and British oil interests in Mexico, see "Investigation of Mexican Affairs" (Report of the Fall Committee), *Senate Document,* No 285, Serial Nos. 7665-7666, p. 2520, *passim.*

* *Los ultimos dias del presidente Madero,* Habana, "El siglo XX," 1917.

correction of the statement.[4] I was officially invited to a lecture by the deputy Jesús Urueta, and when I arrived at the theatre, I found myself in Señor Gustavo Madero's box, which put me in a dilemma: must I withdraw, thus being guilty of discourtesy, or accept, thus alienating public opinion, owing to the evil reputation which surrounded this public personage? Any journalists who called were told, at the porter's box in my hotel, that I "had given orders that they were not to be admitted, as I did not wish to be troubled by the Press." A rumour was actually circulated *sotto voce* that I had received a considerable sum from the Mexican Government. And such was the discredit which began to fall upon the traveller, thanks to these cunning tricks, that I found myself forced to provoke a public explanation.

A precedent existed which I could not forget. When Rubén Darío came to Mexico to take part in the celebration of the Centenary of Independence, an influence was interposed so as to prevent him from receiving the ovations which awaited him. The network of silences and counter-orders which kept the poet waiting on the coast and prevented him from reaching the capital was present in every mind. The Minister of Public Instruction at that time had been Señor Don Justo Sierra, and the Mexican painter Ramos Martínez, who accompanied Darío in these difficult moments, could say something about the manœuvres which were used. Rubén was not a man with an eloquent tongue who might have inflamed the mob in the streets. But he had written the *Hymn to Roosevelt*, he had talked of "letting loose the Spanish lion's whelps,"—his name might serve as a rallying point for national resistance. The Government wished to prevent explosions of enthusiasm which ran contrary to its policy. Hence the effort to prevent his presence; so that the responsibility and faults of those who invited him with one hand, and kept him aloof with the other, fell upon the poet himself.

[4] To the Editor of the *Nueva Era:* "Dear Sir: In an article which your newspaper publishes about me to-day, an error has slipped in which I feel myself bound to correct, since it gives a meaning to my campaign which may be surprising to many. I have not undertaken any 'work in favour of the union of the two Americas.' I believe, on the contrary, that the interests of the two Americas are different, and this conviction is the basis of the lecture which I propose to give under the title of 'We and They.'" *Nueva Era*, January 11, 1912.

Warned by experience, I took advantage of a fortunate occurrence. The Association of Journalists of Mexico was opening its new premises on January 11, 1912, and introduced me without previous announcement, accompanied by two friends, the journalist Don Rodrigo de Llano and the poet Don José de J. Núñez y Domínguez. Señor Ignacio Herreras was in the chair. After listening to the reading of a motion, by which I was not to be given any sort of support, owing to my alleged discourtesy to the Press, I asked to be allowed to speak, and explained the situation fully. Averse to all political tendencies, independent of all parties, I came only to confirm the higher aspirations of the Mexican people, by defending the cause of *rapprochement* and resistance to imperialism. Sincerity is always stronger than intrigue, and the assembly accompanied me in a body to my hotel, thus sealing a compact with the journalists and young men which lasted till the end of my campaign. I only relate these incidents to give an idea of what the atmosphere was like, and because they throw light on the international position of the Government. Will the reader have the patience to accompany me to the end in this involuntary account of myself?

From this time on, the Press was on my side, with the exception of the daily *Nueva Era*, which published the opinions of certain North American personages resident in Mexico.[5] Another paper replied by printing the views of the majority of Mexican deputies.[6]

[5] The Editor of the *Anglo-American* said: "It would seem a strange thing to me that Mexico, a friendly nation, with which the United States have cultivated the most cordial relations, should go so far as to permit the public expression of ideas such as those put forth by this gentleman."

Captain L. W. Mix added, "It is my opinion that the Government of Mexico should deal with Señor Ugarte in accordance with the law."

Mr. Charles F. Yaeger confirmed this: "I consider Señor Ugarte somewhat imprudent in attempting to foment enmity between peoples of friendly nations, which are also neighbours; especially considering that the friendship which unites them is mutual. The people of the United States have always had the best of intentions towards Mexico, without nourishing the least desire to intervene in her internal affairs: on the contrary, they have contributed towards the progress, prosperity, and tranquillity of this country, at the same time respecting all her rights."

[6] "In making his ideas known, Manuel Ugarte is amply within his rights. In an epoch of liberty it would be abominable to try to muzzle a man having

Señor Justo Sierra openly declared to me that the theme which I proposed to treat might give rise to a protest on the part of the neighbouring country, and made it clear to me that this was not only his idea, but that of the Ministry for Foreign Affairs. He appealed to my patriotism to give up the lecture, so as to spare Mexico a humiliation. I replied that the only humiliation for a country was that men should be unable to speak freely within its borders. And since, when I published the conversation, Señor Sierra tried to correct me, I called to witness Señor Ibarrola, secretary of the School of Engineers, who had accompanied me to the interview and entirely confirmed the accuracy of the dialogue.[7]

This incident coincided with the publication of an open letter signed by a number of students. "We do not believe," they said, "that you are capable of selling your silence; at least, we hope not. Would it be possible for a man of your distinction and judgment, and your well-merited reputation, to put himself in such a ridiculous position? If it were so, then there would be nothing to be done. If persons whose position places them above suspicion and beyond attack, and who call themselves the apostles of union, were to pro-

as his point of view fraternity, complete harmony, and a tightening of relations with the great, strong, and noble Latin-American race."

Deputy TALAVERA.

"Not only am I in agreement, but I go further: I wish that Ugarte may be widely heard. His ideal could not be nobler. For us Mexicans it is without precedent."

Deputy CHAPITAL.

"Since the moment when Mexico, in our time, has been able to call herself a country of liberty, Ugarte enjoys a full right to make use of speech."

Deputy MELGAREJO.

"Given the sobriety and discretion which are Ugarte's most essential qualities, it is not to be expected that his speeches will occasion an international conflict."

Deputy ASPE.

"I sincerely believe that Ugarte can be allowed to express his ideas easily and without any reservation. In view of his personality it may be hoped that he will not disturb the tranquility of our territory."

Deputy TORRES TORIJA.

[7] *El Imparcial*, of Mexico, January 23, 24, and 25, 1912.

ceed in this way, there would be nothing to hope for: Latin-American submission would be an accomplished fact." [8]

My answer was: "Have confidence in me, as I have confidence in you."

That same evening I told the whole truth to the reporters who came to interview me. Placed in the uncomfortable position of being reproached for my silence by some, while the others prevented me from breaking it, I had no course left me but to refer the matter to the people. Public opinion was only waiting for the situation to be defined to give its decision, and the first general and lasting observation to be drawn from these incidents is the patriotic impetuosity of the youth of Mexico.

Very early the next day a noise was heard beneath the windows of my hotel. A big band of students came up to my rooms. "To the balcony!" And they drew me to the balustrade. The street was blocked by a mass of young people to which had been added groups of workmen. They were the engineering students who, on hearing the news, had refused to enter the lecture rooms and come to offer their support to the traveller. Above the crowd, borne on the shoulders of the others, rose a silhouette, voicing with vigorous gestures the sentiments of the demonstrators. It was impossible to hear what he was saying. At that moment the students from the art school debouched from the Calle Plateros, and soon after them appeared compact loads of medical, law, and preparatory students, followed by others who entirely filled the avenue and held up the traffic. Above it all was heard the cry of "Long live free Mexico!" An Argentine flag was produced and was saluted with cheers. Several students made speeches from my balcony, with enthusiastic declarations in favour of Latin-American union. The more violent and openly defiant became their periods, the louder the applause with which the assembly received them. Deeply moved, I began to give thanks for the demonstration, using the words "In my quality as a foreigner"; upon which loud protests were raised on all sides. "No!" they cried, "You are no foreigner. You are a Mexican, since you have come to defend our country." When I mentioned Bolívar and San Martín, every head was bared. Never have I felt such emotion. It was a welling-up of all their patriotic instincts, finding at

[8] *Gil Blas,* January 19, 1912.

last a safety-valve in an explosion of wrath against the intrigues of politicians and an oath of fidelity to a militant idealism.

The dykes were now broken, and every element in the country voiced its protest, from the Law Society down to the smallest of the Trade Unions. The Minister of Public Instruction attempted to calm the agitation by closing the students' clubs, but he only succeeded in inflaming opinion. An unexpected incident increased the agitation. The President of the Maderist Constitutional party, who had been prominent for his hostility to my campaign, formulated in the official newspaper a declaration offensive to the students, reproaching them with being led away by a new-comer. At the same moment appeared a leader in *Nueva Era*, spiritedly written by a foreign man of letters who happened to be in the country at the time, but quite inadmissible from the Mexican point of view.[9] These two manifestoes upset the situation completely.

"We cannot ever remember," said a newspaper,[10] "the occurrence of any similar case to that of yesterday. Within the short space of eight or nine hours, the declaration of a party leader on the one hand, and a leading article in a government paper on the other, have provoked a most vigorous protest from the mass of the students, seconded by popular elements." Another paper headed its leader, "Two governments against one man." Knowing that the schools were closed, the young men instinctively gathered together at the premises of a student's society situated in the Callejón de la Condesa, and after a tumultuous meeting, in which the Minister for Foreign Affairs and the official organ received a vigorous drubbing, a sea of young men, from among whom arose here and there, in brotherly union, the characteristic hats of the *pelao*, poured out into the streets of the city ready for reprisals.

[9] The article contained such paragraphs as the following: "The whole of America will belong politically to the Yankees, because they are more civilized; because in Mexico and Central America they are already practically and positively preponderant, or will soon be so, thanks to their commerce, capital, industries, etc.; all that is lacking is for them to transfer the waving banner of the Stars and Stripes, surrounded by an army in parade uniform, and substitute it for the Mexican eagle or the Guatemalan quetzal, thus happily transforming themselves into political sovereigns." *

* The exact date when this article appeared is not given.

[10] *El Imparcial*, January 27, 1912.

It is not for me to report the significant scene which took place at the Palacio del Gobierno. I will quote the words of the local papers. The committee of students which went up to the presidential offices bore Señor Madero to the balcony, and in the presence of a vast crowd which filled the *plaza*, Don Luis Jaso, a student at law, formulated in their name the following questions, which were published in *El Imparcial* on January 27, 1912:

"Mr. President: Are you at one with to-day's declarations in *Nueva Era?* Is there an attempt to prevent Ugarte from speaking? Do you share the opinion of the President of the Constitutional Party on the conduct and merit of the student class and the professorate?"

In the midst of silence the President began to speak in the manner which I also reproduce word for word, with annotations and all, from *El Imparcial* of the same date:

"Gentlemen: I am not at one with these opinions, and I deplore the fact that they should have been put forth in this manner. We are not attempting to prevent Ugarte from speaking. I am unspeakably grieved that a foreigner should have come and reproached me with such a thing, and that he should have misled you. (Protests of "No!" "Long live Ugarte!" "Long live Latin America!") Nor is it true that we are wavering in the defence of our territorial integrity. (Shouts of "Down with Calero!").

The President retired from the balcony and betook himself to his office, where he replied to the delegates Señores Jaso, Buenabad, and Muñoz.[11] As I have said, Señor Madero was a dour man, who would not let himself be intimidated. But this same quality did him harm. His anger led him to make two imprudent statements: that he could not authorise demonstrations against a friendly people "who had supported the revolution," and that the phrase for which they found fault with *Nueva Era* was merely copied from a book of mine, *The Future of Latin America* (*El Porvenir de la America Latina*), only with the omission of quotation marks.*

This confession that the traditional enemy had given patronage to the internal disturbance, and the absurd inaccuracy of the latter accusation, were the last straw. The student Señor Buenabad went

[11] *El Imparcial, El Diario*, etc., of January 28, 1912.

*See the Editorial Introduction.

out on the balcony once more, accompanied by two students, Enrique
Soto Paimbert and Gay Fernández. He ironically reported the upshot of the interview to the people, and the angry crowd started
moving off in the direction of the editorial offices of the official daily.
Somebody tossed down a Spanish flag from a balcony, and there
were shouts of applause in honour of the mother country. Some unknown person distributed Spanish-American and Japanese flags from
a shop on the central avenue. The demonstration threatened to
become aggressive. But students in all countries are the chief
guardians of culture, and one of them rose once more to calm men's
minds.

If the demonstration afterwards took on another character, and
led to extremist action, this was the work of a fresh element.

But did not politics, too, enter a little into all this? In putting
this question, I desire to enlarge the lines of my picture in order to
lead to a better understanding of the situation which we are studying. While these patriotic youths made themselves masters of the
street, delegations and visitors were arriving at my hotel from those
who had been carried away by party passions, and were trying to
convert the movement into a campaign against the Government.
High as was the personal position of the messengers, my invariable
answer was that I could only take part in acts which had as their
object a Spanish-American *rapprochement,* and that I would not be
the spokesman of a demonstration hostile to the authorities, whether
they were directed against the President or the Minister of Foreign
Affairs. And this, not out of any respect for persons, but out of
consideration for the country and for public opinion, which, once
the first impression was past, would be the first to find any such
action on my part misplaced.

Thus these movements took on a widely national character, and
the procession which took place a few days later, in which there
took part the Anti-re-electionist Democratic Party, the Nationalist
Democratic Party, the Anti-re-electionist Club of the Free Workers,
the Santos Degollado Workmen's Club, the Filomeno Mata Workmen's Club, the Right and Labour Club, the Melchor Ocampo
Anti-re-electionist Club, and a number of societies, some favourable
to the Government, and some opposed to it, was a tribute to their

fraternal sentiments towards the sister republics, without any mixture of party.

There was one incident which revealed the tension of the atmosphere. The students who were the moving spirit in this disturbance received a telegram from the Military College expressing their desire to join the movement. The authorities were alarmed to hear this, and resolved to apply disciplinary measures. That evening the school was drawn up in the barrack square, and after a speech, the head of the College gave orders "That the culprits should take two steps forward." And the whole school stepped forward. These sentiments spread to the entire republic, and demonstration followed demonstration—at Guadalajara, Puebla, Guanajuato, Jalisco, etc., in an unanimous rebellion of the soul of Mexico.

I recall these facts quite apart from all vanity, in order to show the state of public feeling. How could any one man flatter himself that he had created sentiments or enthusiasms, which, if we get below their surface courtesy, we find in the depths of all our peoples? Neither in Mexico nor in any of the other countries which I afterwards visited was I anything more than a humble voice of the community. The only merit I can claim is that of having had the firmness to say what I was thinking. In reality I was quite unknown. [12] But the masses, disheartened by the eternal manœuvres

[12] The editor of *El País*, Don Trinidad Sánchez Santos, summed up the psychology of the situation in a leading article: "Manuel Ugarte the eminent Argentine poet, has not yet spoken: but he is applauded, loved, defended, and respected even among the masses least concerned with the greater issues of international policy. Why is this? What is the mysterious reason why so much sympathy is displayed for a man who has not even begun to give the lectures which he has announced?

"Let me try to explain this strange phenomenon, if but in a few short lines. Manuel Ugarte has presented himself as the interpreter of a great idea, which has been latent in the minds of Latin Americans since it was conceived by the great Bolívar: the union of all American countries of Latin blood. But this idea, fine as it is, does not bear within it the elements of a wide-spread popularity, of that popularity which reaches the illiterate masses, and stirs them deeply, waking them from the inertia in which they live.

"What is it that the people have seen behind the ideals of the Argentine writer? What has the infallible popular instinct divined beyond the spirited theory of Ugarte? The people has concluded with the logic of the multi-

of those who had asked them for their votes or their blood in order to grow fat in public offices, were ready to give their whole confidence to anyone who spoke to them for patriotic ends, with no personal interest to serve, with no view to honours, and with no further object than the general safety. Moreover, the opposition which I had met from the Government had something to do with it. The visitor was "the touchstone" which was to "bring to light" as one paper said, the attitude of the new President towards international problems. That which had not yet come to the surface amid the internal struggle suddenly became plain to see. A voice which had no part in the local strife, the ideals of a passing traveller, were all that were needed to make his vacillations evident, and throw into relief proceedings which the nation as a whole repudiated.

The farther the intrigues were pushed, the more agitated did the waves of popular sentiment become. The government refused me the use of the Teatro Arbeu, and next brought pressure to bear on Señor Carlos Peralta, who had offered me the Teatro Hidalgo through the agency of Señor Zaldívar, to withdraw his offer. The same happened with regard to other premises, the owners of which, after attempting a gesture of independence, ended by submitting.

The Minister of Foreign Affairs none the less disowned these acts of authority and alleged his disinterestedness.[18] Even the President,

---

tude that it is certain and fully established that the ideal of Latin-American union bears within it the widely popular idea of anti-Yankeeism, an idea which we might say forms part of the traditions of every Spanish-speaking country of the American Continent, and which in Mexico has come to form part of the very rudiments of our patriotism.

"The fact is, that Ugarte has not spoken, and that he is popular in Mexico. The really unprecedented fact is that Ugarte has come to Mexico to give lectures with the object of convincing our people of a given thesis, and that before he has made his first speech, the people are giving lectures to Ugarte to persuade him of the truth of the very thesis which he carries in his portfolio. We cannot recall any similar situation in all history."

El País, of Mexico, January 30, 1912.

[18] "I find myself compelled to state that Señor Ugarte's good faith has been imposed upon. The present Government has the deepest respect for liberty of thought and of speech, and the public may be sure that neither

attempting to baffle public opinion, declared in an interview that he had charged his private secretary, Señor Sánchez Azcona, to go and "assure Señor Ugarte that in Mexico he might give as many lectures as he liked; and that if his engagements did not prevent it, he (Madero) would have the pleasure of being present at the first";[14] which was absolutely untrue, for nobody had discussed the matter with me in any way.

But public opinion knew what to believe. The newspapers of the United States, which published daily long accounts of the conflict, declared with no beating about the bush that Señor Madero's government was doing all it could to prevent me from speaking. A summary of these reports was transmitted to the Mexican newspapers, and in the very number of *La Prensa* in which the President made his declaration, a New York telegraph could be read which said the absolute opposite.[15]

At last two students brought the good news that the proprietor of the Teatro Mexicano, Don Francisco Cardona, who was friendly to the government, but a man of independence, had offered his theatre to the young men. "He knows to what he is exposing himself," they said to me; "he is ready to pay all the fines, to bear

I nor the Secretariate of Foreign Affairs have intervened either directly or indirectly in matters concerning Señor Ugarte's lectures."

La Prensa, January 29, 1912.

[14] *La Prensa*, January 24, 1912.

[15] "New York, January 23.— The New York *Sun* is publishing intelligence from Mexico, in which it comments upon the political opposition which has been worked up to prevent Manuel Ugarte from holding lectures on Latin-American union. It adds that Ugarte is perhaps the most impassioned champion of Latin-American alliance against the United States. It is believed that the American Embassy has used its influence in Mexican Government circles to put obstacles in the lecturer's way. The night the poet arrived at Mexico City, a number of journalists, writers, and students organised a demonstration, going *en masse* to the railway station to receive him; moreover, a number of prominent politicians went to Vera Cruz to bid him welcome. The police surrounded the newcomer and did not allow anyone to approach him. He was conducted in haste to a hotel, the doors of his lodging were closed to all visitors, and a report was put out that Ugarte was indisposed."

La Prensa, of Mexico, January 24, 1912.

every annoyance, to take full responsibility." The event was fixed for February 3, at eight o'clock in the evening. And the editor of the *Prensa*, Don Francisco Bulnes, published a semi-official leader announcing that all opposition had been withdrawn.[16]

But had all this stubborn opposition really emanated from the government? Madero was an idealist demagogue, as fond of applause as a bull-fighter, and up till that time all his tactics had consisted in flattering the mob. He had even gone so far as to make promises—for instance, that the land should be divided up—which he knew in advance could not be carried out. He was assured that there was nothing in the lecture I was to deliver which might appear to be an attack on another country. As a Mexican, he surely shared the general sentiment with regard to the invader of 1847. Was it admissible that solely out of an obstinate pride, he should set himself up against the whole trend of opinions, when there was no serious international question involved; and expose himself to odium for the first time—he, who had always hunted for popularity, even in the meetings held by strikers in the public *plaza?* On examining these incidents, and trying with their aid to understand the state of the republic, we are met with this first apparent contradiction.

In Cuba, where the Platt Amendment has created a difficult situation, I had been able to give the same lecture at the National University without any unfortunate incidents. At Santo Domingo, at a grave crisis in the life of the country, just after the death of a president, in the midst of a party tumult, I had spoken quite freely on the same subject, pointing from the platform through the open window at the cruisers anchored in the bay. In neither of these

---

[16] "The Government has done and is doing all it can, without breaking the laws, to muzzle a man who has found out that they want to muzzle him, and knows that he will increase in public estimation in proportion as he is determined not to be silenced. The situation is undoubtedly a delicate one for the Government, and since all has now come to light, since every face is laid bare, since all doors are now open, since all the tickets for Señor Ugarte's lecture are taken, and since there is no means by which Señor Ugarte can be turned into a pillar of salt, or of silver, we must hope that he will speak, we must listen to what he has to say, and judge of his ideas in the most fitting manner possible."

La Prensa, January 27, 1912.

two cases did anybody go so far as to think, much less to say, that a mere study of the situation of our peoples in relation to Anglo-Saxon America might give rise to international disturbances. Every year a hundred speeches are made in the United States on the necessity for putting a check on the action of Japan, without any offence being taken by the latter. Why have we got to look anxiously towards the North before saying two calm words about the desirability of co-ordinating the action of the Spanish republics of the New World? What special reason was there in Mexico which put a different complexion on matters? I had no right to question the Government. But was the shadow of some secret Platt Amendment rising up amid the smoke of the revolution, an amendment more serious than the previous one, since it established a right of censorship over the ideas within Mexican territory?

Those opposed to the existing state of affairs—whether out of fidelity to the old régime or discontent with the new—alleged that the change had taken place under the influence of the United States. But in Mexico patriotic disquiet is always awake, and unfortunately frequent use has been made of it during civil struggles. Each party accuses the other of being in league with the enemy, and nobody ever blames anyone else for using this as a weapon of controversy. Señor Bulnes himself in the leading article which I have quoted above,[17] said "Señor Madero's government owes indirectly part of its existence to the United States," adding that everybody, including all the Maderists, is conscious that General Díaz fell owing to the will of three parties: the Mexican people, the people of North America, and most particularly Mr. Taft. In so doing, Señor Bulnes was playing the game of "amicable hostility" so frequent among our turbulent democracies, in which, to use the current phrase, controversialists frequently support the governments as a rope supports a hanged man. I have never believed that either Señor Madero or the majority of his adherents consciously lent themselves to these intrigues. And be it known that in speaking thus I am defending the memory of a man who went so far as to use against me the weapon of putting words into my mouth which I had not spoken.

[17] "The Question of the Government v. Ugarte."
La Prensa, January 27, 1912.

Where President Madero went wrong was not in having a secret understanding with the United States, a course which, then as always, would have been not only a bad action, but suicidal for any representative of the Mexican people; but, on the contrary, in not reckoning with the United States, in not realising how they might profit by the new situation; in not keeping a vigilant watch on external policy. His attention was diverted by the turmoil of the internal situation and a civil conflict which was too much for him. Imperialist policy, more clear-sighted than he, took advantage of the confusion of the strife to assert itself.

For Madero, as for many other elected representatives of our improvident Latin America, the only problem which existed was the internal problem. How to implant a theoretical democracy, when the way had not first been prepared by wide-spread public instruction; how to govern the country before establishing its material and moral frontiers; how to decorate the house before gaining real possession of it. He forgot that for our peoples the problems present themselves in a different order: first, that of integrity, territorial, racial, political, economic, etc., i. e., the real and undisputed possession of the nation by the nation itself; next, that of internal peace, of breaking with the system of boss-rule (*caudillaje*) and violence in order to give stability to the body politic; and finally, that of the organisation of its activities and the exploitation of its wealth. To disturb this order is to sterilise all fruitful effort.

The rash theorism which had led Señor Madero to put forth a profession of political faith worthy of a guerilla chieftain, one-sided and sectarian, was soon awakened to an ingenuous astonishment, by the harsh realities latent in a position of subjection. The wild series of intrigues which followed were the outcome of bewildered improvisations in the face of an unexpected fact, confusing to the mind of the impressionable man who found himself at the head of the government. What! The United States, which had aided in "overthrowing tyranny," were now preparing to impose it in international relations! This upset all his ideas about the "great democracy," about Washington, about Monroe, and about "the generous work of Cuban independence."

But the governments of certain regions of our Latin America frequently start from the basis of the individual, leaving the community to the last. The urgent matter, for a revolutionary *caudillo*, was to keep himself at the head of public affairs, whatever procedure he might be forced to resort to in order to placate an ambassador making representations to him. In the following chapters we shall see a curious contradiction appearing in more palpable form between the principles of North American democracy and its action upon those countries in which it claims to exercise influence. At present I merely wish to insist on the point that my journey was entirely exempt from any immediate political object. It did not enter into my plan to put ideals into effect, but merely to propagate them, and that exclusively in the sphere of ideas. But the personal decision which led me to undertake my tour, without foreseeing the echoes which it might awake in official circles, put me in a position to diagnose how far the morbid condition of our continent had gone.

After a preliminary *contretemps* caused by the cutting off of the electricity (which was put right by the Students' Committee) the lecture took place as announced, on February 3,[18] with a success

[18] "Myriads of people filled the streets, and it was physically impossible to advance a step. The trams which pass that way toward Zaragoza, Martínez de la Torre, and Juárez, had to stop going along those streets; nor was it easy to work one's way through the gaily-coloured crowd which reached from the Chamber of Deputies nearly to the Mariscala. The ex-Minister Garcia Granados was cheered on entering the theatre, with shouts of "Long live Granados! Long live the iron will!"
El Diario del Hogar, February 4, 1912.

"The crowd surged with the force of a hurricane, and rushed the grated windows with intent to tear down the bars. What they wanted was to hear Ugarte. It was a tempestuous multitude which fought for an entry at all costs. Part of this multitude had booked places; the rest were a set of curious individuals who wanted to push their way through, and arrive at places in the theatre by crushing whatever stood in their way. The police were incapable of stemming this human avalanche; the doors were closed and the way was barred, even to those who had the right to enter because they had tickets. The struggle lasted for three hours.
El País, February 4, 1912.

"When we reached the Teatro Mexicano, a roaring crowd was jammed together, and with successive rushes tried to take the theatre by storm rather than enter it. It was with difficulty that Señor Ugarte made his way into the theatre, after being nearly crushed by the crowd, which was in paroxysms

which was not due to the qualifications of the speaker, who was little used to appearing in such conflicts, but to the harmony between the idea which he was defending and the sentiments of his audience.

The Government organ, though it called for the application of Article 33 of the Constitution, referring to dangerous foreigners, had to admit that there was nothing in these words which might appear offensive to a foreign nation. I merely enumerated dangerous precedents and made an appeal for solidarity, without being needlessly provocative. I recognised, on the contrary, that our situation arises rather from our own national faults than from imperialist greed; and that in order to realise to the full the ideals of independence, we must redeem ourselves from these faults.

The younger generation thought they were at the threshold of a great movement, and founded Latin-American Associations and Clubs intended to carry on the work of propaganda and to keep alive the ideal of resistance to foreign influences. How many illusions can be ascribed to this life-giving impulse alone! Nobody dreamed of the complications which were afterwards to arise under

of enthusiasm and attempted to get in at all costs, thus increasing the disorder."

La Prensa, February 4, 1912.

"There were three thousand persons fighting for entry to the theatre and the efforts of the *gendarmes* appeared at times fruitless to restrain this human avalanche. The doors of the theatre, closed and guarded by the police, cracked from time to time under the pressure of the crowd, and many persons felt it could not be long before they fell, to give passage to the enthusiasts who would not be deprived of hearing Ugarte's words. At last the poet descended from his automobile and received an ovation, and by dint of great efforts succeeded in reaching one of the doors. Those who accompanied him remained in the street for a long time in the same difficult position. As yet there was no hope that the entry of the public might become normal, and the riot subside, for this pandemonium was no less when Manuel Ugarte appeared on one of the balconies of the theatre. Silence was obtained and the Argentine prophet announced that the lecture would not begin till everybody had gained access to the theatre, and that he hoped nobody in the street would be left outside. Ugarte was loudly cheered, and after this ovation the struggle to enter the building began afresh."

El Imparcial, February 4, 1912.

that demoralising influence which provokes conflicts, inflames passion, and perpetuates discord, so that everything turns on personal rivalries and the field is left free for a general invasion.

By a curious coincidence, just after this campaign of mine the Secretary of Foreign Affairs, Mr. Philander C. Knox, left the United States to make, in his turn, the tour of all the Spanish-American countries, beginning with the Argentine and ending with Mexico.

It was plainly to be seen that the fraternal character of the visit was a diplomatic *façade*. Only in an idyllic world would a minister put himself out to go and carry disinterestedly gentle messages of tenderness from people to people. The real object was to study on the spot the movement towards solidarity which was beginning to be talked about.*

Mr. Knox was able during his journey to win by various arts the support of certain Presidents, but he could not reach the soul of our people. None the less, his tour had a great influence on the political orientation of the governments of the South, as we shall see in the following chapters.

It is not that there is any lack of capable men in our Latin America. Few regions can show a greater abundance of natural talent, keen, sharp-sighted, and prepared for every situation. But the fact is that it is not these men who govern us. The conduct of public affairs does not as yet belong to the thinkers, but to the men of action. And this is the malady of Latin America, especially of Mexico, the general atmosphere of which we have attempted to indicate by means of an anecdote.

Señor Madero soon afterwards fell, stabbed in the back by that very diplomacy which had brought about his elevation, a scapegoat who had served his purpose for an hour. A large proportion of the younger generation, who had stood with me in defence of our continental ideal, was decimated during the complicated revolutions which followed. Taking advantage of the civil disorder, two in-

* Mr. Knox appears to have visited only the countries of the Caribbean, his tour having occurred between February 23 and April 17, 1912. Cf. *Speeches* incident to his visit, published at Washington, Government Printing Office, 1913.

vasions were let loose in a short space of time one after the other, one from Vera Cruz, the other from the north.* And the disintegration which started after the fall of Porfirio's dictatorship became more and more pronounced up to the rise to power of Don Venustiano Carranza, who put himself at the head of the reaction, and perished tragically. But we shall speak of all this at the end of this book. We will now continue the account of our travels, which will enable us to command a general view of affairs, in order to deduce from the result of our observations the truths which sum up our situation.

On leaving Mexico I carried away the impression of a valiant, spirited, intelligent people, capable of prevailing over fate itself and of struggling with destiny. But this mass of gold was corroded by political ambitions, by *caudillos* fertile in expedients, by a tendency to discord, by incessant military risings, by a vortex of passions which were bound to weaken it. The hatred, greed, and hastiness of certain *caudillos* gave rise to anarchical movements, commercial disasters, summary executions, so much ruin and blood, such waste of audacity and life, that no country's health could bear it. The rock of Mexico stood intact as regards race, and the untouched nucleus of its people. But the confusion sown by cunning reports, fevered ambitions, the arrogance of the leaders, and the attraction of guerilla warfare, were serving as the instruments of its downfall. And the tragic duel of the two races on the banks of the Rio Bravo appeared to me under the aspect of a giant, provided with every modern arm, aided by all human knowledge, and acquainted with every ruse, pitted against a simple-minded dwarf, who instead of preparing to defend himself, was madly tearing out his own entrails.

To these evils, which Mexico has survived because she has a constitution hardened to cataclysms, must be added the two chief errors of Señor Madero, and of many of the political leaders who carried on his work: that of dissolving the strong army created by General Díaz, and that of forgetting that the united economic interests of France, Spain, and England outweigh those of the

* Whatever the results of his policy, President Wilson appears to have been trying to protect Mexico from the economic pressure which Señor Ugarte so much fears.

United States. But in the actual blindness of the moment, all was
subordinate to a philosophy of disintegration, an illusory view of
human unity, which gave little importance to language, religion,
and origin as forces of national resistance, trusting perhaps in the
promised universal fatherland. And in the last analysis this is the
supreme danger for the whole of Latin America.

CHAPTER IV

THE PARADISES OF AMERICA

The tyranny of Señor Estrada Cabrera—The inconvenient traveller —Results of anarchy—The hospitality of Honduras—Our hope is in the South—The youth of San Salvador—The cable foments discord —The protectorate of Nicaragua—The "Statesmen"—Physiology of revolutions.

NATURE has richly endowed our lands with all that it is possible to imagine for human happiness; but for Central America she has reserved everything that is most splendid and most incredible. The lands which extend from ocean to ocean, from the southern frontier of Mexico to the borders of Colombia, overflowing with vegetation and wealth of every kind, full of marvellous views, with mountains which counteract the rigour of the climate, and romantic cities in which colonial usages survive, are so many legendary paradises, where everything seems to have been arranged by God to afford to the human race an enchanted retreat full of serene abundance and spiritual repose. In spite of this, no region in the world has witnessed a greater orgy of acts of violence and extermination, none has been rent by more vicissitudes, as if the vegetation of the region were reflected in men's nature, poisoning them with flowers and fruits of blood, and thus giving wings to tragedy in the very heart of paradise itself.

Before leaving Mexico I had occasion to converse with Dr. Ortega, the Guatemalan Minister in that country, who assured me that the President, Señor Estrada Cabrera, would not offer any opposition to my campaign; adding, in a confidential tone, that if Señor Madero had expelled me, the neighbouring country would have been prepared to offer me its protection. I can still remember his words: "I have sent daily to Dr. Estrada Cabrera full information about the events which have taken place here, and I think I can sum up the situation in one word—Go!"

In the course of some of the controversies to which this journey

gave rise, the Minister had afterwards to contradict in the newspapers [1] the accusations brought by my Mexican friends as a result
of the incidents which obliged me to leave Guatemala. But perhaps
he was the first victim of the tyrant's stratagems.

Señor Estrada Cabrera had the reputation of being one of the
most subtle political intriguers whom Latin America has ever known.
Devoid of scruples, but more than amply endowed with shrewdness,
he had succeeded in controlling the Government uninterruptedly,
sometimes striking terror by his rapid action, sometimes winning
goodwill by his favour and bounty. It is superfluous to say that
he proved more dangerous when he employed these latter weapons;
for if with the former he destroyed men's lives, with the latter he
sapped their wills. He enjoyed unvarying unpopularity throughout all Central America, so that his goodwill was more compromising than his persecution. After the Mexican disorders, it turned
out harder to gain entry into Guatemala than anywhere else; not
that my propaganda was at all local or aggressive in character as
regards this country or its internal régime, but on account of the
submissiveness which Señor Estrada Cabrera had always shown
towards imperialist policy.

The fact of desiring that our race should maintain its position
in the New World; the propaganda which tends to reunite the scattered fragments of the ancient Spanish and Portuguese colonies; my
aspiration towards saving from disaster, by peaceful co-ordination,
those republics which are nowadays forced to tolerate the encroachments of foreign countries; all this signifies nothing that could possibly have a subversive aspect. When I left Paris, I believed, in
my simplicity, that it would meet with no hostility. I reckoned
upon a more or less diplomatic neutrality on the part of the Governments, but I never imagined that anybody in our own lands
would put obstacles in the way of my speaking of patriotism and
future greatness.

A few Guatemalan refugees tried to dissuade me. But I wished
to know all the Spanish-American republics. I wanted to speak
in every capital of the Continent. So, crossing the Isthmus of
Tehuantepec, I set sail from Salina Cruz on February 22, in the
steamship *Salvador*.

[1] *El Tiempo*, of Mexico, March 5, 1912.

Having sent a preliminary telegram of greeting to the President—
a ceremony which is *de rigueur* in the authoritarian democracies of
Central America, I landed at San José and continued my journey
straight to the capital. I remember that I arrived on a Sunday
evening. My first visit was to the representative of the Argentine,
who was at that time Colonel Belgrano. Groups of people were
going slowly homewards along the sidewalks. At the windows were
groups of girls dressed in white, talking with their suitors, a survival of one of the most picturesque customs of our tropical regions. At the end of the street I saw a battalion marching away
with its band in front of it. But something indefinable and gloomy
seemed to weigh upon the flat city with its straight streets stretching out towards the boundary. I learnt afterwards that it was
terror.

On returning to my hotel an envelope with the stamp of the
Ministry of Foreign Affairs was handed to me. It contained a
solemn communication which read as follows: "The Secretary of
State and the Department of Foreign Affairs of the Republic of
Guatemala have the honour to offer their courteous salutations to
Señor Don Manuel Ugarte, and request him to be so good as to
come to this Secretariate to-morrow at eleven."

At the hour indicated, I presented myself at the Ministry. The
Minister, whose name I do not remember, so ephemeral is the
character of these temporary dignitaries, who have no importance
other than that which they draw from the office which they mo-
mentarily occupy, was a thin little man, ceremonious and insignificant. He waved me pompously to a chair with a melodramatic
gesture, full of the importance of his mission.

"Guatemala is proud," he said to me, "to have in her midst a
writer of your stamp. We have learnt with the most lively pleasure of your presence in this capital, and I have hastened to summon
you in order to offer you my greeting in the name of the Government. Your literary lectures will meet with our delightful appreciation."

"I regret to have to undeceive you, Señor Ministro," I answered,
after thanking him for his opening courtesy, "but it is not my purpose to give a discourse on literature. In view of the situation of
our Latin America, I felt that a writer free from all diplomatic

responsibility could do a useful work, quite apart from official organisations, in spreading certain ideas of co-ordination which are in the air. This is the cause of my journey. The subject of my lectures cannot be other than that which occupies the minds of our peoples."

The Minister maintained a disapproving silence.

"Mr. Knox's voyage," he declared after a moment's reflection, "and the peculiar conditions of our politics, prevent us from viewing with favour the treatment of this subject."

"I neither ask for nor expect the intervention or support of the Government, in any form," I replied. "I only desire to set forth and study certain given questions in a popular and youthful atmosphere."

"You will not be able to do so," he said shortly.

"In that case, Señor Ministro, I shall give myself the trouble of leaving to-morrow; but as I shall some day have to write an account of this journey, I shall be obliged to put words on record."

Nothing surprised me more during my tour than the ingenuousness of certain men who believe their stratagems to be infallible. As I went out, chance, which is the god of Guatemala, would have it that I met General Enrique Arís, a soldier of some culture and the President's right-hand man. He said that he wished to invite me to a luncheon. I can still see the open window before which the table was laid. The guests were the Argentine Consul, José Santos Chocano, General Arís and the writer of these lines. As coffee was being served, the General, strange to say, was called up on the telephone, and after a moment he came back, saying:

"I have just been speaking to His Excellency; he is at present at home, and as I told him that we were lunching together, he expressed a wish to know you. We will go presently."

The one thing that was necessary to maintain my prestige in Central America, if I could not give a lecture in Guatemala, was that I should *not* see Señor Estrada Cabrera. The reputation which the President had for liberality, taken together with my silence, might lead people to suppose that I had voluntarily given up speaking as the result of a corrupt bargain.

It was impossible to forget the example of what had happened on my arrival in Mexico. So the situation presented itself in these terms: if I were able to give a lecture, it was a matter of indifference to me whether I saw the President or not; but if I were unable to speak, it was absolutely indispensable not to see him. Moreover, I could not consent to the interview taking place, because it might furnish a cunning pretext for the prohibition which might ensue. And it was this which I courteously gave the friends who accompanied me to understand. None of them could suppose that a question of formal courtesy, invoked in consequence of a preliminary step taken by the Consul without my consent, could be the real obstacle.

From this moment I realised it was inevitable that I should leave the country.

"But public opinion?" the reader will say. This was a very different situation. There were not in Guatemala, as in Mexico, turbulent masses ready to be lashed into fury by a gale of liberty. There were no press, no public meetings in the *plaza*. It was impossible for a man to go out into the street and loudly proclaim his convictions, for in this atmosphere of intimidation and reserve, everything was under the tyrant's thumb. The leading newspapers had sent reviewers and photographers to my hotel the evening before, but this very morning they had even suppressed my name in the list of travellers arriving on the previous day. The orders were final: silence was to be maintained. The only person who broke the silence after my departure was José Santos Chocano, in spite of his understanding with the Government of Señor Estrada Cabrera.[2]

[2] "This Man—thus capitalized—is hurrying off on his Pegasus, on his Clavileño, towards his native Pampas, from which the *gauchos* strike out under the prancing hoofs of their fiery steeds sparks which are called San Martín, Belgrano, Mitre, Sarmiento . . . The fertile Argentine will hear the watchword from the lips of one of its greatest minds. Oh, if she would band together as one whole and attempt by a great and active propaganda to create the great Fatherland!

"Manuel Ugarte is a poet, and like a poet, he sings. Let us not forget that the song of the lark is the herald of dawn. Shall we awake?

"Away goes this champion of the ideal—my great and true friend in art—following the course of that romantic bark which we all know.

"He will find a race sad and pale as Rubén's Princess; but let him not forget, for his satisfaction, that the thorn is the elder sister of the laurel."

José Santos Chocano, Guatemala, March, 1912.

As for students, the country well knew that those who had managed to escape being shot were at foreign universities. None the less, the nucleus that was left, the Law Society, offered me its support, and a group of young men published a typewritten broadsheet containing a manifesto, interesting for the situation which it revealed.[3] In spite of all its excesses, in this cry was contained all the soul of Guatemala, oppressed and stifled, but spirited to the point of rashness—for it is not difficult to guess to what its authors were exposing themselves.

I have already said that Señor Estrada Cabrera was a past-master in the art of tracking down his victims and forcing them into a prescribed course of action. The repugnance with which his first invitation had been received exasperated the dictator. I was nothing but an isolated traveller. Every abuse, every outrage could be heaped upon me with impunity. But I had one weapon, which, as we could see in the course of my tour, averted the attacks of many: I could relate what happened to me. The President of Guatemala was careful of his propaganda in Europe, and wished to avoid a similar fate to that which had been promised to his minister.

Two hours after General Arís's invitation, the Argentine Consul received a letter under the President's own hand and seal, in which he said he would receive us the following day at five in the evening.

[3] "The Latin has out-distanced the Anglo-Saxon. Manuel Ugarte has outstripped P. C. Knox. Thought is lighter than the eagle.

"Our brother arrived in our home, and we cast him forth from it; the false friend is coming, and we shall receive him on our knees. The city is decked out as it has perhaps never been decked before, and millions of pesos are being spent on fêtes and banquets; while the Indian, like a beast of burden, is hungry because he has not eaten for three days.

"Ugarte's thought, like our quetzal,* cannot live where there is no liberty; for this reason he could not stay among us. The eagle of the North is coming to make the acquaintance of his flock.

"The people of Guatemala protest vigorously against the ignominious exit of Ugarte and the reception of Knox.

"If the Press here had not been muzzled, we could have placed our names at the foot of this protest; but no newspaper would have published it; no printer would have printed it. In countries where liberty does not exist, what is anonymous is not to be despised; it is we Guatemalans who should be despised for tolerating slavery."

* A brilliant tropical bird, the national emblem of Guatemala.

Since his tactics had not changed (those of creating a vacuum about me, and allowing me no way out but an interview with the Dictator) I took train for the port of San José, leaving the invitation dangling. My plan was to sail that evening for San Salvador. But I was really turning out to be rather an undesirable visitor in the eyes of those governments, just at this time, when Mr. Knox's visit was arousing the wrath of Central American patriots. The bewildered chancelleries were making unheard-of efforts to hold in check the protests which were being foretold, and to hide the true state of feeling. Their national anthems, their interlaced flags, and their banquets could not prevent rebellion from being hatched among the masses and the young. Even beforehand these rejoicings provoked a natural reaction of bad temper in these unruly countries, where men seem to be born with a tendency to opposition; and this might be worked up into demonstrations if the opportunity offered.

In these circumstances, the arrival of a writer who stood for a doctrine opposed to Pan-Americanism, and had just occasioned demonstrations in Mexico, was bound to prove inconvenient, above all if we consider that more than one of these governments existed merely by the support or on the sufferance of the Anglo-Saxon republic; though it naturally concealed from the people the commitments which had been made in its name.

Hours before I set sail for San Salvador, I received these unexpected telegrams: "Come in spite of everything, and do not be impressed by intrigues," said the students. "The artisans of Salvador will defend you," affirmed the workmen. I realized that some unpleasantnesses were arising in the Republic of Salvador as well. Shortly afterwards arrived other telegrams which threw light on the matter.[4]

4 "San Salvador, February 29, 1912: I have pleasure in reciprocating your courteous and affectionate greetings both in the name of the *Diario Latino* and for myself. We are ready to receive you here after March 15. I do not think it would do for you to come before then. Yours most affectionately, MIGUEL PINTO, Editor of the *Diario Latino*." "San Salvador, Feb. 29, 1912: I am highly gratified at your affectionate greeting and reciprocate it. You will be very well received by our Government after March 15. Impossible before. RAMÓN MAYORGA RIVAS, Editor of the *Diario Salvador*." "S. S. Feb. 29, 1912: I reciprocate your courteous telegram of this date and notify you that we should be pleased to see you

I was asked to postpone my visit on account of that of Mr. Knox, and the scruples which prompted the Government to avoid difficulties during the stay of the North American Secretary of State in their country seemed to me worthy of all consideration. In view of this, I decided to remain at the port of San José till the date indicated. But the Government of Guatemala did not see it in this light, and General Arís's reply to a telegram from me was final.[5]

Señor Estrada Cabrera wanted to be sure that I should not be on Guatemalan territory on the arrival of Mr. Knox.

So that when I set sail on the *City of Panama*, I really did not know where I was going. North American policy was master of the whole of Central America, both by land and by sea; and the Latin-American traveller, who was defending Latin-American interests on Latin-American soil, seemed to be fated not to set foot on any coast, and to be turned back from every port. Life was paralysed, either by the memory of Mr. Knox's visit, or by the presence of Mr. Knox, or by the expectation of Mr. Knox, who landed, commanding and cold, surrounded by official committees, without being greeted by any popular cheers or homage, in spite of the efforts which the governments had made for this purpose.

When we consider the situation, it is only fair to take into account the fantastic disproportion between, on the one hand, the power of subjugation exerted by the United States—masters of a formidable navy, the arbiters of American commerce, the purveyors of war supplies to every revolution that might happen to suit them —and, on the other hand, the material and moral weakness of those who govern these little republics, having no foundation in public opinion, no economic or military powers of defence, and being exposed to the insurrections of opponents who do not hesitate to invoke the aid of Washington in "regenerating their country." To accuse

here from March 15 to 20, or onwards. Your humble servant, M. Castro, Minister for Foreign Affairs." "San Salvador, Feb. 29, 1912: I shall be pleased to receive you from March 15 onwards, Manuel E. Araujo, President of the Republic."

[5] "San José de Guatemala, March 1, 1912: Your friend and admirer allows himself to point out to you the advisability of taking advantage of the boat which sails for Salvador to-day. I do not doubt that there too the perfect gentleman and talented writer will receive an enthusiastic welcome. General Enrique Arís."

them of cowardice is to underrate the element of courage in the Spanish-American soul. The only thing for which they can be blamed is for having profited by the evil instead of rebelling against it, and contributed towards perpetuating the harm instead of combating it. If these men, clinging to power and intent on nothing but keeping it, were afraid. of rebellions fomented from abroad, it was because, in the majority of cases, they had themselves employed the same system for dislodging their predecessors. From the circumstances of their elevation, too, perhaps arose the point of view which made them underestimate the efficacy of moral forces well applied. Faced with the dominating colossus, all that they had ever done was to measure their comparative power of resistance, to reckon up their artillery, leaving in the background that moral mobilisation of right and justice which also has its weight in the balance of historical solutions. I recognise—and here we touch the true reason of Central America's weakness, and of the weakness of Spanish America in general—that these factors can be made use of with some probability of success in stable democracies (Belgium, Switzerland), which entirely avoid the reproach of anarchy, and conquer the respect of other nations by encouraging peace and progress. In order to proclaim to the world "I am the victim of an injustice!" it is necessary to have won the consideration of other nations. And unfortunately, in the greater part of our territories, and especially in those which I was then visiting, the blood, wealth, and future of the nation have been thrown away in insane struggles which have tired the patience of the world.

But these struggles have been provoked by the United States? That is even worse. Those who joined in this discord in order to favour foreign interests are more guilty than those who took advantage of it; and so are those who, seeing themselves placed in the necessity of choosing between their country's advantage and their own, accepted, in order to triumph in an internal contest, the arms or financial support offered them from without by an imperialism interested, like all imperialisms in history, in dividing in order to rule in the end by imposing themselves as a civilising element. Even if the men who governed were right at a given moment in the evolution of Central America, in the history of the aggregate of these countries they would never have been right, because the cause which placed them in irremediably subordinate positions was precisely their disintegration, their life of anarchy, their lack of far-sighted solicitude, their selfish greed, all that they and their predecessors had fomented and enjoyed the fruits of, since the fall of the great leaders of Independence.

The state of affairs made manifest by this particular and significant coincidence of Mr. Knox's simultaneous journey was the result of a long disintegration brought about throughout long years by the heat of those revolutions, which had disorganised the finances, destroyed the lives of the best citizens, hindered the development of natural wealth, and divided Central America into small states. Political blindness, the desire for rule, every base passion, had prevented them from flourishing normally, and turned their energies towards nothing but the conquest of power, with no plan or programme save that of the conquest of power itself, in such a way, and with such rude intensity, that the great business enterprises, the exploitation of their vast resources, the life-blood of the nation, were in foreign hands. From this arose a painful, ironic situation. In the pursuit of power, some of them had in reality only been running after its shadow; for the real governors are those who have in their power, not only diplomatic influences, but loans and Damocles' sword of intervention, keeping in severe tutelage those who cherish the illusion that it is they who are ruling. Thus this region, marvellously endowed by Nature, and inhabited by men full of intelligence and worth, which seemed destined to be an earthly paradise, has been slowly committing suicide.

If my reproaches are harsh, it is because I feel myself so much identified with the fate of these nations, that I almost feel myself personally cheated of my rights. I am well aware that our countries are not accustomed to the truth. I am well aware that my frankness is bound to irritate conceit and thin-skinned vanity. But heretofore their errors have always been fostered and acclimatised by adulation and deception. And the best proof of my support which I can give to these countries is consciously to risk the fulminations which will be launched against me in some quarters for having committed the unpardonable fault of rendering them a real service.

The coasting steamer which was carrying me southwards was to touch at every harbour in Central America. The first was Acajutla, on the territory of Salvador, where Señor Don Ramón Mayorga Rivas awaited me as the official messenger of President Araujo. He told me that the young men were in a state of excitement, that demonstrations were being prepared, with the flags of the Latin-American countries, and that in view of the approaching arrival of Mr. Knox, my visit might give rise to unfortunate incidents. In support of this plea, he handed me a letter from Don Estebán de Loqui,[6] the Argentine Consul in San Salvador. All this seemed to me as worthy of respect as it was well meant. But there remained the problem of finding out where Mr. Knox would allow me to land.

After a few days, a telegram at last arrived from Honduras which cleared up the situation. It came from the Minister of Foreign Affairs and read as follows: "In the name of the people and Government of Honduras, I give you hearty thanks for your courteous greeting, and inform you in advance of our sincere gratification at your visit to this republic, where you are well known and appreciated for your praiseworthy work in the cause of Latin-American solidarity. Accept, with our cordial greeting, the assurance of our esteem." This noble gesture on the part of the smallest and weakest country effaced the impression of all my mishaps.

After touching at La Unión, where I was met by delegations of

[6] The Argentine Consul said in his letter, dated February 29: "I believe that your visit at the present moment is not very opportune. Tomorrow the anniversary of the rise to power of the illustrious first magistrate of this progressive and industrious nation is to be celebrated with due rejoicings. The natural excitement which will be produced in this loyal people by the celebration of this anniversary might, on the pretext of your arrival, produce an effervescence at this solemn moment, so anxious for Central America, especially on the eve of the arrival of the Secretary of State, Mr. Knox.

"I have before me the telegram of the excellent President, Doctor Don Manuel Araujo, in answer to yours, which he has communicated to me unofficially. As I am unaware whether for one reason or another the said telegram has reached you, I reproduce it as follows. It says: 'I shall be pleased to receive you from March 15 onwards.'

"As you see, my honoured fellow-countryman, the President of the Republic's telegram is sufficiently explicit and requires no comment. I merely say to you, defer your journey, as they ask you to do, till next March 15; for I can guaranty that you will be received with affection by this people, which has on every occasion displayed admiration and love towards our country."

young men who insisted on my landing at all costs, the *City of Panama* arrived at Amapala, a port of Honduras from whence Mr. Knox had just departed *en route* for the North. The streak of smoke from the boat in which he was disappearing could still be seen on the horizon. We anchored in the splendid Bay of Fonseca, which is perhaps the most extraordinary natural harbour known, and in which, to use the expression of a North American admiral, all the fleets of the world could be contained. It is bounded by the shores of the republics of San Salvador, Honduras, and Nicaragua, and forms a great common outlet on which the three countries converge on the side facing the Pacific.

Nothing could be more picturesque than the journey up to the capital. It can hardly be called modern and comfortable. But Nature is so prodigal of vegetation and views among the parallel ridges of the mountains which rise between the sea and Tegucigalpa, that one forgets the discomforts, and the three days which one spends on mule-back seem too short to gaze upon these marvels. From San Lorenzo to Perspire, Noramulca, La Venta, Sabana Grande, Sauce and Loarque there is a constant gradation of flora, fauna, and changing horizons which succeed each other as the road rises above sea-level, skirting the hills which appear as one proceeds under a clear blue sky.

Tegucigalpa is a little city of the pure colonial type, which has maintained its character, its distinctive features and its appearance without appreciable change since the time when the mining industry made of it a prosperous centre of Spanish commerce. The capital of a republic of half a million inhabitants, which reckons its revolutions by the years of its independence, it has not been able to accomplish its own renovation or cultivate progress, agitated as its life has always been by political disturbances. But I met there a group of men ready for my ideas, and a brilliant group of young men who were aware of all that was going on in the world. I will mention Froylán Turcios, Rafael Heliodoro Valle, Salatiel Rosales, José Cruz Sologaistoa, Enrique Pinel, Samuel Laines, Ramón Ortega, Adán Canales, Edmundo Lozano, Alonso A. Brito, Manuel A. Díaz, Gustavo Alemán Bolaños, Esteban Guardiola, Juan María Cuéllar, Federico Miltón, Joaquín Bonilla, Manuel A. Zelaya, and Norberto Guillén.

The politicians seemed to me to be resolute and wide-awake. The President, Don Manuel Bonilla, was a dour, cautious man, somewhat silent, but strongly in favour of what concerned the integrity of our Latin America. The Minister of Foreign Affairs, Don Mariano Vázquez, had the happy inspiration of recalling, in his reply to Mr. Knox's speech, the phrase of Mr. Elihu Root: "We consider the independence and equal rights of the lesser and weaker members of the family of nations to be deserving of as much respect as those of the great empires." * And Señor Bertrand, the Minister for War, afterwards President of the Republic, said to me at my first interview: "It is to be wished that there were more patriots like you in America."

The chair was taken at my lecture by the Rector of the University, Dr. Rómulo E. Durón, the Athenæum devoted one of its meetings to me, the Club of Tegucigalpa gave a ball in my honour, and though the semi-official newspaper *Nuevo Tiempo* maintained an attitude of reserve, it may have had its reasons, and one detail need not take away from the significance of the whole.

What Salatiel Rosales said in the article in which he bade me welcome, was confirmed by the facts: "When our guest recalls his tour through Spanish America, he will say that there is in this country a handful of representative young men with some pride in their hearts and a spirit open to great ideals. He will say that this is a country swarming with politicians. But at the same time he will relate that there is a new generation, with broad views, vital and healthy, which will not imitate its predecessors in criminally dismembering the republic by those ridiculous squabbles which have laid claim to the name of revolutions. He will say that Honduras leaves its fields untilled, that it is devoid of railways and factories; that one progresses along its roads at the measured pace of the Biblical ass; but he will also draw attention to the fact that a younger generation is arising, energetic and optimistic, which believes in its ideals and has a lively faith in the future." Let us set aside his estimate of the politicians of his country. As regards the younger generation, his impression is most accurate. And I confess

---

* Cf. *Speeches Incident to the Visit of Philander Chase Knox . . . to the Countries of the Caribbean*, p. 72. (Washington, Government Printing Office, 1913.)

that I have seldom felt such emotion as in that little city, very Spanish and yet quite indigenous in character—above all, essentially *ours*—the humble capital of an undefended country, exposed to every kind of material and moral reprisals, and yet so independent in its bearing. And be it said that when I speak thus I am not only calling to mind their tributes and their laurel wreaths; for the best laurels for him who had set out on this difficult journey were the impersonal acceptance of his ideals. All flattery apart, I allude to the readiness of that people to understand and experience lofty impulses.

Two telegrams which I received from the President of San Salvador [7] on my return to the coast seemed to show that the atmosphere would continue to be propitious. While retracing my steps on the way which Mr. Knox's tour obliged me to travel twice, and while once more turning the prow of my ship towards the Central American republic with the tiniest area and the densest population, it was natural to call to mind the peculiar situation of this country.

San Salvador shares with Costa Rica the merit of having had fewer revolutions and drawn more profit from its natural wealth than other countries of Central America. This industrious activity began with the first missionaries, who drew from their religion a sense of discipline and a taste for manual labour. Salvador, with its forty inhabitants to a square kilometre, has since developed this original tendency vigorously, and is to-day in proportion to its population, one of the most civilised and European republics of tropical America.

The committee of politicians, which insisted on making me land at the port of La Libertad and carrying me off in an automobile to the capital, was doubtless unaware that a popular reception had been organised at the next port, Acajutla, whence there is a

[7] "President's House, March 24, 1912: I send you my affectionate greetings. I have the pleasure to inform you that the commandant of the Port of La Unión has orders to wait upon you in due form. If you desire to embark from La Unión, he will hold a launch at your disposal. Your most affectionate friend, MANUEL E. ARAUJO.

"President's House, March 25, 1912: The steamer *Jalisco* is on its way to this port. Commandant Montoya and the captain of the above vessel have received instructions to receive it and wait upon it. Your most affectionate friend," MANUEL E. ARAUJO.

good railway up to the centre of the country. Perhaps it would be unduly suspicious to suppose that it was their intention to play a trick on the students. But something must have happened, none the less, since the demonstration, which had been prepared for eleven in the morning on the 28th, had to be improvised at eleven at night on the 27th, on account of a special train which could not have been foreseen. It was perhaps on this very account that the crowd was greater and the speeches more violent.[8]

Speaking in the name of the students, Salvador Merlos,* who was afterwards to publish a book entitled *The Yankee Peril** recalled the invasion of the pirate Walker in 1856 and the burst of feeling which roused all Central America against him.† Leopoldo Valencia, in the name of the Workmen's Federation, said that at that moment "the hands of our forbears are being raised, those indomitable leaders who would rather die fighting than see a scrap of the land which they inhabit fall into the power of the conquerors." The representative of the Society of Artisans, Joaquín G. Bonilla, spoke of the "task of continental defence which falls upon the new generations." And Rubén Coto Fernández said in conclusion: "In other ages we were attacked with bayonets, but now with the dollar. But we have realised that superiority lies in education and we have begun to create in every school a machine-gun."

In official circles the fact that I abstained from occupying the carriage which the President sent to the station was interpreted as a discourtesy. But I must here set forth a point of view which applied to matters of this sort in every country through which I travelled. My journey was strictly personal, and was nothing but the visit of a writer to the young people and the masses who might propagate his ideas. I was not speaking in the name of any government, nor was I asking for official favors. If on my arrival I

---

[8] "The rejoicings of those taking part in the demonstrations at this great moment were indescribable; their hearts overflowed with joy, filled with the enthusiasm of divine patriotism, and their heads were held high, as if to fix their thoughts on the lofty summit of our future destiny, whose defence the famous Argentine writer has come to preach with the voice of a Titan."
El Independiente, March 28, 1912.

* *América latina ante el peligro.*

† Cf. W. O. Scroggs, *Filibusters and Financiers*, (New York, 1916), p. 108 ff., for the exploits of William Walker,

paid my respects to the presidents or ministers, I did it as a tribute to the official representatives of the nation in the hope of obtaining by this demonstration of respect a certain tolerance of my propaganda. But I was far from having any ulterior pretensions or interests, and aspired to no honours save those which arose from the enthusiasm of popular assemblies. It was obvious that I was bound to acknowledge the courtesies of the national representatives. But it was not my object to be received by them while omitting to fraternise with the people in general. And I must sadly confess that in order to arrive at the latter result, in the majority of cases the best thing to do was to keep at a respectful distance from the authorities, who did not always enjoy an overwhelming popularity.

The President of San Salvador was a democrat, and was far from being the man who aroused the most visible resistance in Central America. But the crowd begged me to accompany them on foot as far as my hotel; and to the hotel we went, amid shouts of "Long live the Argentine!"

These cheers for my country, and the blue and white flag which floated over every gathering, in countries holding no communication whatever with Buenos Aires, for whom I was one of the first to visit their country from the Argentine, produced in me a double sensation of gratification and of sadness: of gratification, because of their significance with regard to the prestige of my nation; and of sadness, because they drew attention to the negligence of Argentine diplomacy, imprisoned in the formulas of fifty years ago, and therefore cut off from the atmosphere in which it should move in Latin America. All these countries had their faces turned toward the South, straining their eyes for the appearance of a light which ought logically to arise within the bounds of the political ideas of the Continent. They were waiting for that Latin-American mass which was triumphing at the southern extremity of the Continent,—in a climate similar to that of the United States and with a like inflow of immigration—to make a sign, to send forth a voice to the kindred groups which were ranged between it and the tropics; to proclaim a united policy, with no hostility against anybody, but in the full communion of a family. This aspiration was in the air, as a result of the affectionate admiration with which they were all following the rise of the sister nation. In every cheer for the Argentine there

was a cheer for our family of kindred nations, as and how it should
have developed, had not influences and accidents interposed themselves, born of the geographical situation or derived from external
agencies.   In every cheer, too, there was a cheer for their own
sacrifice; for everybody understood that what had made the development of the peoples of the South possible was, to a certain extent,
the body formed by those of the North.   I frequently heard it said
that the A B C could only advance behind a rampart formed by
these suffering states.   And perhaps those who said so were right.
We in the South, from the very beginnings of our development, have
never experienced the pressure of powerful neighbours.   There was
nothing but the sea between us and Europe.   We have been able to
breathe freely and draw in oxygen from the four cardinal points,
while other republics were struggling against the dominating influences radiating from an enormous empire upon their frontiers.
In these cheers for the Argentine there was a cheer for the past, a
cheer for Morazán, and also a cheer for the future, for all our hopes.
If Argentine diplomacy had had any higher aim than its morbid
obsession with its immediate frontiers, if it had lifted the veil and
caught a glimpse of the continental panorama, the position of the
other countries of Latin America would surely have been different,
and different too would be our prestige.   But let us reserve these
reflections for the moment when we shall speak, in one of the following chapters, of the peculiar position of the republics of the
South, and the responsibilities which rest upon them.

In spite of this atmosphere of enthusiasm, within a few days what
was to prove a constant struggle till the very end of my journey
began to take shape again.   After a visit to the President, I found
myself obliged to write the secretary of the Students' Committee a
letter giving up the lecture which had been announced.[9]   The young

[9] "To the Secretary of the Students' Committee, Don Miguel Coto Bonilla:
My dear friends, Nothing could be more flattering than the invitation
which I have received from you to give a lecture in this capital, which has
ever been distinguished for its lofty spirit and serene patriotism. I have
always had the highest respect for youth and democracy. and there is here
such a close union between the students and the workmen, that I accepted the
idea with the liveliest pleasure.
"Unfortunately, an obstacle has arisen.
"I have selected a theme, which is, to my mind, not only the most living

men replied in a Manifesto, begging me to address them in spite of all.[10]

Disquieted by the turn which matters were taking, the President wrote a letter authorising the lecture, to which I replied in the respectful tone which my situation demanded. As in Mexico, the affair was assuming the appearance of a battle, and I had to meet the attack in the open, relying upon the people and the young men to counteract the intrigues which were being hatched in the dark.

In this bright and smiling city, where the central *plaza* was filled towards evening with groups of lovely women promenading round the bandstand, and where an atmosphere of idealism and distinc-

question of the day, but the one which has the strongest claims upon our attention at this critical moment from the international point of view, namely: 'Latin America face to face with Imperialism.'

"In a call which I had the honour to make this morning on the President of the Republic, I was notified that I must not treat this subject, because it is untimely to canvass such questions.

"This is not my opinion; but my position as a foreigner prevents me from commenting on the decisions of the Government.

"I deplore what has taken place, and with my deepest gratitude for the welcome extended to me by the young men and the people, I beg them to accept, with a warm shake of the hand, the expression of my most friendly feelings."

San Salvador, March 28, 1912. Manuel Ugarte.

San Salvador, March 29, 1912.

10 "Dear Friend, We have made ourselves acquainted with the ideas expressed in your letter.

"The result of your interview with President Araujo was what we had expected. But it is not the will of the Chief-Executive which should take it upon itself in this case to check the right of assembly; nor is it his function, in spite of the powers at his disposal, to imprison thought and stifle the voice which imperiously summons us to the defence of our race.

"Protected by our Constitution, and without claiming to overstep what is legal, we call upon you in no wise to respect the notification which you have received.

"For our part we will do all that is within the bounds of possibility to prevent the principles of our fundamental charter from being overthrown by means of those political subtleties which lay our sovereignty at the foot of the steps of the Capitol at Washington.

"The people of Salvador yearns to hear your voice.

"The people of Salvador ardently loves its liberties.

"And interpreting the sentiments of our fatherland, we again call upon

tion diffused itself, I understood better than anywhere else the strangely dual character of certain peoples of our Latin America. On the one hand, we have illusion, pliancy, and inaction, on the other, spirit, resolution and firmness. In that mild climate, beneath a cloudless sky, surrounded by the prodigality of nature, man does not feel himself stung by an eagerness for constant activity, and easily allows himself to drift into love of ease and idle distraction. But this tendency does not destroy the mainspring of his activity, and when the occasion arises, all his native ferocity and Spanish pride blaze up in unison. And so we saw when, finding all the theatres closed, my lecture was arranged to take place in the garden of an old convent; when the workmen received me at their headquarters; when, on April 11, a demonstration took place in honour of Latin-American solidarity; and in all the incidents arising out of my stay in the country. It was further proved, above all, when, four months later, without the presence of the "agitator", popular pressure and street demonstrations forced this same President Araujo to protest against the invasion of Nicaragua and put himself at the head of a joint protest of the Governments of Central America.

I have not yet cared to mention the surveillance to which I was subject from the very beginning of my journey. But in view of my antecedents, the character of my propaganda, and the disturbances to which it gave rise, it is hardly necessary to say that my every act was watched, not only by local agents, who were fulfilling their regular functions within their own frontiers, but also by special emissaries of the United States.

Those who are acquainted with the procedure of imperialist states and the importance which they attach to direct intelligence will not be surprised. But as my tour assumed wider proportions, this observation was transformed into hostile intrigue.

Pretexts which might give rise to damaging interpretations were you in no wise to desist from the project which has brought you into our midst.

"We remain your obedient servants and friends,

"J. Arturo Gómez, Oliverio C. Valle, Martín S. Pineda, Manuel J. Argueta, Juan A. Serpas, Leopoldo Valencia, A. García, Miguel Coto Bonilla, Salvador R. Merlos, José A. Canas, J. Leonardo Godoy, Salvador A. Jirón, Marcos R. Escobar, Benjamin Valencia, Federico Azucena, Alejandro Meléndez, J. A. Yanes (260 signatures follow)."

seized upon. By the aid of stratagems which passed unnoticed by the majority, my path was beset with snares, false intelligence was spread, and I was discredited in every way, sometimes by word of mouth, sometimes by the aid of the inspired Press. One day I was accused of touring in some commercial interest, another of being an eccentric millionaire, supposed to be subsidised by Germany. It is impossible to imagine what prudence, perseverance, energy, and diplomacy it was necessary to use in order to meet these emergencies. They afterwards went so far as to intercept my letters, oppose the circulation of my books, and blacken' my character unscrupulously; and I felt the pressure of severe reprisals. But at the time when these activities began, I believed I should have a fair fight. I was surprised at the atmosphere and the plane on which I had to manœuvre.

My greatest difficulty lay in communicating with the outside world. I only received what passed the censor, or the North American cable, so that I was frequently ignorant of the atmosphere of countries before my arrival or after my departure. Thus the New York *Times* of August 18, 1912, was able to print an absolutely inaccurate report, which was copied by *El Día* of Havana and various Latin-American papers, without my hearing anything about it until I arrived at the end of my journey. And so the most abominable reports of my tour were cabled to Buenos Aires.

All this brought clearly to light—to pass over the sphere of personal affairs, and to return to those of international interest—the power which newspaper intelligence may have as an agent of discord. When it is not a case of remote lands, but of adjacent ones, the results are generally grievous. Many of the collisions which have taken place between our republics have originated in malicious intelligence. And the cable foments estrangements and enmities even when the peace is not broken. Every time I tried to defend Mexico in Buenos Aires, I had to begin by destroying the hostile impression created by the press agencies. Nothing is harder than to reaffirm the truth in a *milieu* impregnated with a constant flow of tendencious information. When we consider that in the majority of cases our nations have to make use of the foreign cable even for their official communications, we can measure the degree of efficiency to which government action is likely to attain, even in internal matters, when it tries to carry on diplomatic action in disagreement with that very power which holds in its hands the essential source of information.

The month of April, 1912, was not the most propitious time at which to arrive in Nicaragua, for the treaty which was to prove fatal to its autonomy was then being carried through against the will of the country. As an inevitable result of this, a fresh revolution was in the air.

It will suffice to recall what had gone before,[11] to understand the tragedy through which this people was living. The administration of Señor Adolfo Díaz, a continuation of that of Señor Juan Estrada, had just contracted a new loan with the house of Brown and Seligman, of New York, secured by the customs, accepting the nomina-

[11] The North American Government, interested in preventing the possible construction of a new inter-oceanic canal through Nicaragua, sent a squadron into Nicaraguan waters in April, 1908, composed of the cruisers *Washington, Colorado, South Dakota, Albany*, etc., with a contingent of about 4,000 men and instructions to avail themselves of a pretext for landing. The President of Nicaragua, who was at that time Don José Santos Zelaya, tried to temporise with Captain Moore, head of the squadron. But shortly after, on October 10, 1909, Mr. Moffat, the North American Consul at Bluefields (on the Atlantic coast of Nicaragua), supported an insurrection led by the Governor of this region, Señor Juan J. Estrada. Mr. Knox, in a note which aroused much comment in Latin America, declared the revolution legitimate, and handed Señor Zelaya's representative in Washington his passports. In the course of the struggle, General Toledo, who commanded the lawful Nicaraguan forces, had shot two American subjects, Canon and Groce, whom he had caught in the act of trying to dynamite the Government's ships. This threw light on the character of the revolution, and the leader of it himself, Señor Estrada, took it upon himself to confirm this later, by declaring in the New York *Times* of September 10, 1912, that this movement had received financial aid from North American companies, mentioning the firms of Joseph W. Beers, which contributed $200,000 and Samuel Well, who gave $150,000. Convinced that the revolutionaries would receive every sort of aid from North America, the President of Nicaragua, not to prolong the struggle, thought it patriotic to resign, and left the country on board the Mexican gun-boat *General Guerrero*, after handing over his powers, in accordance with the Constitution and by the consent of Congress, to Dr. Don José Madriz, a jurist having no connection with politics. This Government was recognised by many nations, but not by the United States, which continued to support the fictitious revolution. When Señor Madriz

tion by the bankers of a North American collector, and handing over to them the railways. The situation was such that the Nicaraguan Congress, which ought to have met in January, had postponed its sessions, at the request of the *chargé d'affaires* of the United States, till the arrival of a special envoy from Washington with the mission of introducing amendments to the Constitution. In spite of the fact that the cities were occupied by North American troops, public opinion openly protested. When they alleged the Nicaraguan debt in justification of this intervention, popular enthusiasm surged up, subscriptions were opened, and as much as possible was collected in order to redeem themselves and safeguard the independence of the country.[12] This did not fall in with the plans of the Government, which was bent upon signing the famous Knox-Castrillo convention, against the wind and tide of public opinion.

When the *City of Sydney* arrived at the harbour of Corinto, a police official intimated to me that I could not land.

"Why not?" I asked in surprise.

"I am not going to give you any explanations."

"All the same, it is your duty to give me them."

The official hesitated for a moment, and with visible annoyance finally said:

"There is a law prohibiting the entry of anarchists into the country."

gave orders to attack Bluefields, he was met by the fact that the harbour was defended by North American sailors, and that the cruisers of that country were blockading the coast. Realising that it would not be a civil but an international struggle, he renounced his mandate on August 26, 1910, and left for Mexico, where he died shortly afterwards. So the U. S., under the presidency of Mr. Taft, took possession of the customs of Nicaragua, and thus was started the régime which still continues to-day.

12 Nothing could be more painful and moving than these lists, in which were to be seen the tears of a nationality. The newspapers of Nicaragua of March, 1912, set aside wide columns in which the most humble offerings could be read side by side with the contributions of the moneyed classes: Samuel Gavarrete, his whole possessions; Laura Delgada, the proceeds of the sale of her bed; Juana Gutiérrez, the house where she lives; Laura Roque, her sewing-machine; Manuel de Aragón, day-labourer, the value of twelve days' work; Ramón Robleto, his cart with two oxen; Joaquina Velásquez, licensed mendicant, her day's collection, 20 centavos.

Without answering, I drew up then and there, in the saloon of the ship, my telegrams of greeting to the Press; and as soon as I had written them, I called a steward to take them on shore.

The official then intervened again:

"You have been cut off from all communications," he said, "and cannot send letters or telegrams."

"Not even to the Consul for my country?" I asked.

"Not even to the Consul for your country," he repeated harshly.

It is superfluous to say that I managed to find a traveller who saw the Argentine Consul, Don Marcial R. Candioti, that very morning, and told him what had happened. Candioti was a man of energy, formerly a *caudillo* of the province of Santa Fé, where he had headed a few revolutions in his day, and, continental doctrines or no, he came that very evening with the sole intention of showing courtesy to a compatriot who had been arbitrarily detained. He offered to talk to the Minister of Foreign Affairs, and assured me that the boat should not leave before I had succeeded in landing.

The look-out men attracted the attention of the workmen on the quay, and it was they who put me in communication with the newspapers of Nicaragua and León, thus upsetting the plans of the Government. On the following day the commotion broke out. The *Diario de Nicaragua* had interviews on the subject with the Minister of Foreign Affairs, the Minister of the Interior, the Minister of Finance, and the Minister of War, Señor Mena, who had afterwards to bow before the revolution. The *Diario Moderno*, of León, protested violently, and the whole Press took the matter up. This outrage, as was natural, was better propaganda in favour of my' ideas than a dozen speeches. Two telegrams [13] and a letter [14] con-

[13] "Managua, April 21, 8. 15 A. M. : I could obtain no result last night from my investigations as to the subject of my telegram. The under-secretary of Foreign Affairs pledged himself to telegraph to me to-morrow here, where I shall arrive by train at mid-day. Greetings to you."

M. R. Candioti.

"Managua, April 22, 6.55 P. M.: No reply up to the present. I am sending an official protest against this discourtesy to me in my capacity of Consul. I shall report it to my Government. Greetings to you."

M. R. Candioti.

[14] "Managua, April 23, 1912: Distinguished fellow-countryman, I have the pleasure to introduce to you Señor O. S., who, with his charming wife, will

vinced me that the resolution was irrevocable, and in spite of the severe interdict laid upon me, I sent to the papers a protest [15] upon which they commented in emphatic terms.[16]   One significant detail may be noted: the dock-labourers to whom I have referred came opposite the boat that day to make a silent demonstration, grouped round the national flag.

be your travelling companion; he will be delighted to have your company.

"To-morrow I will send you word from Managua touching your affairs; I shall go in person and demand an answer to my telegram of to-day. Your affectionate friend and obedient servant." M. R. CANDIOTI.

P. S. "On leaving your boat I was asked for my name. I suppose that to-morrow they will not let me see it. Vale."

[15] "To the youth, the intellectuals, and the people of Nicaragua. From the port of Corinto, where I have been prevented from landing by order of the Government and where I am watched and not allowed to communicate with anybody; from this beautiful spot of Nicaraguan territory, whose natural beauties ought to soften the harshness of its politicians, I formulate an indignant protest and call upon the honourable citizens of all parties in the name of the dignity of our republics.

"I am neither an agitator nor a demagogue. I stand outside party. I know nothing and I wish to know nothing of the internal conflicts of the republics through which I pass. And my calm propaganda of union and concord within Latin America, my reasoned plea in favour of the co-ordination of our republics, can only appear subversive to those who have lost all notion of patriotism and high spirit.

"I know that the young men, the intellectuals, and the people of Nicaragua, whose reputation for hospitality is well known, will be the first to condemn severely the attitude of the authorities; and it is for this reason that I formulate my protest. In closing their gates on a writer of the same race, who speaks the same language and defends the common interests of the Latin peoples of the New World, the Government has made evident the pledges which bind it to the foreigners. It is you who must now give judgment. I do no more than indicate the position of affairs, convinced that the Nicaraguan people is high-spirited, that treachery cannot prosper in Latin America, and that we will go so far as to tolerate in our republics every crime of the politicians except those harmful to the flag and the fatherland." MANUEL UGARTE.

On board the *City of Sidney*, April, 1912.

[16] "To refuse entry to the country to a Nicaraguan, without just cause, i. e. without a previous sentence condemning him to expatriation, is an offence frequently committed here; but it is rare for this to happen to a foreigner, still less when it is an important person, worthy of particular consideration.

"Even barbarous peoples are as a rule hospitable; for hospitality is a

In this book of calm exposition there should not be a single violent word against anything or anybody, and I abstain from passing judgment on the politicians who accepted as a loan from the foreigner funds secured on their own customs, whereas the conventions signed by them were so irregular that the very Senate of North America rejected them as abusive and contrary to international law. We are observing the panorama of a continent; and with such wide horizons before us, direct criticism of the conduct of individuals is hardly suitable. What is painful to our Latin-American patriotism is the impression which certain attitudes must produce in Washington, and the unjust generalisations which can be made by attributing to a whole nation or a whole continent tendencies only concerning those who were guilty of them.

Costa Rica is the republic of Central America in which public instruction is most widely diffused, in which peace has been the least frequently disturbed, and in which all fruitful activities have accordingly developed to the best advantage. All the same, on my arrival, the accustomed difficulties arose. The President did not answer my telegram of courtesy, and the interview which the correspondent of *La Información*, of San José, had with me at the har-

---

human sentiment, it is a bond of fraternity between men, placed by nature in their hearts, like a seal of union and of solidarity among them. This hospitality cannot be denied without a serious reason of great weight which may so justify and excuse the act that it is not deserving of a universal anathema.

"When dealing with such a person as Señor Ugarte, even if the President had had reasons for prohibiting his entry, he ought to have discussed the matter with his Ministry, seeing that the consequences affect not only the President and his Cabinet, but the whole country, to which he is exhibiting himself as deaf to every principle of civilisation and humanity."

Diario de Nicaragua, April 25, 1912.

"The previous protest needs no comment. A hazardous minority which guides the destinies of the republic, which receives the foreign conqueror on its knees, which kisses the hand that strikes it, so long as this hand contains gold, is not, and never will be throughout all time, capable of any notion of patriotism, pride, or dignity.

"Manuel Ugarte's written page remains as an eternal stigma on a Government which, having treated the flag of their fatherland like a rag, feels ashamed and afraid to hear the words of a free man."

Diario Moderno, April 25, 1912.

bour was intercepted by the administration,[17] together with various communications addressed to me. All this, as in San Salvador, contributed towards gaining me a popular reception.[18] For the success of my journey was really the work of the Governments, who by opposing me revealed to the people a subservience and so aroused the national pride.

In this republic, which had always had a reputation for hospitality to the political refugees of neighbouring nations, there had gathered together that brilliant group of Nicaraguans which afterwards, under

[17] "On the arrival of Señor Ugarte at Puntarena, we commissioned our correspondent at that port, Don Hector Guevara Santos, to obtain an interview with the famous Argentine lecturer, and wire us a thousand words on his impressions of Central America.

"Señor Guevara Santos obtained the interview and handed it in at the telegraph office. But it was not transmitted, owing to orders from a high quarter.

"This case is unique under the present administration and the recent ones which we have had in the country, and we cannot do less than deeply deplore that by an act which was perhaps not considered in connexion with its high and transcendent significance, a dark and sultry shadow has been thrown across the luminous and beautiful panorama of the liberties of our democracy."　　*La Información,* May 3, 1912.

[18] "The train stopped and the students gave thunderous cheers for Ugarte. A hundred persons at once invaded the carriage, in which the celebrated poet and notable author arrived, to pay him their respects.

"With great difficulty, owing to the compact mass surrounding the carriage and crowding the station platform, Ugarte was able to get out to the street."　　*La Información,* April 30, 1912.

"A concourse of more than a thousand persons crowded on to the platforms of the Pacific Railway station to cheer our famous guest and prove to him the hospitality and sympathy of the people of Costa Rica.

"In the midst of a delirious crowd the defender of the Latin race was conducted to the Imperial Hotel, and more than once had to bow his thanks on hearing expressive cheers for the Argentine Republic."　　*El Republicano,* April 30, 1912.

"When the train stopped, a unanimous cry of enthusiasm announced with a clamorous shout that the poet was about to descend from it. Ugarte greeted the people and the young men with pleasant phrases. Afterwards he was accompanied to the hotel on foot, an attitude unknown to the dollar diplomatists who inopportunely arrive in the country."　　*La Prensa Libre,* of same date.

the leadership of Julián Irias, and working in accord with General Mena, set on foot the last revolution for liberty, which broke out a few months later. It was there that I made the acquaintance of General Zeledón, who died at Massaya, at the head of the patriots, in a fight with the regular troops of the North American Army; of Alejandro Bermúdez, who was afterwards the best champion of the defensive policy in Central America, and was followed with such implacable persecution; of José D. Portocarrero, Alceo Hazera, Felipe N. Fernández, Ecateo Torres, Leonardo Montalván and other *émigrés*. Among the men of reflection and action with whom I had dealings, I remember Guillermo Vargas, editor of *La Republica;* Skinner Klee and Augusto Coello, editors of *La Prensa Libre;* Napoleón Briceño, editor of *El Noticiero;* Ricardo Coto Fernández, editor of *El Republicano;* Lesmes Suárez, editor of the *Hoja Obrera;* Fernando Borges, editor of *La Información;* Joaquín García Monje, José Fabio Garnier, Justo A. Facio, Joaquín Barrionuevo, the poets Lisimaco Chavarría, José M. Zeledón, and Omar Dengo, and a group of organisers of the labour movement, at the head of which was Don Gerardo Matamoros.

The President, Don Ricardo Jiménez, showed himself extremely reserved, and gave no sign of that spirit of opposition which, report had it, had led him to fulminate against imperialism in Congress a few years previously, when he stated that "a stone thrown into Wall Street would be bound to fall on the head of a thief."

But if the first representative of the people had his reasons for making a show of prudence, the people did not share them. With Panama on its frontiers, the republic of Costa Rica had been, so to speak, an eyewitness of the dismemberment of Colombia, and felt itself more directly threatened than its Central American sisters by the conflicts which this proximity was bound to cause it. So that my idea met with a favourable atmosphere. I received enthusiastic telegrams, supported by hundreds of signatures, from the most distant villages of the republic. Of course, hostile acts were not wanting, and I had to beat off a street attack with my stick. But from the Athenæum to the workmen's organisations, including the Students' Association, public opinion was favourable to the lecture, which took place in the pelota ground of Beti-Jai, with no more disturbances than are inseparable from all large assemblies.[19]   The thesis was taken up once more some days later by the Venezuelan General, Rivas Vázquez, who took occasion to attack the President of his own country, thus giving Bermúdez, the Nicaraguan, a chance of raising the debate, in his turn, to the international level, by his decisive answer.

"A poet's journey!" said some.   "The journey of an idealist who on his way to an ideal world will come to grief on the rocks of the world as it is!"

"A logically necessary journey!" I replied, after I had sounded the truth of the situation in half of Latin America.   For in Costa Rica, too, the germs of dissolution were already fermenting, which were to bring this country a few years later, in 1917, into the painful situation summed up by Don R. Fernández Guardia, their own Minister in Washington, in an official note to Mr. Robert Lansing, the North American Secretary of State.

[19] "Those who expected to find in Ugarte a tumultuous orator, an incendiary and a raiser of storms, were disappointed. His speech does not smack of the barricades or the political demonstration; it is calm and serene, its object being to give a lesson in patriotism, not to promote rebellion or disorders.

"In accomplishing his pacific and redeeming mission, moreover, Ugarte is discharging his right function. His discourse is the result of a propaganda of civilisation and education. A writer by nature, his popular addresses may err on the side of a literary and artistic quality too high for the public, but his nature cannot be belied. He is before all things a literary man, an artist, a poet, and even in his efforts to remain on the level of the crowd, he discloses the lyrical wings which spring from his shoulders."

La Prensa Libre, May 15, 1912.

"It was after the exit, at the corner of the Teatro Circo, that the police intervened. At the moment when a numerous band of young enthusiasts was surrounding and cheering Ugarte, the Commandant of Police, Señor Ricardo Monge, cleared a way to the lecturer and notified him that he must prevent his companions from shouting, as a public demonstration was prohibited.

"Ugarte raised his voice and proclaimed this to them, advising them to disperse, so as to avoid trouble.

"The enthusiasm of the students was delirious. From among the dense mass of police, excited cheering could be heard and the ovation continued till the lecturer had been escorted to the door of the Imperial Hotel."

La República, May 16, 1912.

"In these few words of convincing eloquence," says the official document, "is admirably summed up the doctrine of non-intervention. Costa Rica takes her stand on them to claim, in the name of the right of small nationalities to existence, that she shall be allowed to live her own life, in conformity with the freely-expressed will of the majority of her people. For intervention exercised by means of armed force is not the only kind. In dealing with a small and weak nation, an unfriendly attitude on the part of a great and powerful nation is all that is required to produce the effects of intervention to a greater or less degree."

Certain elements in our Latin America have lived in a state of oscillation between a denial of the existence of any danger, and wrath after acts of violence have taken place. The words "foresight" and "negotiation" do not exist in the dictionary of those *caudillos* who, fertile in expedients, believe they are saving their country by their presence in the Government. Either "the United States are our best friends," or "we must bow before what they impose upon us." The idea of seeking a middle course between these two attitudes rarely presents itself to the minds of our "statesmen."

It is perhaps for this reason that they insisted that I was talking like a "man of letters" with "no previous knowledge of international affairs" and with no knowledge of "American politics." It is obvious that neither in Costa Rica nor in any other republic did I fall in with the limitations, simple-mindedness, compromises, vainglory, and narrow local outlook which keep Spanish-American politicians revolving in an artificial cycle of insignificant parochial rivalries, disproportionate pride, and puerile credulity, far removed from any wide vision or redeeming impulse. In the judgment of those who had the direction of affairs in these little cities—who had never left their native corner of territory or acquired any ideas beyond what they had learnt in the forests ordering people to be shot—I "had no understanding of diplomacy." It was they who knew how to govern; they who had caused Mexico to lose, in California and Texas, half her territories; they who had not foreseen the results of the Panama Canal; who tolerate a guard of foreign sailors round the government buildings at Managua, who play the part of Greek chorus at the Pan-American Congresses, who, from north to south, have led our Latin America into all her dangers and humiliations. If a policy is to be judged by its results, they have certainly been inimitable politicians.

The most serious malady of Central America is that of revolution.

All these peoples have had upheavals, when some necessary change was resisted by the governments, and no way but that of violence could be found to effect it. Forces useful to the well-being of the body politic, finding themselves obstructed, became disorderly and overturned the obstacle. It was in this sense that the emancipation of the Spanish colonies in the New World a century ago was inevitable, after an economic, political, and social evolution which had outgrown the Spanish administrative system and forms of government. It had been prepared by general interests, and such deep causes, that it may be considered as a collective effervescence unaffected by the whims of the mob and the ambition of the leaders.

Unfortunately, the same cannot be said of the revolutions, insurrections, *coups d'etat*, seditious outbreaks, and *pronunciamientos* which have succeeded one another since 1810 without logic or moderation, paralysing the advance of the Continent and casting discredit upon a great number of the Latin republics. For this reason it is interesting to try to find out what have been the primary causes and contributory conditions, in the sphere of sociology and politics, which have brought about this morbid liability to convulsions, and this endemic state of anarchy in territories exceptionally favoured by Nature, where man can find without effort all that is necessary to life. When we examine the past, we see that Latin America is overshadowed by two atavistic tendencies to anarchy: first from the Indian side and afterwards from the Spanish side.

It is a very widespread error to regard the primitive inhabitants of South America as a homogenous body. The New World, like Europe, was divided at the time of its discovery into numerous distinct groups or communities, which were unknown to one another, hated one another or made war with one another. There were some more numerous, warlike, progressive, and audacious tribes which dominated the others, and the spirit which reigned over these territories was the negation of solidarity. With the exception of the two great combinations formed by the Inca and Aztec empires (which were founded on the subjection of great masses to a governing group, exacting tribute and service), the Indian tribes lived in a state of perpetual hostility, constantly preoccupied with revenge, arising from the injuries and traditions which formed their rudimentary history. This is what made possible the subjection of so many millions of men, and the conquest of such vast territories by a handful of Spaniards. Pizarro and Hernán Cortés were not only lucky fighters, but subtle politicians, who took advantage of grudges, revenges, rivalries, and ambitions, fomenting division and doubt, and by recruiting among the Indians themselves the allies necessary to beat down the strongest resistance, succeeded in the end in imposing their domination. But this victory, obtained by means of anarchy, had not destroyed it and was in its turn to be rendered fruitless by its means; for it was the Indians who formed the mass of the armies in the separatist revolution, in which they thought for a moment they saw the instrument of their own vengeance.

To this foundation of corrosive hatred was added the proud individualism and jealous arrogance of the new comers. When we recall the discovery of South America and the three centuries of Spanish domination, we are surprised at the frequency with which, in the midst of the most heroic deeds, the leaders fight between themselves or their subordinates rise against them. The discord and armed struggles between the captains who lead the expeditions are so intermingled with their prowess and success, that at times we ask ourselves if the chief secret of their victories should not be sought precisely in this independence and exaggerated tendency to personal assertiveness. Once it had taken root in the colonial régime, we meet with the same spirit of haughty pre-eminence and tenacious love of command, throughout the interminable disputes between the military, civil, and religious authorities which frequently obliged the mother country to send over emissaries—whose decrees, dictated in the name of the king, were not always respected. What was a strength during the conquests, when every soldier thought himself a captain, and every captain a sovereign, only produced weakness in the Spanish colonial régime, and degenerated in the new states into an inexhaustible source of conspiracies and dictatorships.

The South American revolutions are not chance phenomena. However it may be in regard to the historical antecedents which we have just recalled, they are obedient to well-defined general causes, seeing that we meet with them under a similar form in territories having no communication with each other, and find them diminishing or disappearing gradually in certain regions, when the germ which makes them fatal has decayed or died.

Among the causes arising within Latin America (we will speak afterwards of those which come from outside) we must mention, above all, the bewilderment of the indigenous masses, mocked by a separatist movement which in the majority of cases meant no more to them than a change of servitude. The new republics, governed by an *élite* in which the descendants of Europeans predominated, were organised on the basis of the economic and social principles of the mother country and always pushed aside the original masters of the territories. Banished from these brand-new organisations, the aborigines formed an exasperated mass in which political adventurers used to seek the elements with which they effected their interminable revolutions. But these revolutions would not have taken on the character of continuity which constitutes their special feature, if it had not been for three conditions which have particularly favoured them.

The first of these is the disaggregation of the ancient colonial administrative areas into twenty or so organised bodies, whose irrational frontiers, relatively small population, and lack of size, places them at the mercy of every bold enterprise. The absence of an adequate regular army, the violence of ambition, and the inexperience of the men in casual possession of power, make surprise attacks easy. For a change of authorities to be brought about in a *milieu* which is still unstable and lacks a basis in tradition, it is sometimes enough that a minute group desires to change the established order.

The second cause is the illegal origin of these authorities, which have nearly all come into existence by means of a *coup de main* or a sham election. Such a basis for the institutions standing for order is not best calculated to impose respect, and it frequently happens that the sight of the success achieved by a government based on revolution encourages the hopes of a revolution aspiring to transform itself into a government.

As for the third condition, it is to be found in the weakness or absence of commercial interests, industries, economic enterprises—those forces of social equilibrium which are interested in maintaining order.

There exists, without a doubt, in these countries—even in those which seem to be the most rent by discord—a majority which disapproves of violence, and desires to put an end to this fruitless agitation. This majority may be divided into two categories: the first and more numerous is composed of those who, having no political aim in view, are obeying a personal desire for security and rest; the second and more important is formed by an *élite* of intellectuals capable of realising the painful consequences of anarchy and the harm which it does to the future of the country. The abstention, the silence, or the complaisance of these more peaceful and cultivated elements are to be explained by the fact that in communities in process of formation, and sometimes as yet unorganised, defects make themselves more easily felt than qualities; and the reasons which lead to pre-eminence are sometimes the opposite of those which good sense demands to ensure a healthy government.

Wherever, in the South American republics, the elements which work or reflect feel themselves immune from unscrupulous conspirators, and are aided by a real national organisation, a legal basis for their electoral systems, and a profitable exploitation of the wealth of the soil [violent] changes in the established order become difficult, or have completely disappeared. Profiting by their gradual rise and increasing prosperity, the masses have widened their views, and professional exploiters of discontent have found themselves forced to confine their petty ambitions within the normal democratic forms.

Survivals of this evil persist, however, in the form of rivalries or frontier controversies with neighbouring republics. Except in some isolated cases, no essential reason, touching vital matters, can separate these countries, because they are concerned with territories having no divergency of interest and with practically no communication between them. In spite of this, we have seen some nation, which has not yet succeeded in exploring its own territory, embarking rashly on fratricidal conflicts in order to wrest from another country regions which are sometimes sterile, to the detriment of a group of the same composition and the same language as itself.

They thus waste their combative instincts over a frontier question, just as the republics about which we spoke before squandered them in struggles for the Presidency. Latin America, one in its history and interests, but blinded, like all weak regions, by the hopes and ambitions of powerful nations, has thus seen its forces diminished by an incessant unrest which has constantly set at odds the different parties in each republic and the different republics within the larger aggregation, to the grave prejudice of the interests of these communities, whose riches have to a large extent fallen into the hands of foreign companies.

The mutual hatreds have been so violent that, in order to combat a rival party in internal affairs, or a neighbouring country, in external affairs, they have often gone so far as to accept foreign aid. Such is the origin of those factors making for disorder to which we have alluded in former pages.

In using these general currents of feeling in order to forward their own interests or widen their influence, the imperialist nations have done no more than follow tactics as well-known as they are ancient, and we will not insist upon the moral aspect of their action. But it is none the less sure that in overthrowing governments not favourable enough to their course of action, and elevating to power men pliant enough to serve them, these powers have for more than a century had a share in producing this anarchy, while never ceasing to represent themselves as the natural allies and guardians of peace. Revolutions have been backed by financial aid, by sending military supplies, and even by military intervention, so often as this has been useful to the end which they were following. On the other hand, their diplomacy has frequently complicated the quarrels between our peoples, in order to forestall coalitions for purposes of resistance, and so assert their hegemony by setting themselves up as arbiters.*

By the influence of such manœuvres as these, they have prolonged the nervous tension of the masses, uncertain whose leading

---

* One cannot avoid wishing that Señor Ugarte would give specific instances supported by documents. Are the documents inaccessible? Señor Ugarte also fails here, as elsewhere, to distinguish between official acts and those of private individuals or companies.

they ought to follow, and have increased the dislocation of their forces. These constant revolutions, which, far from serving the cause of liberty, contributed towards strengthening dictatorships, have proved their best auxiliaries in subjugating our people and favouring the success of imperialism.

It is in this way that the republics of Nicaragua, Santo Domingo and Haiti have arrived, after an innumerable and confused series of internal cataclysms, at the point of pledging their customs and accepting a protectorate. The same methods led to the separation of Panama, to the detriment of Colombia. And it is with the aid of similar factors, though in the face of greater difficulties, because the resistance is vigorous, that the work of weakening Mexico is being carried out.

Attempts have been made to explain this constant agitation by pointing out that these are young nations, and that peoples have to pass through some trying stages before attaining to balance and maturity. But this theory is contradicted by the example of the United States, who are still a young nation, but have not had more than one revolution, caused by a serious disagreement about slavery. It is also rendered doubtful by the normal, pacific life of certain of the republics of the South, which have undergone a reaction against these errors for some time past. So we have to admit that it is not a question of an unavoidable evil, but of an occasional tendency which can be modified or overcome by the aid of an ideal, namely, the good of one's country; and by two weapons, namely, the railway and the school. The much-abused word inexperience is purely correct as applied to these phenomena, but on condition that it is interpreted, not in the sense of youth, but of lack of knowledge. And perhaps this is the kindest interpretation; for though peoples cannot grow old at will, yet the acquisition of enlightenment and judgment may depend on their own efforts.

It is not going too far to foresee that a moment is at hand in the visible development of our nations, tried by innumerable difficulties and admonished by voices on all hands, when their interests will rise above internal politics and foolish quarrels with their neighbours, in order to face their real problems in the wider sphere of international life, and examine the favourable or unfavourable conditions which must be encouraged or combated in order to ensure their full development. The true problems of Latin America do not consist in knowing the name of the men or groups of men who ought to govern them, nor in disputing with their neighbours over a frontier zone before they have fully exploited their own heritage. The groups which quarrel for power all have the same programme, or rather lack of programme. Every one of these republics is capable of supporting a population a hundred times denser than at present. Their preoccupation with internal politics and their sensitiveness with regard to frontier questions are fated to pass into the background, in face of the necessity for determining the economic organisation which shall develop the resources of their lands both on and below the surface, and the urgent need to ensure an autonomous development which may check foreign influences.

There are some who, while recognising the logic of this process, put forward an objection. "What we have, above all, to root out," they say, "are those tyrants whom we cannot get rid of, and who can only conceive of opposition in exile." Unfortunately it cannot be denied that in certain republics pride, ignorance, and fear seem to work together to perpetuate a situation which cannot be tolerated. But in this connection a saying of the French Revolution comes to one's mind: "Tyranny does not exist because someone represents it; it is represented by somebody because it exists." If the atmosphere continues the same, it is highly probable that if the tyrant is overthrown, it is not democracy, but another and greater tyrant that will arise. But there can none the less be no doubt that the régime of irresponsible authority which oppresses some republics constitutes an obstacle to harmony between the different countries, and keeps up a continual incitement to disorder.

But a solution must be hoped for from the conditions with which Latin America is necessarily bound to be faced in future from the point of view of international politics. Popular pressure will become more powerful as it becomes more pacific. I do not say that revolutions will suddenly cease. Before disappearing, the system will inevitably make aggressive reappearances. But promising symptoms are not lacking. The younger generations have a tendency to form organised parties. European immigration brings with it a less violent conception of the struggle. The masses who provided the inflammable material for these holocausts are showing themselves less ready to respond. And, as civilisation spreads, the bosses whose sole programme was their own ambition are beginning to appear an anachronism. Something of the same sort has got to happen with regard to those artificial dissensions which have separated these republics, born of the same movement and promising a parallel process of development, in a continent divided into two halves by its racial composition, its language, and its two types of civilisation. Illness has to end either in a cure or in death; and in like manner these dissensions must end, either in a vital recovery of the groups of which they are the scourge, or in a national abdication before a foreign power. "Nations live so long as they have the will to live."

CHAPTER V

THE NEW ROME

The policy of weak peoples—"Anti-imperialism" in New York—The wiles of the conqueror—Roosevelt's "gesture" and the silence of Latin America—The methods of advance—Had we but known!

"WHY do you not go and put forward these ideas in New York?" a man said to me one day, thinking that he was sarcastically expressing an impossible idea.

His objection was due to ignorance of the nature of the United States, whose external action on the peoples conterminous with them becomes an abuse and a tyranny rather by the fault of those dominated than of those who dominate; but whose internal life, thanks to the censorship exercised by public opinion, allows scope for every sort of controversy. Imperialist policy might expel me from Nicaragua, by the agency of subservient and obsequious persons who punished thought with the penalties of an act of violence; but it would not venture to oppose my entry into New York, thus assuming direct responsibility for the guilt. In course of time the United States may end in becoming the only country in which we are allowed to speak with perfect freedom against the policy which they are themselves carrying out in Latin America. So there was no temerity about my journey to New York, since the ogre is nowhere less dangerous than in his own domain.

And how easy it is to travel to the United States from the coasts of the Caribbean and the Gulf of Mexico! It is as if all roads, material and moral, led to the new Rome. An easy road, a gentle declivity, draw towards this metropolis those in search of knowledge, those longing for pleasure, those in pursuit of fortune, and, what is more serious, those who are ambitious of government. For just as it is the United States to which people resort in quest of a university degree, a gay life, a fashionable dress, a profitable business, so too, it is sometimes there that they go to seek the presidential baton.

123

Many popular causes, candidatures, and elections are made in the White House rather than in the country interested. To be a minister plenipotentiary in Washington is to have ninety-nine chances out of a hundred of becoming a president. It is there that the bonds are created which begin by being political, then become social, and end by becoming economic. It is there that men lose touch with their own nationality, and are saturated with alien ideas, so that it is the usual thing for them to return to their own country as commissaries, delegates or proconsuls.

And it must be confessed that the recantation and defection of those who leave the little cities of the old colonial courts at an early age, to fall suddenly into this portentous Babel, this unprecedented super-city, which has no peer in all the ages, is to a certain extent explicable. To come to New York is to live in the future of the world, to inhabit those planets constructed in dreams by the imagination. However hardy may be one's patriotism, there is a moment in which it is overcome by a human impulse of wonderment at this progress, and a selfish sentiment of its comfort.

From the huge, fantastic harbour to the enormous, splendid hotel, passing down avenues crossed in every direction by tramways and railroads; from dazzling shops to the advertisements and newspapers; from the fabulous businesses, juggling with unheard-of figures, to the seas of people pouring out on the streets from the sky-scrapers; from its spectacles to its catastrophes; everything when we arrive in the United States speaks to us of something vast, be it heaven or hell, of something paradoxical and disconcerting which arrests us and strikes us dumb. The writer had lived long years in Europe,. and arrived fresh from the sight of Paris, London, and Berlin; but this was the capital of capitals, the summit of the most formidable of civilisations. Even I too, as a man, felt proud that the human race should have been able to scale such heights, and I applauded the victory with all the enthusiasm of my soul. But as a Spanish-American patriot I experienced a deep sensation of disquiet and sorrow on seeing the contrast between this stronghold of domination and the miserable forlornness of our weakness.

My hostility to imperialist policy,—or rather, my natural and patriotic desire that Latin America should oppose it,—has often been misrepresented and wilfully depreciated, by perverting it into hatred or underestimation of the United States. I have tried to destroy this impression in numberless articles and speeches, but I now insist on it once again, and perhaps not for the last time, for wilful errors have amazing vitality.

I have never blamed Cæsar for dividing Gaul against itself in order to subdue it. Cæsar's manœuvre was a sign of his superiority. But it is legitimate to deplore the fact that the Gauls were not astute enough to frustrate it. It would be insane to consider the policy of Hernán Cortés in Mexico as a crime. In the whole of time there is no record of a greater deed of prowess than that accomplished by him. But it is reasonable to consider that if the twenty millions * of inhabitants who constituted the mighty Aztec empire had not come to grief through internal dissension, their subjection could not have been effected. To rail against the conquest is a futile task, given the predestined course and irrevocable nature of human events, the morality of which is that formulated by the conqueror. So much so, that it may be said that a race definitely conquered is a race definitively dishonoured; since victory destroys military and moral values, sweeping away even the most legitimate glories and distinctions. My object has been to call the attention of the Aztecs and Gauls of my time and my family of nations to the possibility of avoiding suicidal dissensions, in order to develop a vigorous power, increase the health of their community, and co-ordinate it, in view of what is the supreme aspiration of every living species: development and survival.

The United States have done and will continue to do what all the strong peoples in history have done, and nothing can be more futile than the arguments used against this policy in Latin America. To invoke ethics in international affairs is almost always a confession of defeat. Lamentations have never had any weight in the government of the world, unless they have been taken up by some other powerful body which hoped to profit by them. It is no use to say "this is a bad state of affairs." We must place ourselves in such a position that we can say, "This cannot be allowed to happen." And to effect this, it is as useless to invoke right, morality, and reason, as to have recourse to appeals, imprecations, or tears. Peoples which

---

* These figures appear to be too large. There is, of course, no means of ascertaining the exact number.

expect life or a future from a legal abstraction or the will of others are doomed in advance to become victims. It is from within ourselves that we must draw the elements of life; foresight to see our dangers, fortitude to face our difficulties, stoicism to withstand failure, all which arises from the life-giving vigilance of the organism itself, whose first necessity is to breathe. When self-defence ceases, whether in men or peoples, the throbbing of that very life which causes them to endure in nature or in history also ceases.

To hate the United States is a sentiment of inferiority which leads nowhere. To depreciate them is a sign of insensate parochialism. What we ought to cultivate is our own self-love, anxiety about our own existence. If we seek to stir the collective will by denouncing the external and calling up the memory of former disasters, let it not be taken as an accusation brought against the attitude of others, but as an attempt to find our own bearings. What it is urgent to consider is not what our adversary has done to harm us, but what we ourselves have failed to do to counteract his aggression, and what we shall have to achieve to-morrow if we do not wish to be annihilated.

Six days in New York sufficed for me, without any difficulties or obstacles, to converse with important men, to arouse the interest of public opinion in favour of my cause (as far as is possible in such an enormous community), to deliver a lecture on the imperialist danger at Columbia University on July 9, 1912, the Argentine National festival,[1] to have it translated into English, published in

[1] In introducing the lecturer Professor Fitzgerald, in the name of Columbia University, made a significant speech, of which we reproduce this paragraph. "Columbia esteems herself peculiarly fortunate in being able to offer her hospitality to the distinguished gentleman who is her guest this afternoon. A poet, prose-writer, orator, and publicist who is known and respected throughout South America and Europe, he has many claims upon your attention, and upon our interest. Despite a widespread opinion to the contrary, we of the United States have an especial affection and admiration for an idealist; and on this ground, more even than on those already mentioned, our guest compels our affectionate regard, for, at an age when many other young men are wasting their substance and their time, he is giving his substance and himself to the promulgation of an idea and the maintenance of an ideal."

pamphlet form,[2] and distributed to clubs and institutions. The newspapers discussed the problem dispassionately, judging the controversy to be natural. The *Tribune*,[3] in a leading article headed *"Not 'Shocking,' "* raised its voice against those who sympathised with my campaign, and tried to prove that the Nicaraguan loan was a legitimate negotiation. The *Daily People* [4] said "Mr. Ugarte has been surnamed the apostle of Latin-American union, and the hostility which was shown him by some governments has enormously contributed to increase his popularity." The New York *Herald* published a long report under the heading of "Poet voices cry of Latin America against injustice." [5] The *Sun*,[6] under the heading, seven columns wide, of "Stop Baiting South America Says Ugarte," devoted a page of intelligence to the lecture and its author. Naturally a paper was not wanting which used the affair for political ends.[7] But in contradistinction with my experience at the beginning of my tour, I had no dealings with the police or with official personages. I conversed only with journalists, workmen, students, and university professors, as is fitting for one submitting a thesis for reflection and controversy. And they all assented or dissented on the high plane of a theoretical debate. It has since come to my knowledge, in the course of a conversation at Madrid in 1921 with a North American professor, that Columbia University was requested by the government at Washington on this occasion to cancel the invitation, arguing that it ought to avoid as far as possible lending

---

[2] This pamphlet was distributed at the entrance to the hall in which the lecture was given and was printed at the works of *Las Novedades*, 26 City Hall Place, New York, in 1912, with the title of *The Future of Latin America*.

[3] July 22, 1912.

[4] July 8, 1912.

[5] July 10, 1912.

[6] August 8, 1912.

[7] The Albany *Argus* said in its issue of July 10: " 'A journey I have just made through all Latin-American countries,' says Señor Ugarte, 'convinces me that the blind restlessness and disquieture [sic] that besets our people is organizing and crystallizing into an alert and vigorous movement against the imperialism of the United States.' True Democracy is not in sympathy with imperialism. There are hundreds of thousands of independent Republicans who do not sanction imperialism, and the only safe thing for them to do next November is to vote for the Democratic national ticket."

its authority to my propaganda. It appears that a Secretary of the United States Legation in Chile, who happened to be on a visit, represented to the White House how great an impression such an act would produce in the Republics of the South. But Columbia University replied that the intimation surprised them, for they had never been subject to government inspiration [supervision?]. And this attitude, which our Universities would perhaps not have taken in a similar case, is another proof of the apparent contradiction between the atmosphere of liberty which reigns in the United States and the oppressive influence diffused by imperialism among the people of the South.

I say apparent contradiction, for this lack of connection, or difference of plane, between morality and action had been characteristic of imperialist powers in every place and time. They adopt one morality for their home consumption, and make use of another for the peoples which they desire to subjugate, citing in justification of this dual policy, sometimes the difference in social conditions, sometimes political exigencies.

Thus the liberty of the Press, which is an inviolable and sacred right in the United States, is converted in many of the Latin-American republics into something paradoxical and non-existent, not only at the will of the petty local tyrants, but as a result of the representations of North America, who at the slightest signs of independence in pronouncing judgment on international affairs, formulates indignant protests or resorts to every form of intimidation.* A rise in the price of paper, or the withdrawal of advertisements by North American firms serves to exert pressure when the governments do not take action against the unruly newspapers. A disinterested offer of capital or machinery serves to purchase their support in other cases. If it be so foolish as to resist, a boycott is organised against it, or it is disparaged in some way or another. The newspapers of the United States may say as much as they like, even what is most wounding to the feelings of our republics. The Latin-American ones may sometimes not even defend the interests of their country. And for this reason it is needful to say that the light

* For Henry Lane Wilson's attempts to modify the tone of the Mexican press, see *Papers Relating to the Foreign Relations of the United States* (1911), pp. 359–361.

of liberty in New York casts by contrast a shadow of discredit upon the intelligence of the South.

Much the same thing happens in politics. Progressive institutions, the right of the people to self-government, submission to the exigencies of public opinion, all these are essential axioms in the great republic of the North. But in the countries which are more or less obscurely attached to its influence, this same great republic contributes towards corrupting the vote, fomenting anarchy, keeping despots in power when they are in favour of imperialist expansion, and counselling the worst acts of violence against the local constitutions.

It is clear that the fundamental error does not spring from those who profit by the evil conditions of our atmosphere, but from the greed or hurry of those who in order to exalt themselves accept support, interference, or censorship damaging to the respectability of their country, or pretend to ignore them. Imperialist powers have always claimed the high mission of preparing peoples for civilisation, without ever intending to accomplish this aim except in so far as it is useful to them, by converting the group which they have deprived of sovereignty into a servant or auxiliary of their own wealth or power. To believe in the paternal desire of a state to serve another state disinterestedly is a negation of the philosophy of history. Governing powers which are so ingenuous as to attempt it are either deceiving others or themselves, and in both cases they compromise the future of the country which they rule. The process is well known. It begins with a loan and ends in a sorrowful abdication of sovereignty. In this game with those who are blind to their detriment, to all but their own ambition, and allow themselves to be made use of to further the ends of a policy which they do not understand, imperialist powers do not go beyond what all the powerful peoples of the world have done. Those who are responsible are the people who lent themselves to these ruses, or those who look on at them without a protest.

The peculiar power of suggestion which the great republic of the North exerts over the South is a strong contributory cause of this. Even in independent spheres and in those which have nothing to do with the rotation of the governments, there is a constant uneasiness which makes everything depend on the North. Even the most determined opponents of the United States follow their internal politics, hoping from them a change in international perspective. Each presidential campaign arouses a new anxiety in the Latin republics. They look to a lottery for their salvation. They are simple enough to believe that the triumph of one or the other candidate will bring about a modification in what is really a national aspiration and a necessary outcome of history. And this childish belief would be a fit subject for irony if it did not carry with it this danger: that we identify ourselves to a certain extent with the life of the dominant people; and if it did not confirm the unavowed submission of communities which look at the foreigner for all good things, including their own liberty.

It is obvious that this applies in a varying degree to the different regions of our Latin America. Some of them have left their early errors so far behind them that nothing in a normal and well-balanced era now recalls them. But in the situations to which I allude, unskilfully exaggerated and generalised, is none the less to be found the origin of the world's indifference in the face of the pressure and vexations of which certain republics are the victims.

It is not because these states are weak. Holland, Switzerland, and Belgium are also weak, as measured against the rest of the world, but they have been able to make themselves invulnerable by their clear-sightedness and honourable character. Helplessness arises from the poor reputation attaching to these groups rather than from their actual smallness. The attention of the world is arrested by the most striking phenomena, and so it judges them severely, extending to vast territories the evils occurring in some cities; and it accepts the view that all acts of violence are the result and the penalty of unpardonable faults.

It is against this state of mind that we have to arouse our young men for the good of all, by making the truth about Latin America known to the general public, and by exerting influence on our countries so as to modify mistaken tendencies. From north to south, we have all committed errors. The error of the republics which have encouraged anarchy has lain in their ignorance of the fact that, in every civil war, foreign interest creeps in. That of the countries which have got beyond the critical stage has lain in perpetuating misleading egoisms, thus retarding the birth of a world policy, in the absence of which no country, be it large or very small, can have a voice in the world's councils.

In the new lease of life which has been obtained by the great oppressed nationalities, as one of the consequences of the late war, in this hour when Ireland, China, and Egypt are reasserting their personality, Latin America has also a word to say in the presence of the United States and of the world. But if this word is not to be lost in the void, it is necessary that it should emanate from a recognised and coherent organism. The weakly parts of America must rise to a higher level, taking as their goal those regions which have achieved a normal state of development. And these latter must arrive at a vision of their destiny, grasping it in a vast panoramic view which shall give rise to a policy of solidarity. Only thus can the evils of which we have spoken be remedied. Only thus can there remain any probability of maintaining our material and moral integrity in the present and in the future. Only thus shall we cease to be confined to a position of insignificance in international politics. Only thus shall we be able to make our voices heard in the discussion of great affairs. But if Latin America is to have a voice in these assemblies, she must begin above all by establishing her moral authority, and showing that she has a political mind of her own.

The absence of this political mind was precisely what struck the eye on arriving at Panama.

If the United States have treated us with such scant respect, it has perhaps been owing to the obsequiousness with which we have always bowed before them; and also because of the egoism which has caused us to place the good of our community second to the immediate interests of a man, an oligarchy, or a region. Force is a decisive factor. But the moral factor must also be reckoned with. Every injustice requires at least a pretext to gloss it over, and a complicity which is ready to forget it; and the skilful course for us to have taken would have been not to offer this pretext or to extend this sanction.

In the Panama affair the pretext was offered by Colombia's lack of foresight. The absence of communications, the deplorable sanitary conditions, and the pitiful state of neglect in which the isthmus had been left, explain the discontent of this region, which was afterwards taken advantage of by those who trumped up a sham separatist movement. This, followed by the opening up of the new means of communication, led to the greatest victory ever achieved by a people in the struggle for world domination.

But the sanction was also offered by us when we left Colombia to protest alone, and hastened to recognise, at the prompting of Washington, the new state which had just been artificially founded. No example exists of greater precipitation in covering up a surprise and making it irremediable. And it had not even the excuse of being imposed by circumstances. There was no obligation upon us to do so. If, from one end of the Continent to the other we bowed to events, it was out of a naïve humility, which brought us no profit, which was not extorted by fear of reprisals, but was due to the blind attraction exerted over us by the prestige of this hypnotic power.

It is true that in certain places this abdication was cloaked by the invariable formulas of "progress" and "civilisation." The imperialist tendency sometimes seems actually to have as many adherents in the countries which it injures as in the nation which uses it as a weapon. I have heard it more spoken against in the United States than in certain Circles in some Spanish-American republics, in which the men who govern confine themselves to drawing from the customs or from loans the money necessary to keep themselves in power. This epidemic of obsequiousness has had the effect of making the younger generation sympathise with the old tyrants of Latin America, such as Porfirio Díaz, Cipriano Castro, or Santos Zelaya, who amid many blunders and acts of savage violence, always defended autonomy. The rage with which imperialist policy attacked them till it had overthrown them proves that, though they represented a primitive and possibly uncultivated Latin America, they at any rate upheld amid their stubborn barbarism the pride of their flag and of their authority.

As I landed in Colón, I recalled the words pronounced by President Roosevelt at the opening of the St. Louis Exposition: "We have begun to take possession of the Continent." In the republics of Spanish America there is as yet no general idea of what is portended by that mighty stronghold between the two oceans, raised by the greatness of a people and the decisive action of a statesman.

For though Roosevelt's action has been ill-fated for us, for the United States it has been providential. At the moment when the diplomatists of that country were wavering before their opportunity, he found the necessary energy for facing and deciding the situation without appealing to formulas or treaties, but with exclusive regard to the interests of his country. Roosevelt must have said to himself: "In a continent where so many artificial republics have been created, which arise from no historical necessity and have no rhyme nor reason, I can very well improvise one which may at least be of use to us." His arbitrary and dictatorial manner made the policy of the United States take a great stride, by means of which Mexico and Central America have been surrounded, the Pacific dominated, the absorption of the Antilles insured, and the dominion of the United States over the Caribbean coasts guaranteed. Thus the new Rome has rounded off her Mediterranean in the very heart of the New World, and advanced her centres of influence half-way along the route to the South.

A North American writer once expressed to me the astonishment which he felt at a certain Pan-American historical congress in which it was impossible to study any of the history of our Latin America, owing to the fact that all the delegates were paralysed by different local views and quarrels about precedence. It was inconceivable to his mind, that in cities where the most distant events of Europe were examined closely, it should not be the proper thing to open a calm debate upon our own antecedents, and should be dangerous to trace the lines of a general conception. His surprise would be greater if he learnt that a matter of such transcendent importance as what happened at Panama, an event which affects the whole of Latin America in its most vital and radical interests, gave rise among us—apart from the posthumous protest of the country injured—to nothing but newspaper paragraphs and the comments of spectators, less full than those which are habitually devoted to a fire in London or a change of government in Bulgaria. The United States have studied the matter in its every phase, and one has only to turn over the leaves of a library catalogue or a file of newspapers to find every shade of North American opinion endorsed by the most authoritative signatures. What Latin-American statesmen have dared to approach the subject? And yet there is no question of greater importance to us. The silence of Latin America at the gravest moment of its existence since the epoch of independence is one of the results of our lack of higher ideals and definite policy. It is impossible to believe that the men who were at that time directing public affairs in the different republics were so lacking in experience of human affairs and elementary foresight, that they failed to recognise the transcendent importance of what had just happened. Probably they all felt the shock which was bound to echo down the future. But anxiety for their own personal position within the party which had raised them to power, the interests of that party in the vicissitudes of internal politics, little frontier rivalries, the futile strife between the parts of the same aggregate, paralysed all speech and action. Those who were bolder and less compromised resolved to keep silence also. How could they risk a *démarche,* given the disloyalty and possible defection of the neighbour republics? Even abstention would have been significant, for imperialist policy did not ask for silence; it demanded that everyone should without delay recognise the legality of what it had decided. And countries which, in other circumstances, had delayed for a prudent space of time the recognition of new governments, had to admit *ipso facto* the existence of an illusory state, closing their eyes and ears to the protests of Colombia and to the truth. Never had our chancelleries displayed such activity. Those whose custom it was to let the most harmless questions slumber in their offices for long years, felt themselves seized by a feverish activity, and in a few days all our republics, with the exception of three countries, had entered into relations with the new entity born of expansionist policy.

Mr. Taft, who was Mr. Roosevelt's Minister of War, and afterwards President of the Republic, expounded in *McClure's Magazine,* of New York, the technical reasons which decided the choice of the lock-system for the construction of the canal and the political reasons which induced them to create a republic *ad hoc.* "It was not possible," he says, "that after such an effort, diplomatic, scientific, material, and financial, we should place the *entrepôt* for the ocean traffic of the world under the jurisdiction of degenerates, and make use of a directing body which would speculate in the shares and destroy the *matériel* of the undertaking." After which he added, to close his article: "Perhaps the day is not distant when

three banners of the Stars and Stripes will mark the extension of our
territory at three equidistant spots: one at the North Pole, one at
the Panama Canal, and the third at the South Pole; the whole
hemisphere will be ours *de facto* as in virtue of our racial superiority
it already is *de jure*." [8] *   The majority of our presidents, who often
read nothing but the local paper which sings their praises, were ignorant of all this.

These circumstances would also explain why Mr. Elihu Root, the
lawyer for several trusts, and especially for the Standard Oil Company, was received by our countries as the idealist messenger of
continental concord, while non-imperialist North Americans, like
the ex-ambassador Sherrill,† could hardly gain a tolerant hearing.
It is our ignorance of world-conditions that is most prejudicial to
our continental policy, and our morbid obsession with what immediately touches us.   Mr. Sherrill said in his speech at the Middy
Club: "I am fully convinced that it is not the business of the
United States to direct the policy of Latin America; and that the
sooner this idea becomes widely spread, not only among our neighbours, but also among North Americans, the more our international
reputation will increase."   Why do we despise words which are favourable to us?   Why do we not seek the support of those elements
which square with our interests?

I well know, and I have said it in previous pages, that it is not
precisely these men who are most listened to in the United States;
and it remains an established fact that the politics of the mass obey
laws of growth and hypertrophy alien to the individual will.   But
are we to neglect the arguments which North Americans themselves
give us for our defence?   Are we to silence those words, both in our
papers and in our souls, which offer a support to our claims?   Mr.
Wilson, before he became president, expressed himself in these words:
"Rome was supreme and unique in history.   She imposed herself on
the world by the glory of her warriors, legislators, philosophers,
writers, and artists.   She taught humanity to read and to think.
In pagan times she ruled from the Capitol in the intellectual and

[8] *La Estrella de Panama*, August 24, 1912.

* The Panama journal misquoted Taft. He said nothing of the kind.
(See *McClure's Magazine*, May, 1909, p. 3 ff.)

† See Sherrill's *Modernizing the Monroe Doctrine*. Boston, Houghton
Mifflin, 1916.

material spheres, and in the Christian Era she has ruled from the Vatican in the sphere of conscience, first with the eagle and then with the dove of the Holy Spirit; while we have no other title to the respect and love of men but our free institutions and the fact that we have offered an asylum to the oppressed of the earth. If we are now to turn ourselves into miserable caricatures of the Caesars, we shall be betraying the ideals of the fathers of our country and working for our own ruin." *

We cannot, however, forget that Mr. Wilson was later to set aside his wholesome inclinations and land troops in Santo Domingo in prosecution of the traditional policy. We cannot, then, place our hopes either in men or parties. They both grow out of the time and surroundings which determine them. But our task is to take advantage of circumstances to appeal to declarations of principle, to manœuvre for position—in fine, to set our ship in motion in such a way as to prevent it from being overwhelmed without remedy by the winds and waves. Faced by imperialist policy, we have stood for immobility; and immobility in international policy, as in war, spells defeat.

In Panama I found yet another proof of the limited outlook which renders our Latin America incapable of conceiving a general plan of action. There were not a few who stigmatised me as a secret agent of Colombia.

"Do you want the isthmus," they said, "to relapse once more into poverty, backward conditions, and yellow fever?"

The mistake should not have surprised me, since my propaganda was interpreted in Cuba as an aspiration towards the return of the island to Spanish domination, in Mexico as a move in internal politics to bring about the fall of the Government, in Guatemala as an intrigue of San Salvador, and in San Salvador as an intrigue of Guatemala. By the same line of argument I was afterwards to pass for an adherent of Ecuador in Peru, as an enthusiast for Peru in Chile, and in the Argentine as denationalised, and inimical to the splendid isolation of my country. Each group was dazzled by its

---

* I am unable to find this statement in any of Wilson's published writings or speeches. That he held such sentiments, however, is well known. See, for instance, his address at Annapolis, June 5, 1914. (*Addresses and Messages of Woodrow Wilson*, Hart ed., p. 38.)

immediate preoccupations, and so attributed to local motives that higher aspiration which should be concerned with them all.

When a newspaper asked me whether it was true that in New York I had expressed a harsh judgment upon Panama, I answered that I had always condemned separatist movements. But I made it clear that I ought not to be reckoned amongst those who despise and insult Panama for her attitude. Everybody made mistakes in this affair. The Government of Colombia, by neglecting the administration and well-being of the province; the province, by allowing itself to be entangled in an adventure, without calculating the consequences; and the whole of Latin America, for evading responsibility by abandoning this region to its fate as if it were a thing which had no bonds of intimate connection with the larger whole. Panama can no more detach her evolution from that of the rest of the Latin continent than Latin America can cease to interest herself in the fate of Panama. In the isthmus lies the pivot on which the future will turn.

The railway which takes us from Colón to the capital, skirting those stupendous constructions which open a communication between the two oceans, is, of course, completely North American; just as the Canal Zone, the hotels, the troops, and the flags which wave over them all are North American. To the passing traveller the Republic of Panama does not exist. It is, moreover, a fact that the new state, in addition to being of minute size, is divided into four zones cut off from communication with one another: namely, the fringe of land bordering on Colombia, that which touches Costa Rica (separated from each other by the North American zone, which stretches from ocean to ocean), and the cities of Panama and Colón. Nobody would suppose, as he goes from the boat to the hotel, and from the hotel to the railway, hearing nothing but the metallic ring of the Yankee pronunciation, that he is in a state Spanish in origin, in a republic having its parliament, its president, and its autonomous life. If we stop to observe, we see that there is not, and cannot be, in reality, more than the simulacrum of a Government, since everything is in the hands of the powerful nation, and must breathe through her and for her. Hence the amazement which appears on people's faces so soon as one speaks of opposition to imperialism. Interests are so far subordinated to it that the little local life, the survivals of the old province of Colombia, the remains of what aspired to become the Panamanian republic, would be extinguished in a minute if the United States were to withdraw; for everything emanates from the masters of the Canal, or is drawn into harmony with its designs.   And yet these regions began to bear fruit under the inspiration of the Latin genius.   In one quarter, on a height dominating the sea, there is a statue of the French engineer, Lucien Bonaparte Wyse, the promoter of the Canal works, who seems to stand and proclaim to the world the miserable *débâcle* of that which might have changed the history of America.

Señores Obaldia, Amador, and Huertas perhaps sincerely believed, when they originated the policy of separatism, that the region would derive great advantages from its submission to the United States. They imagined that the new entity would enjoy the benefit of the profits from the enormous commerce brought about by the new line of communication.   But, except for the sanitation of the towns, the old province of Panama has not seen its hopes realised.

Prosperity has been canalised by the protecting nation, leaving no room for any progress really beneficial to the original inhabitants. Señor Guillermo Andreve, then Minister of Public Instruction, to whom I put the question, could not answer in the affirmative.   In the school which he took me to visit, to show me a specimen of local progress, I found in the hall an enormous North American flag. This was symbolic of the situation.   The young and assimilable elements of the population were attracted by the encroaching force, thus confirming the transitory character of this political body, which is destined to-morrow to fuse the white elements composing it with the dominant mass, leaving the others confined to the subordinate status of Indians or Jamaicans.   For the superior cleverness of imperialism in this and other regions has lain in splitting up the original group, by offering some of them the prospect of being able to identify themselves in future with the invader.

Thus the maintenance of an apparently autonomous government is an expedient for bringing about an era of gradual transition, by simplifying the administration of the subjugated regions during the time for which their classification or subdivision in accordance with the methods of imperialism is delayed.   The existence of a president, a parliament, and a flag stand for no more, from the practical view-point of modern conquerors, than the acquisition of an opportune concession and a formula for avoiding responsibility. If finance, foreign affairs, and the higher direction of matters of internal policy are subordinate to the will of the ruling people, the essence of the colonial system is achieved in its full virtue, without effort and without expense, within the bounds of an apparent respect for possible local susceptibilities and the public opinion of the world.

The flexibility of North American imperialism in its external activities, and the diverse forms which it adopts according to circumstances, the racial composition and the social conditions of the peoples upon which its action is exercised, is one of the most significant phenomena of this century from the point of view of political science. Never in all history has such an irresistible or marvellously concerted force been developed as that which the United States are bringing to bear upon the peoples which are geographically or politically within its reach in the south of the Continent or on the shores of the sea. Rome applied a uniform procedure. Spain persisted in a policy of ostentation and glittering show. Even in the present day, England and France strive to dominate rather than absorb. Only the United States have understood how to modify the mechanism of expansion in accordance with the tendencies of the age, employing different tactics in each case, and shaking off the trammels of whatever may prove an impediment or a useless burden in the achievement of its aspirations. I refer equally to moral scruples, which prohibit the employment of certain procedure in certain cases, and to considerations of *amour-propre,* which in other cases habitually impels nations to overstep the bounds of what is expedient to themselves. North American imperialism has always succeeded in dominating its dislikes and its nerves. Even respect for the flag has been considered by it rather as an efficient agent of domination than as a question of *amour-propre.* At times imperious, at other times suave, in certain cases apparently disinterested, in others implacable in its greed, pondering like a chess-player who foresees every possible move, with a breadth of vision embracing many centuries, better-informed and more resolute than any, without fits of passion, without forgetfulness, without fine sensibilities, with-

out fear, carrying out a world activity in which everything is foreseen—North American imperialism is the most perfect instrument
of domination which has been known throughout the ages.*

By adding to what we may call the scientific legacy of past imperialisms the initiative born of its own inspiration and surroundings,
this great nation has subverted every principle in the sphere of
politics just as it had already transformed them in the sphere of
material progress. Even the European powers, when confronted
with North American diplomacy, are like a rapier pitted against a
revolver. In the order of ideas with which we are dealing, Washington has modified the whole perspective. The first conquerors, with
their elementary type of mind, annexed the inhabitants in the guise
of slaves. Those who came afterwards annexed territories without
inhabitants. The United States, as we have already insinuated in
preceding chapters, inaugurated the system of annexing wealth,
apart from inhabitants or territories, disdaining outward shows in
order to arrive at the essentials of domination without a dead-weight
of areas to administrate and multitudes to govern. The interplay of
internal forces in the life of a community is of small importance to
them; still less the external form under which domination has to be
exercised, provided that the result offers the maximum of influence,
benefits and authority, and the minimum of risks, commitments or
cares.

Thus there has arisen within their spheres of influence an infinite
variety of forms and shades. The new imperialism, far from ap-
plying a formula or a panacea, has founded a system of special
diagnosis for every case, taking into account the area of the region,
its geographical situation, the density of its population, its origin,
predominating racial composition, level of civilisation, customs,
neighbours, whatever may favour or hinder resistance, whatever may
induce assimilation or alienation by reason of affinities or differences
of race, whatever has to be brought about with a view to future
contingencies. The higher motives of force or healthy activity
which give direction to expansionist energy, watch particularly over

* From the official viewpoint, this appears to be an exaggeration of both
our capacity and our vices. Do our diplomats and our administrators
possess the training, the system, the foresight here attributed to them?

the racial purity of the group and reject every addition which is not identical with it. To annex peoples is to modify the composition of one's own blood, and the invader who does not desire to be diluted, but to perpetuate himself, avoids as far as possible any impairing or enfeebling of the superiority which he claims.

Imperialist policy might with no effort have doubled or tripled in recent years the official area of its territories, but it saw the danger of adding to its original community great masses of different origin. The complete occupation of small territories inhabited by a sparse white population offers no difficulty. But the conquest of vast zones of a character hard to assimilate entails dangers which are obvious to those possessing the most elementary foresight. Hence arises the opportunist solution of reigning without a crown, beneath the shadow of other flags which the unavoidable force of realities ends by making illusory.

That species of action which makes itself felt in the form of financial pressure, international tutelage, and political censorship admits of every advantage with no risk. In the development of these tactics imperialist policy has given evidence of that incomparable dexterity which is admired even by its victims. In the financial sphere its tendency is to control the markets to the exclusion of all competition, to take upon itself the regulation of any production to which it attaches any value, and to lead the small nations on to contract debts which afterwards provoke conflicts, give rise to claims, and prepare the way for interference favourable to the extension of its virtual sovereignty. In the sphere of external policy it appoints itself the defender of these peoples, obliging the world to accept its intervention in treating with them, and drawing them as satellites into its orbit. In the internal order it encourages the diffusion of whatever increases its prestige, forwards the ambitions of those men who favour its influence, and opposes the spread of all influences of a different nature, blocking the way peremptorily to those who, from a superior sagacity or patriotism, try to maintain their nationality unimpaired.

It is in this last sphere of action that we can best observe the commanding ability of imperialism. Is subtle intrusion into the private affairs of each people has always in consecrated phrase invoked peace, progress, civilisation, and culture; but its motives, procedure, and results have frequently been a complete negation of these premises.

It is obvious that the point of departure and the fulcrum on which to rest the lever is the unceasing political effervescence of our peoples. But the use which has been made of this circumstance is so prodigious that it seems incredible. Profiting by the clash of factions, and by the trend of men's ambition, taking advantage of the instability of governments in these unruly and impressionable democracies, it has created within each country a higher power, sometimes hidden, sometimes apparent, which confuses, enmeshes, combines, weaves and unweaves events, bringing about solutions favourable to its interests. Here it foments tyrannies, there it supports attempts at revolution, always constituting itself the conciliator or the arbiter, and indefatigably pressing events in the direction of the two ends which it sets before it: first in the moral order, to increase anarchy, so as to bring discredit upon the country; and second, in the political order, to get rid of national representatives who are refractory to the dominant influence, till they meet with a weak or not very enlightened man who, out of inexperience or impatience, will make himself the accomplice of its domination.

Our ambitious men know that the ideal of imperialism consists in governing through alien hands, in accordance with their broad policy of aloofness; and more than one of them has mocked these calculations by stooping to opposition in order to arrive at power by outside support. But even by following the tactics of Sixtus V, who consented at first in order to resist later, the same miserable result is produced; because the door is thrown open to a series of similar actions, which, though they do not give imperialism directly what it is aiming at, prolong the effervescence and disorder, dissipating the national strength and creating by their multiplication in the body politic an endemic unhealthiness, which is bound ultimately to end in submission.

The greatest triumph of this system has consisted in the fact that it has come to be a cause of success within our own life. As the source of expedients in our civil struggles, as the dispenser of favours in official life, it has driven not only those who are impatient, but even the most incorruptible and upright to the utmost limit of what

can be granted without abdication.   In this manner it has proceeded
to create subconsciously, in the countries it has "manipulated", a
peculiar state of mind, which admits the collaboration in its civil
struggles of forces not arising from their own surroundings, and
allows an element of foreign life and interest to enter into every
national act or project.

Hence arises the phenomenon that in a continent over which there
hangs a foreign pressure unprecedented in history, there should be
so few men who openly speak out against it.   They all seem to
tolerate or to be ignorant of the secret force which makes itself felt
at every turn: some because their supreme aim is success; others
because they think it clever to hide their feelings.   Nobody, with a
very few exceptions, talks of submission.   But all these grades of
complaisance are like a musical instrument brilliantly played upon
by the invader who naturally stresses those notes which are most
grateful to his ears, insensibly playing chords in harmony with his
own preferences.   I do not say that in this way a sort of auction is
opened in which power is granted to those who are most complaisant.
The pride of our people would not consent to this.   But no case has
as yet occurred in our republics of a known adversary of imperialism
arriving at the presidency.   Even those who have risen by grace and
favour of Washington fall so soon as they display any tendency to
resistance.   The axis of politics, then, does not lie between those
who attack and those who submit, but rather in the degree of submission and the intensity of subservience.   In this way popularity and
prosperity has more than once been improvised for secondary figures who did not seem intended to govern a people.   And in this
way good statesmen, who constituted a danger by their clear-
sightedness and capacity, have been sacrificed.   Metternich's motto
in one of Austria's critical moments—"We must forward the
ambitions of X in France, because X is a great rogue, and with him
we know where we are"—has more than once been applicable in
Latin-American politics.   Our native shrewdness, which sometimes
takes the place of talent, has taken it upon itself to frustrate some of
these bold calculations.   But the general rule has been to advance
those who are less capable, more because of the mistakes which they
commit of their own accord, without anyone's prompting, than for
the concessions that can be extorted from them.

Those who, once they are in the government, oppose this policy, even by the most courteous and diplomatic means, soon see the cloud arising, either on the frontier or in the neighbourhood of the capital, which is shortly to sweep them from the heights. Even if the insurrection can only reckon on sparse supporters at first, it will soon increase, because it will be supplied with all the material it requires. And even if the government has sufficient power and popularity at its disposal to dominate the disorder, it will never succeed, for at the last moment foreign ministers will intervene, appealing to the necessity for defending property or preventing butchery, and foreign troops will be landed. In spite of the divergent interests of France, Spain, and England, the diplomatic corps in our Latin-American countries is a series of *wagons de luxe* drawn by a locomotive carrying the American flag.

Moreover, the world only hears what the United States choose to say about Latin-American affairs, for they impose on world opinion the dominion of their cables. Deserted even by his partisans, the representative of the people who persists in his resistance will find his supplies, movements, and utterances cut off. This explains the rapidity of some politicians' fall in countries where civil wars used formerly to last for long years; and it enables us to understand, if not to justify, what we might call the official terror.

The procedure is even more drastic when the resistance comes from individuals, whether merchants, soldiers, or writers. A wind blows from a new quarter; and friendships are broken, opportunities vanish, the atmosphere becomes rarified. Nothing appears on the surface, but it is as if a curse had fallen on their heads. The merchant sees his credit impaired, the soldier sees his career marred, the writer sees his reputation diminish. It matters little that before taking a stand on the matter the merchant was courted by the banks, the soldier belauded for his knowledge, the writer respected for his works. The mere enunciation of an idea not in harmony with the dominant will closes the way to their future. And the case is none the less serious when this subterranean action confines itself to checking the growth of a force. It frequently happens that on some casual pretext which has apparently nothing to do with the opinions he has expressed, the merchant is ruined and goes to prison, the soldier loses his career and leaves the country, the writer is accused of the basest actions. To this is to be ascribed the opportunist hedging of those who, carried away by the stream, try to reconcile their patriotism with Monroism.

The fall of Porfirio Díaz, Cipriano Castro, and Santos Zelaya, the sacrifice of the Alfaros in Ecuador, the death of Araujo in San Salvador, Miguel Gómez's end in Cuba, the immolation of Dr. Madríz in Nicaragua, and of Madero and Carranza in Mexico, the tragic end of Zeledón and Perdomo Herrera give the timorous reason to suppose that a strange fatality pursues all those who attempt an attitude of resistance, if only for the moment of its inception. On the other hand, fortune favours those who, like Señor Chamorro in Nicaragua, sing the praises of Pan-Americanism.* Possibly Washington is ignorant of the degree of virulence attained by this system in some regions. The interests of certain financial companies which overstep the bounds set by the national interests, or the initiative of agents who exceed their instructions, may exaggerate the abuses. But, taken as a whole, all that happens is in obedience to a deliberate policy. Matters are so arranged that for Latin Americans action becomes difficult and success impossible, so long as they fail to come to terms with that influence which lays its iron hand on interests and consciences, rendering all hostility impotent. And here we are faced by the eternal question: does the ultimate responsibility for this state of affairs rest exclusively upon imperialism, which in our time, as at all others, is wont to extend its ambitions until it meets with an atmosphere of resistance which blocks its way? Is not greater blame to be attributed to our rulers, who, though enlightened by earlier catastrophes, instructed by similar situations in other countries and epochs, and put on their guard by warnings from every quarter, cannot manage to rise superior to their limitations in order to embrace a wider view and achieve a broader vision?

We all know the faults of imperialism, and there is nothing to be gained by an angry repetition of them. What we have got to bring into prominence are our own errors. Not in order to provoke discord once more by their means, but to make an end of discord, by patiently building up again what has been destroyed by thoughtless action.

* Here again the reader will long for more evidence. There may be much truth in these assertions.

My visit to the President of Panama, Don Belisario Porras, enabled me to grasp the state of mind of certain national representatives. I have never believed in the bad faith of our men. If they have resorted to false manœuvres, it has been, in the majority of cases, because they have not been able to react against a formidable impulse from without. Weak outposts, isolated in the night, have surrendered more or less openly, through lack of higher co-ordination, or through the material impossibility of resistance. But though this may save the honour of the soldier, it does not reflect credit upon the foresight of the leaders, who were unable to guard against the gradual enveloping movement. In this century of operations, in a battle which has lasted since the days of independence, our leaders are still so adrift, and give proofs of such an absolute incapacity of will, that it may almost be said that whatever is still afloat in Latin America has been defended up till now rather by geography, distance, and climate—by the irresponsible action of Nature—than by man.

Señor Porras expounded his point of view to me with sincerity and at length:

"The position of Panama grows constantly more difficult," he said to me; "my Government cannot establish any real authority. I lack means for carrying out its decisions. I meet with difficulties even in arming the police properly, and they are frequently the victims of mysterious outrages. Persons come from the Canal Zone, assault my police agents, and return with impunity to North American territory, after committing breaches of the laws and municipal ordinances. If a political insurrection were to break out to-morrow on Panamanian territory, I could not suppress it unless the United States authorised me to equip troops and transport them from one division of our country to another."

As he spoke, Señor Porras kept arranging his eye-glasses, with a certain nervousness which he controlled with difficulty. When he referred to what tropical America expected of those nations in the south which, like the Argentine, Chile, and Brazil, are lit up by the resplendency of hope, his eyes took on a changed and optimistic expression:

"If you were only willing . . ."

I was forced to apologise to this Spanish American for the sordid character of our politics, which were still absorbed, as I told him, in making their own foundations secure. I did not hide from him, however, that we, too, in the South were committing the greatest of errors, namely, failing to interest ourselves in the fate of kindred peoples. But if the Latin America of which we have so far spoken is already deploring its faults, to-morrow, when it has achieved safety, it will have to expiate those which it has accumulated by its lack of foresight and its narrow local views.

In speaking of the separatist movement in Panama, Señor Porras uttered these words, which were a revelation to me: "If we had only known!"

In them was revealed the philosophy which has underlain the whole of Central-American policy in recent years, the summing up of the work of three generations of governors. After such a series of blunders, what irony appears in that mild exclamation, "If we had only known!"

It was an open secret which everybody in the world was repeating, and only the presidents and ministers continued to be ignorant of it, until the malady became a scourge. It lay in the incapacity of the politicians, and their stubborn hostility against those who warned them; it lay in their self-sufficiency and boasting; it lay in the greed and disorder which the invader found among his auxiliaries; and yet not one of them had any idea of what he was doing. During a century of imperialist madness every symptom of the *conquistador* spirit had been exhibited in Latin America. Every sign had foretold shipwreck; but the men at the helm, those who were responsible for the ship, had not seen the storm coming. In consequence of these wrongs history to-morrow will perhaps have to say: "There was once a race which possessed the most lovely territories of which any race has ever had the mastery, with the most fertile lands, the most abundant rivers, the most richly-stocked woods, the most fabulous mineral wealth, every type of climate and produce, in the hands of warlike, intelligent men carrying on glorious civilisations; and by the indolence of those who governed them, by a morbid weakness of their political system, and by base passions, all this incalculable treasure, all these hopes, all these memories, were swept away and annulled by another race. And to-day nothing is left of all this but the memory of an irreparable disaster, which will not even be remembered for a moment, because the legend would have to be written in a foreign tongue."

When we consider the work of imperialism in America as a whole, it is impossible to refrain from a certain admiration for the magnitude of its effort and the clearness of its conceptions. Never in all history has such subtlety been seen, combined with such a capacity for sustained action. It is evident, I repeat, that from the Spanish-American point of view we have to do with a policy which we ought all to work together to check. A good number of us have been writing and speaking in this sense without intermission for long years. But if we are to stem the advance, our most urgent task is to arrive at a full knowledge of the truth, and to give up vain speech-making. Every strong people extends its ambitions as far as its arms can reach, and every weak people lasts just so long as its energy for defending itself endures. In sacrificing doctrines in order to favour its present and future greatness, the new Rome believes itself to be accomplishing a duty, since it is thus preparing that world dominion for which it considers itself to be set apart. By developing to its full volume and protecting itself against these risks, Latin America would preservè its personality. History does not reckon with lamentations, but with results. And it is by results—not by words or theories—that we must try to rise to the level of events.

CHAPTER VI

THE TOMB OF THE LIBERATOR

Bolívar and San Martín—The position of Venezuela—Political and economic mistakes—Necessity for direct investigation—Colombian patriotism—Rational education—Racial problems—Destructive tactics.

THERE are men who are to their country what rivers are to a land: they perform the function of arteries, and animate the inert landscape: the vitality, initiative, and force which they bear with them fertilise vast areas, shorten distances, and enable the energies of a people to realise their possibilities.

Such a man was Bolívar. His triumphant audacity set in motion the latent energies which produced Latin-American emancipation in spite of all the factors making for immobility which stood in the way of the necessary transformation. We all owe him so much, that we can hardly find words to express our gratitude. Yet, when we review his activities, we find that his disillusionments were more numerous than his deeds of prowess; and that when the final balance is made up, the benefits which he lavished upon Latin America are outweighed by the acts of ingratitude which Latin America heaped upon him.

When he retired, conquered and abandoned by his friends, Bolívar declared in a proclamation: "My last prayers are for the happiness of my country. If my death contributes towards the cessation of party strife and the consolidation of union, I shall go down in peace to the grave." And in these simple words is perhaps summed up the whole effect of that saturnalia of disorder which reigned from North to South, from the first shout of independence to the fall of the great *caudillos*. The moral content of this phrase embraces every aspect of that tempestuous ebullition which disintegrated the forces of the old colonies, until, by sacrificing the ideals of those

149

who initiated the movement, the fragmentary organisation of the present colonies was reached.

The first apostles of separatism in Mexico, New Granada, and the Río de la Plata, had perhaps twice erred by an excess of imaginative exaltation. Firstly, by allowing themselves to be fascinated by political systems, while relegating to the background the economic situation and the real prospects of the viceroyalties with regard to their financial capacity or the possibility of self-support. And secondly, by their ignorance, or their failure to gauge the full importance and scope of the foreign support which had aided the insurrection. But a similar lack of foresight is to be found at the origin of every movement; and at the time when the revolution took place, it had not that importance which it has since acquired. Taking into consideration the wealth of Latin America, the condition of the United States at the time, and the state of world politics, the initial conception was perfectly reasonable and feasible in every region. The factor which intervened to upset their legitimate hopes and the conclusions from which they had started, was the refractory and turbulent character of the masses which they were attempting to inspire. If we establish a parallel between the revolutionary activity of the English and Spanish colonies respectively we find, on the one hand, solidarity and discipline; on the other, anarchy and disunion: on the one hand, a racial ideal; on the other, a preoccupation with local conditions: there, a far-sighted care for the future, here, an irresponsible greed for immediate gain. While the English colonies were consolidating their existence and fitting themselves to play a part in world affairs, the Spanish colonies were exhausting themselves in sterile struggles, forgetful of any higher aspiration. But this fact, the result of those peculiar idiosyncracies which we have referred to in another chapter—throws into relief the greatness of the *caudillos* who were at once its heralds and its victims.

Few heroes have given so many pledges of their disinterestedness as Bolívar. His personal fortune, and the consideration he enjoyed within the colony set him above all suspicion. He launched out on his historic adventure under the guidance of an imaginative exaltation emanating at once from the French Revolution, from North American emancipation, and from his Greek and Latin culture, heightened by a recent visit to the Acropolis. In his heart there was something of the philosophic vigourism of the 18th century, and an after-taste of Napoleonic grandeur. He desired to found a great modern state, and dreamed of becoming the Washington of the South. He knew that his aspiration was not overbold, for he was conscious of his own merit and had a vision of historical possibilities. He had faith in his star, and the future of the Continent. He had at the service of his dream treasures of ability and energy. And yet there was something lacking. It was not the workman. It was not the tools. It was the material upon which he worked. Not that it was inadequate or inferior; for few peoples at that time, and in such a region, offered better conditions, either in point of the masses or the men of distinguished ability. Not that the people lacked understanding, either. Nor was it hostile; for, in spite of a certain momentary resistance, the Liberator was in agreement with the fervent aspirations of the community. But in such an atmosphere of anarchy, agreement did not imply adherence, understanding did not signify support, gratitude did not involve respect. There was something refractory and indocile which was opposed to all leadership or to any programme, something obscurely atavistic which prevented them from taking an ordered part in any activity.

Our Latin America has always been lacking in that lofty faculty for admiration which is a sign of superiority in men and peoples. Paradoxical in its passion for equality, instead of levelling things up to the heights, it has sought to bring them down to the plain, overthrowing all individual superiority, and so, at the same time, making all collective superiority impossible. Removed from a life-giving emulation with other peoples, a mute internal struggle has gone on from the very beginning between its own component elements, which have been determined, not to surpass themselves, but to abolish all grades of honour, careless of the fact that, by giving free rein to their instincts, they were condemning the whole community to an inferior status.

When in 1830 Bolívar wrote: "I have never looked with a favourable eye upon insurrections, and I have lately come to deplore the one which we made against the Spaniards," he was perhaps concentrating in a phrase the tragedy of his fate. Few men have felt as he did the lash of hatred, intrigue, and calumny. He had to bear

everything, from treachery and mockery to the most infamous insinuations, his eyes ever fixed on the work he had undertaken. And
his greatest sorrow was to see that the result was not commensurate
with the effort. "I hope for no salvation for my country," he said
in another letter. "This sentiment, or rather this inner conviction,
strangles my desires and drags me to the most cruel despair. I
believe that all is lost forever, and that the fatherland and my
friends are submerged in a sea of calamities. If I had only one
sacrifice more to make, and it were my life, my happiness, or my
honour, which were in question, believe me, I would not falter.
But I am convinced that this sacrifice would be useless; for one man
can do nothing against a whole world. And since I am incapable of
making my country happy, I refuse to govern it. More than that:
my country's tyrants have taken it from me, and I am proscribed;
and so I have not even a fatherland to which to make the sacrifice.[1]

In undisciplined and fierce societies, evil always has the advantage
over virtue; not that the national character inclines to favour injustice, but because the instinct of discontent and opposition adopts
and applauds in good faith whatever may be harmful to a third
party. Lacking in that calm and discernment which are necessary
to see through intrigues, make a mock of plots, and confine envy or
vengeance within their own limited and proper sphere, our democracies fell from the very outset into an orgy of destruction. Accusations of treason, dictatorship and breach of faith, not to speak of
direct attacks on persons, always found the masses greedy to back
them up and repeat them. Thus was created the atmosphere which
made possible the triumph of this malady of chronic revolution, and
with it the triumph of inferior abilities. And thus were stifled the
hopes of those who brought about the insurrection.

Dominated as she finally came to be by men of second-rate ability,
who waged war upon the heroes and dispossessed them, our Latin
America was bound to be for a time an America of second-rate
importance. Nobody has a greater enthusiasm for Spain than I
have. But perhaps all this was nothing but the logical outcome of
a historical tendency, and Latin America was bound to sacrifice her
great men, just as Spain had sacrificed Columbus and Cervantes,
by the fatality of the same suicidal temperament. It is sufficient to

[1] *El primer centenario de Bolívar*, national section.

recall the attitude of the masses towards their leaders, in order to measure how great is the divergence between the paths of Anglo-Saxon and Iberian America. Those who founded the United States died in an atmosphere of admiration almost amounting to an apotheosis; while the founders of our fatherlands, with hardly an exception, died in ostracism and exile. And so violent is this tendency, that even after an interval of a hundred years, we still seek new motives of discord in the memory of the very apostles of union, and carry on an exasperated debate about the figures of Bolívar and San Martín, prolonging what we might call a useless civil war between the dead.

As a native of the Argentine, I have never found any reason to qualify my admiration for Bolívar. I believe that the *caudillo* of New Granada and the *caudillo* of the Río de la Plata are complementary to each other, if we embrace in its entirety the vast plan of action which they succeeded in developing. There is no clash between them, either in their ideals or their mode of realising them. They might have made war on each other, and yet they placed the general welfare above their own *amour-propre*. When they met at Guayaquil, it was not to squabble over precedence, but to consider the future of Latin America. In trying to prove one of them superior to the other, certain commentators have disparaged them both, because, in the spirit of our history, they both contribute towards the same work and are the instruments of the same ideal. Both had to struggle against the anarchical tendency of our lands, and this similarity is enough to group them together in the course of our history, were they not also united as victims of ingratitude by the memory of the island of Santa Marta and the vision of the humble lodging-house at Boulogne-sur-Mer. How great Latin America might have been, if, instead of raising gorgeous statues to these her best sons, whom she had exiled, shot, or [and] sacrificed in every way, she had let them carry out in their lifetime the plans which they had made for a general victory.

I was once asked who were the great men of Latin America at the time when we were speaking, and, at a loss for a correct answer, I had to confess that in our land our only great men have always been dead. The people of the Argentine only understood the full greatness of Alberdi and the magnitude of his sacrifice when they measured his personality and his work at the distance of half a century.

And the malady of the past is likewise the malady of the present. If the Government of Nicaragua, which spent enormous sums on the funeral of Rubén Darío, had given the poet a pension during his lifetime, he would not have been tormented by the worries which forced him to seek an always scanty remuneration from writing in the Press. His fate was also that of José Enrique Rodó and of Florencio Sánchez, whose departure from their country made no more stir than his, and who might have lived for long and fruitful years on the price of the coal burnt by the war-ships which afterwards brought their bodies back to their native shores. But perhaps it is right that things should happen thus; for their figures are set off by a dark background, thanks to the false values seen by a community which can only perceive the radiance of their glory in a cemetery.

It is superfluous to mention that the reflection which the traveller might have made upon the past and the present, on landing at La Guayra, did not fall in with local prejudices. The President of the Republic of Venezuela was then, and still is, Señor Juan V. Gómez, whose rise to power led to such comment. It will be remembered that this statesman, as Vice-President, was the colleague of Cipriano Castro during his long period of domination. When the dictator set sail for Europe for the good of his health, a speedy *coup d'état* overthrew him in his absence, and entrusted the government to Señor Gómez. Some have explained this occurrence by alleging the oppressive policy of this *caudillo*, others by recalling the resistance of Castro to certain international hints. Was it internal reaction, or a diplomatic penalty? The writer of this book does not feel at liberty to take part in civil differences or in the particular conflicts of each republic; and he naturally leaves the task of elucidating these questions to the Venezuelans themselves; but he cannot omit to record that what he found in Venezuela was a palpable atmosphere of tyranny.

The difficulties which the Government of Caracas placed in the way of holding lectures, by refusing to allow me the use of the theatres for which I applied,[2] and the silence with which the President re-

[2] "Caracas, October 4, 1912. Honoured Sir, I have the pleasure to acknowledge the receipt of your application, dated the 26th September last, to which I have not replied before, for reasons which I will now explain."

ceived my request for an audience, might seem to influence my judgment. But as a matter of fact the moral sphere in which the
government of Venezuela revolved, with regard to the continental
problem, seemed to me to be the same as that of the majority of
the republics which I had visited. A wretched preoccupation with
local and party interests led them to avoid every action which might
have displeased the powerful nation in the North. Their chief object was to maintain the position which they had acquired, without
extending their views, in point of geography, to America as a whole,
or in point of time, to the future.

The spirit of the people was different, as I had occasion to verify
during the demonstrations made by the young men, who organised
lectures, went with me to lay wreaths on the tomb of Bolívar, and
filed by in silence, hat in hand, before the statue of the hero, in
one of the most heart-stirring ceremonies at which it has ever been
my lot to be present. The young men were not ignorant of the risks
which they were running in acting in opposition to official tendencies,
under a régime which showed little favour to divergent opinions.
But the memory of Miranda and the moral presence of Bolívar sustained their resolution and averted reprisals. I am bound to confess
that the Government committed no direct acts of coercion, at least
during my stay in Carcacas, and that the telegrams in which I was
invited to continue my propaganda in the provincial capitals reached
me without accident.[3] Among the people, where official suggestion is

It so happens that the Teatro Municipal, like the Nacional, is at present
under repair, and these operations, which I believed would be short enough
for it to be possible to make use of one of these theatres for the purpose
which you desire—will take a long time. So that I regret to say I cannot
comply with your request owing to these insuperable obstacles. Your
obedient servant, *V. Márquez Bustillo*, Governor of the Federal District."

[3] "Maracaibo, September 28, 1912. We send you our greetings to welcome
you on your arrival in our beloved country. Everybody desires to hear
your advocacy of Latin fraternity. Kindly advise us of your visit so that
we can prepare a tribute from your friends." *Jorge Schmidke.*

"Maracaibo, October 4, 1912. Zulia* awaits you. The Press announces
your visit. Intellectual circles enthusiastic. *Udon, Pérez, Eduardo López,
Guillermo Trujillo, Jorge Schmidke, Yepes Trujillo, Medina Chirinos, Evelio
Oliceros, Butron Olivares, Jambrina.* Messages to the same effect arrived from
Valencia, San Cristóbal, Tocuyo, Coro, Maracay, etc."

* Zulia is a province of Venezuela.

always less strongly felt, the support of certain groups was of course more visible, and it is certain that my propaganda would have met with a more and more sympathetic response. But if I had accepted one invitation I should have had to accept them all, and my journey could not be prolonged indefinitely. Moreover, my object was to record an idea and observe an atmosphere, and for this it was sufficient to visit the capitals.

Caracas falls under the generic type of Spanish-American cities, but it has an indefinable charm arising from its slight elevation above the level of the sea and the picturesque vegetation which surrounds it. From the balconies of the hotel Klindt I could see the Plaza Bolívar and the bright streets, edged by lines of clean houses of two or three stories, above which rose from time to time a building of greater proportions. A flourishing intellectual life was represented by newspapers, reviews, and famous learned societies. I had occasion to make the acquaintance of and to have dealings with men of ability in various institutions, especially in the Academy of History; for Venezuela, after making the history of a good part of Latin America, had devoted herself with particular good fortune to studying it.

Even the Government seemed to wish to listen to the voice of the intellectuals. But was the brilliance of this little centre and restricted group sufficient to enlighten the republic? Was the culture and Europeanism of an *élite*, which lived with its thoughts fixed on the great capitals, strong enough to impose lasting tendencies on the people as a whole and create a national atmosphere?

Let me analyse the sources of national energy. In Venezuela I. had come upon what I had already seen in the countries which I had visited before. In the first place, a governing class, composed of generals and small *caudillos*, professional politicians, all creatures of the existing régime, surrounded by a court formed by those who were soliciting sinecures and minor posts. In the second place, an intellectual class, of European distinction and mentality, standing aloof from the general atmosphere in virtue of their own superiority, and occasionally used by the first group as a temporary auxiliary. In the third place, a commercial class, composed for by far the most part of foreigners, whose interests, independent of those of the country, and sometimes antagonistic to them, are carried on by the agency of international societies, or banks, which determine the prosperity of German trade, English trade, or North American trade, while there exists no truly national trade, in the widest and most lasting sense of the word. In the fourth place, the masses, discontented and confused, who hire out their muscles to the foreign contractor for a negligible remuneration, or make a present of their blood to the ambitious politician in exchange for an illusion; doubly sacrificed, they never find an opportunity to retrieve their position. It is difficult to see behind these disunited groups, as a solid, organised body, the image of a nation in the vital sense of this conception. What is lacking is the binding together and interweaving of these varied elements by means of a higher aspiration which shall intensify and co-ordinate their energies in view of common ends. Imprisoned in the complications of their internal order, the component parts of society have not recast themselves in one mould. The community has not given birth to that diversity of activities with a single aim, which is the distinctive characteristic of complete peoples. And all because of the state of anxiety kept alive by civil wars and political intrigues, which have made endemic those disturbances which ought to have been occasional. To govern and to fight were the same thing. Courage and military success often seemed to furnish a sufficient fund of distinction to rule the destiny of peoples; and this system, which was bound to give such bad results from the political point of view, has given even worse results from the economic point of view.

The governments, carrying on a state of war into times of peace, have continued to look upon the customs as a source to draw upon; and, as in colonial days, these countries have continued to exchange their raw materials for manufactured products, with no reflection, and no regard for the precepts of modern political economy. How can a satisfactory explanation be given of the anomaly that nations exporting gold are raising foreign loans, and that the wealth of Latin America is, so to speak, running through our fingers, without, in some cases, leaving in our treasury even the paltry trace of an export duty? And when, in combination with this inexperience, we find a tendency to let everything pass out of our hands, from our produce to our mines, from our lands to our works of public utility, some light is thrown on the puzzle of our financial difficulties.

The fact that the richest countries in the world are forced to-day to beg for borrowed money in order to pay the interest on their debts —we refer to all Latin America in general, caught in the machinery of an eternal deficit—is due to their inability to construct the solid framework of a true nationality. When, on our own territory, we make use of a railway, get into a tramcar, build a house, or buy a pair of shoes, we pay an indirect tax to the foreigner. For these enterprises, constructions, or manufactures have their headquarters, or send their profits, out of the country. I will not speak of the banks or insurance companies. which annually extort fabulous sums. Our economists maintain that we must have capital. As if wealth was not in itself a form of capital. The theory has been, to say the least of it, badly applied, and what may have been expedient in the beginning has been transformed into a system. In the majority of cases we have not contracted debts in order to put our riches in circulation—which is a logical commercial operation, in the national as in the individual sphere. These riches have passed out of our hands, and their exploitation is the task of other countries. Mines, great plantations, vast enterprises of industrial transformation, cables, transport by land and sea, flourish so far removed from our sphere, that we are sometimes powerless even to impose upon the companies respect for our national law. The loans contracted by the governments have only very rarely been applied to the exploitation of financing, on their own behalf, of what ought to be the sources of national prosperity: gold fields, petroleum deposits, etc. In the majority of cases they have been raised merely in order to cover the cost of the public administration, or to repair the ravages made by disturbances, when the yield from the taxes and customs has been insufficient. And it is difficult to see to what issue this system can lead, seeing that if the money lent does not produce a higher interest than what is paid on it, the operation is inevitably bound to be ruinous. Such is the genesis of those "mortgaged countries, rich for others and poor for themselves," spoken of by the Mexican writer Don Carlos Pereyra.*

On leaving Venezuela I received, through a letter brought me by a traveller, the news of the patriotic expedition of the Nicaraguans resident in Costa Rica. From a port of that republic had set sail

* See Editorial Introduction.

Julián Yrias, Rodolfo Espinosa, Alejandro Bermúdez, and General Zeledón, bent on claiming the rights of their country. The letter was an echo at once of their hopes and of their disillusions. The national insurrection, set on foot by the aid of General Mena, would have overthrown the existing régime with the greatest ease, had it not been for the landing of North American troops. Taking up the defence of the bewildered government of Señores Estrada, Díaz, and Chamorro, they bombarded the city of Masaya and made an end of the generous enterprise. The death of Zeledón [4] put an end to the last death-struggle of sovereignty, and the protectorate has lasted from then till the present, in fact if not in name, and is confirmed by the presence of garrisons in various cities of the country.

Three things above all strike the eye of one who considers these events. First, the strange conception of politics which can induce a minority to solicit the armed aid of the foreigner against its own fellow-countrymen, making the very existence of the nation subordinate to party hatreds. Second, the indifference and calm of Latin America in face of events with whose significance and scope nobody can fail to be acquainted. The protest initiated by Dr. Araujo, President of San Salvador, did not even manage to find a platonic support, and thus, just as they had been silent in face of a treaty placing Nicaragua under an economic tutelage, so too the

[4] The battle began with sustained artillery fire, (North American) which the marines kept up for twenty-four hours against the light and improvised fortifications protecting the town of Masaya. An assault was afterwards made on them. The resistance was weak owing to lack of munitions, especially for artillery. The fight was continued in the *plaza* with the aid of the forces of President Díaz, and after a few hours, Zeledón gave it up, as his munitions were exhausted. Owing to Mena's surrender he had not been able to receive those he expected nor the re-enforcements from Granada. Zeledón was pursued, overtaken, killed. How? The patriots maintain that he was captured and assassinated. Those on the other side say that he died of his wounds. History, which will take possession of the victim's name to honour it as it deserves, will clear up this point; for we do not wish to take this task upon us, even with the documents before us, for the fear of being blinded by admiration for the hero and indignation against those who were the executors, both of him and of his country"—*Doctrina Wilson*, by Policarpo Bonilla, ex-president of the republic of Honduras.*

* An English version of Bonilla's work was published in New York in 1914.

sister republics were mute in face of the acts which placed her under a foreign military domination. The third circumstance which surprises us is the ignorance in which the opinion [*sic*] of the Continent remained, and still remains, with regard to these events. Apart from a few intellectuals who were interested in the affair, nobody was aware of the attack. It is, moreover, certain that the telegraphic agencies, so prodigal of details in other cases, were silent with one accord.

The importance of the cable as an agent of suggestion and an instrument of control is so decisive that it need not be emphasised. We are not now speaking of cases in which information is suppressed. The actual power of presenting facts, even without comment, brings with it the capacity for directing men's sympathies, influencing their wills, and governing their consciences. This is speaking generally. In the case of Latin America, the situation is more serious. A weak community, which feels the pulse of the world and draws its intellectual breath through the medium of the standards of the imperialist group, is foredoomed to be a community in danger, even if no other circumstances intervene. It is even worse when we are dealing with our own Latin-American life, about which we only know what they are pleased to place before us. This explains the atmosphere of contempt which has been created in the Argentine, Chile, and Brazil with regard to the other Spanish-speaking republics, and from this many of the conflicts which weaken us gain their significance. The docility with which our Southern Press announces a "grave situation in Mexico" every time that imperialist policy makes known through the medium of its telegraphic agencies its need to have new moral powers for its activity given to it, is one of the things which are most surprising. To base an inter-American policy on the inspiration drawn from these sources is a proof of naïveté. The first step towards a *rapprochement* between our countries ought to be the creation of our own sources of information about the realities of our life, and also about North-American life, since the agencies of the United States never convey to our republics more than a limited dose of truth. And yet we are faced with the paradox that a community of eighty million men, having great cities and powerful newspapers, lacks its own sources of independent intelligence, which should regulate the fluctuations of public opinion in accord with its own interests.

A telegram from the President of Colombia which I received at La Guayra [5] reassured me as to the favourable atmosphere reigning in that republic, mutilated by the realist genius of Roosevelt. Even in official circles, which are always anxious to temporise, the resentment and pain which had been caused by the attack on them were at that time displayed quite unambiguously. General Pedro Nell Ospina, then Minister for Colombia in Washington, had just addressed a note to Mr. Huntington Wilson, Under-Secretary of State to the United States, *apropos* of the proposed visit of Mr. Knox to Colombia, which ran: "There are perhaps reasons for believing that the visit of His Excellency the Secretary of State may be considered inopportune under present conditions, owing to the circumstances that Colombia still finds herself placed by the United States in an exceptional position, as the sole member of the numerous family of independent nations disseminated over the surface of the earth, with which, in spite of her constant petitions, the United States refuse to submit to arbitration questions having reference to the interpretation of public treaties, and the fulfilment of obligations by the universally recognised principles of International Law." Señor Don J. A. Gómez Recuero, Governor of Cartagena, had for his part said in a recent proclamation: "Let us break the old tables of political fanaticism, and engrave the gospel of our rights on the sacred bronze which conveys our gratitude to the founders of the Colombian nationality, showing ourselves to the civilised world as a people which prizes and loves its liberty, and deserves it, because of the rational use which it makes of it; and let us sacrifice all rather than curtail it for our brothers or lose it to foreigners." The sentiment of protest, which assumed a veiled form in high places, poured forth tumultuously in the Press and in the speeches of the young men, with no check save the culture and good taste of this particularly well-balanced people.

[5] "Bogotá, September 14, 1912. Official. I reciprocate the greetings of the illustrious authority on Latin-American affairs, and hail his proposal to visit Colombia, where his efforts in the interest of the Continent and the race will be appreciated as they should be. *C. E. Restrepo.*"

But it is also true that the wound could not be deeper. According to the treaty of 1846, "The United States guarantee positively and efficaciously, . . . the perfect neutrality of the . . . isthmus, with the view that free transit from one to the other sea may not be interrupted . . . in any future time . . . ; and, in consequence, the United States also guarantee in the same manner the rights of sovereignty and property which New Granada has and possesses over the said territory." * The separatist rising hatched by elements attached to President Roosevelt, might for a moment surprise the good faith of a few simple-minded politicians of the isthmus, but to-day nobody has any doubt of the conspiracy, either in Panama, or in Colombia, or in the United States. The North American writers Mr. Alexander S. Bacon and Mr. Leander T. Chamberlain, in publications as authoritative as the *North American Review*, have said all that was needful about what they courageously call "a page of national dishonour"; and they have given a full account of the great responsibilities which rests upon the Government at Washington.†
When shall we give definite expression to that which rests upon men and institutions in Panama, Colombia and the whole Continent, with regard to the same affair? Apart from what has been said about the matter by the Mexican diplomatist Isidro Fabela, General Jorge Martínez, and a few more writers, we only know of desultory comments which make no contribution to our knowledge of the truth. And it is high time that Latin America should know, with dates and names, what passed in what we may also call, plagiarising the Yankee publicist, "a page of our dishonour." For we must refrain from indignant exclamations, and recognise that there were culprits on both sides, with the sole distinction that those on the enemy's side committed an offence in order to serve their flag, whereas those on our side committed it in such a way as to humiliate ours.

The reception which was given me in Colombia was so enthusiastic, that the memory of it is still fresh in my mind. At every port during my journey I felt the throbbing soul of the wounded nation, which hailed in the traveller its own ideals. Before I arrived in

* Quoted from Malloy, *Treaties*, etc., and not translated from Ugarte's Spanish.
† *North American Review*, February, 1912, contains Chamberlain's article.

the country, telegrams, of which I quote a few by way of illustration,[6] revealed to me the national atmosphere: After visiting the flourishing coast town of Barranquilla and historic Cartagena, those centres of prosperity and culture which are the gates of Colombia towards the Caribbean Sea, I started for Bogotá by the picturesque route of the Magdalena.

Few journeys offer such attractions. Hurried tourists, who think of nothing but covering the greatest number of kilometres in the shortest time possible, sometimes find fault with the slow pace at which one approaches the capital, and do not take into account the fairylike attractions of nature, dazzling in its orgy of colour, in the

[6] "Bogotá, November 3, 1912. I hasten to greet you. The capital of the nation which has been the principal victim of imperialist voracity, is anxiously awaiting the arrival of the noted propagandist of Latin-American fraternity."
Laureano Gómez, editor of *La Unidad*.

"Cartagena, November 5, 1912. The Executive Committee of the Cartagena Club sends its greeting in advance to welcome the illustrious propagandist of the union of the countries of Latin America, and has the honour to invite him to the fêtes which will take place in this centre of social life on the occasion of the anniversary of the independence of this city."
Simón J. Vélez.

"Cartagena, November 5, 1912. In the name of the Second Division of the Army I salute in you the soul of the American race and fatherland."
Luis Maria Teran, officer commanding.

"Cartagena, November 6, 1912. Press of Cartagena sends you a cordial welcome, and takes the liberty of inviting you to visit this city, which desires to make your acquaintance and hear the brilliant words of the illustrious writer on subjects of American importance." *El Porvenir, La Época, Rojo y Negro, El Autonomista, El Caribe, El Penitente, Informaciones, La Patria, Menfis, Alma Latina, El Mundo Nuevo, La Prensa*.

"Medellín, November 7, 1912. I greet the valiant and indefatigable defender of our race. His heroic labour will one day vanquish all obstacles. Come to Medellín." *Francisco Suárez*.

"Nemucón, November 8, 1912. The existence of the South American republics as independent nationalities is bound up with their perfect union. Welcome to our country, as the apostle of this redeeming idea. We greet you with enthusiasm. *José V. Acevedo, Alejandro González Torres, Abel Garcia, Luis M. León, Polidiro Uribe, Julio C. Lezmez, Alberto Latorre, V. Samuel Bravo, Braulio M. Gaitán, J. Alberto Martinez, Nicolás Barrera, Marco Emilio Fonseca, Lorenzo Herrera, M. Pontom, Juan N. Silva, Francisco Latorre, Luis Rodríguez*.

gradation of its flora and fauna, from the torrid zone to the frozen mountain tops; nor do they realise thoroughly the exigencies of the climate, which varies according to the height. Nor do they remember with what forethought the cities of the colony were built, at a period when, in obedience to the law of security, they sought above all for positions difficult of access. Bogotá, like Quito and La Paz, stands at such a great height above the sea, that the traveller sometimes feels oppressed by the mountain summits, as in the Swiss Oberland. The most astonishing thing is that a centre of civilisation and of modern life can exist at such a distance from the sea and at such an unheard-of elevation. From Barranquilla, passing through Puerto Viejo, Calamar, Bodega Central, Puerto Nacional, Puerto Berrio, as far as Dorada and Honda, a series of landscapes, a recurring change of views, make the traveller forget the discomfort inherent in such a long journey. From Honda by way of Guayabal, San Lorenzo, Lérida [Mérida?] and La Unión, as far as the Upper Magdalena, we follow the changing moods of nature, which gradually becomes more solemn, more gloomy, and, perhaps for this very reason, more impressive The upper plateau is crowned by Girardot, where a convenient railway carries us in wide curves up the mountain-side, across bridges and through tunnels to the capital of Colombia.

The demonstrations at Barranquilla and Cartagena had revealed what enthusiasm my journey aroused, but I could not have foreseen what happened on my arrival at Bogotá. [7] My pen halts as if faced

[7] "On learning by telegram that he had entered the train at Girardot, posters began to appear in public places inviting the public to go and welcome him at the station of La Sabana. Among these posters we saw those of the newspapers *La Unión, El Liberal, La Nación, El Artista, Sur-America, Gil Blas, Commentarios, Gaceta Republicana, El Tiempo, El Diario, El Republicano, El Nuevo Tiempo* and others. The same invitation was issued by the Society of Authors, the typographical guild, and various industrial and workmen's unions." *El Nuevo Tiempo,* November 26, 1912.

"The crowd was enormous, and the enthusiasm such as had never before been seen. Persons of every class of society, of every age and position, frantically acclaimed the illustrious champion who with easy speech and elegant phrase recalled the memories of the past glories of the country and its recent sufferings, in order to kindle patriotism, uplift the national soul, and raise indignation against a deed of felony."

El Republicano, November 27, 1912.

with an obstacle when it tries to start on this subject. But I should fail in my aim of portraying a moral state and an atmosphere if I kept silence upon certain facts which are the best data for judging a situation. These ovations were not given to the man, but to the idea, and for this reason, setting myself aside, I may say that I have never been in the presence of greater enthusiasm. The protest of the *chargé d'affaires* of the United States referred exclusively to the action of those groups which went off at nightfall to that country's Legation. But it is certain that the rally of a republic round a principle of resistance made more impression on the diplomatist than the inoffensive outburst of a few excited persons. What was surprising was the unanimity of the impulse, and, at the same time, the serene firmness of that country, raised high upon its mountains.

The lecture took place with the goodwill of everybody.[8] The depths of our peoples—I refer to Latin America as a whole—are so strong and sound, that what amazes us is the small purpose to

"Both when he found himself carried away by the crowd on leaving the train, and when he saw the carriage in which he was travelling almost borne aloft by the human torrent which advanced with thunderous cheers, Ugarte must surely have felt the throbbing soul of Colombia, and measured the force which still resides in this indomitable people."
El Diario, November 27, 1912.

[8] "The crowd which filled a great space in the Parque de la Independencia, near by the Teatro del Bosque, was enormous. It had been proposed to hold the lecture inside the theatre, but it was necessary to hold it in the open air, since the accommodation, though considerable, did not suffice. Every class of society was represented in this crowd of at least ten thousand people." *Gaceta Republicana*, December 2, 1912.

"Señor Ugarte's lecture does not admit of a simple eulogy; it is something abnormal and unique, made to temper men's souls and forge heroes; these are lofty words which go straight to the heart."
El Tiempo, December 3, 1912.

"Ugarte descended from the platform amid a thunder of applause. May the beneficent seed scattered by him take root and bear fruit in the depths of the soul of Colombia." *El Nuevo Tiempo*, December 2, 1912.

"An enormous, enthusiastic, and deeply-moved multitude listened to the orator with religious attention, in the midst of a respectful silence, which was hardly broken when the enthusiasm which filled every breast burst forth imposingly in a enormous shout of exaltation."
El Diario, December 3, 1912.

which this unsurpassed material has been turned. But if we examine Latin-American life, however superficially, we shall understand that the origin of the evil is to be found in the ideas and methods of our education.

We do not only allude to instruction in its direct and applied forms, but to the higher points of view which inspire the general course of action within a community, creating collective tendencies and directing even those who have not passed through the schools. A plan of education is a programme of action in view of future development. And the greater error of Latin America was to transplant to its own soil the forms of antiquated methods. A virgin continent, with fabulous wealth to exploit, born of novel conditions and divergent social factors, in the heat of democratic ideas and in a century of economic strife, required to confront life from the point of view of experimental and practical standards, in order to create citizens capable of rising to the efforts demanded by circumstances. Instead of this a routine was introduced drawn from those peoples who had already realised their destiny. Latin, literature, erudition are the rich elements of a higher culture. But they could exercise little or no influence in the development of societies in course of construction, which ought, in their struggles with the barbarism of Nature, to give their main attention to defending themselves, establishing their position, and making themselves masters of their heritage by virtue of their foresight and muscular strength. All our difficulties have risen from this opposition between our actual necessities and our empirical instruction. They begin by a conflict between the urban population, with its pretentious literary education, and the rural population which, though illiterate, performs the most useful labour; and they end in stagnation and financial dependence.

Life has its imperious necessities which cannot be solved by quotations from Horace; our communities, prepared for all save the *rôle* assigned to them by destiny, left their riches to slumber, or handed them over to others. And let it be borne in mind that by riches I mean not only the exploitable treasures above and beneath the ground—mines, forests, petroleum deposits, etc.,—but also the functions for which the community offers scope, and which constitute a source of profit—transport construction, public works, sanitation, equipment, alimentation, etc. It may be said that in these varied spheres it rarely happened that the natives squarely faced the needs which it was urgent to satisfy. Not through laziness, as has been said; for the laziness arose subsequently, from their loss of illusions and lack of guidance. The cause was literary arrogance, which alienated some from all practical reality, and the lack of technical preparation, which rendered it impossible for others to develop a fruitful activity.

Even those who devoted themselves in early days to agriculture, stock-breeding, and other activities bound up with the first manifestations of a people's life, did so without any theoretical notions or knowledge of the progress which had been achieved in the world. They carried on the methods of the most backward regions of Spain, or took the customs of the Indians as their guide. In the majority of cases, they had to proceed as if humanity were at the beginning of its career, as if there had not previously existed a nucleus of universal knowledge about these affairs; and to find their way by means of successive calculations which had afterwards to be transmitted by oral tradition.

Instruction, which did not take even remotely into account either time, place, social conditions, or the needs of the community, tended exclusively, in its elementary form, to the diffusion of old precepts or auxiliary processes such as reading and writing, or, in its higher forms, towards the cultivation of vain traditionalism within a parasitic body. And thus the situation was prepared which was to oblige us to have recourse to the foreigner every time there was a question of making a road, laying a railway, or constructing a bridge, in order to obtain capital, technical knowledge, and labour.

By cultivating an education worthy of the "floral games," Spanish Americans have handed over the usufruct of their lands and created tributary nations. These riches were systematically extracted, appraised, transported, exploited, manufactured, and sold by enterprises, capital, specialists, and men of affairs who brought with them the mode of activity and the spirit of distant communities. Personal necessities—costumes, household utensils, victuals, etc., the necessities of every social group—tramways, telephones, street-paving, etc., and those of the nation as a whole—railways, telegraphs, armaments, etc., were supplied by other nations. Every people has need of other peoples, and exchange is the basis of universal vitality. But that wealth which is confined to the chance fertility of the soil and the powers of consumption of the population is not of a lasting character. Commerce is only nationalised when the natives take it in hand. A nation is only prosperous when in true possession of its resources, it makes what it produces in abundance pay for what it lacks.

And so these tendencies in our education, unsuitable for arousing enterprise, initiative industry, and a flourishing life, led us to pay a tax to the foreigner in every movement of our daily life: when we get into a train, when we enter a cinematograph, when we take a telephone receiver off the hook, when we take out an insurance, when we get into an automobile, when we turn over the leaves of a book, when we turn on the light, when we go up in an elevator, when we transact business at a bank, when we buy a bicycle, when we walk on a carpet, when we use eye-glasses, when we consult a clock:—because all these objects, commodities, or mechanisms come from without the country or are under the control of foreign companies; and because the very paper of the newspaper which we read every day, the very pen with which we write our letters, the very stuff of which our flags are made, the very hat which we wear on our heads, all have been made or financed outside our boundaries and, what is worse, have often utilised raw materials which went out of our own country without bringing it any profit.

What Latin America purchases, in the majority of cases, is not produce, but scientific superiority, skill in manufactures, the commercial capacity arising from an education which she is herself capable of implanting and diffusing with no more trouble than that of conceiving a plan and having the energy to carry it out. We are so accustomed to our dependence, in some regions, that the very idea of emancipating ourselves from it surprises us. But the present situation is not something stereotyped and removed beyond the will of men. The idea that we shall be able at some time to build our ships, manufacture our arms, control the railways which run through our territories, extract the gold from our mines, run our own cold-storage plant, etc., is beginning to take root in the minds of our young men, who desire to develop an economic initiative and activity suitable to a continent crying out, above all things, for initiative and labour.

A prejudice born of this same deceptive education appears to set us apart from all material efforts and grants us, in exchange, a decisive superiority in the realm of spiritual matters. The Anglo-Saxons are the masters of practical life—repeat some—but we have a greater artistic capacity. The absurdity is so evident, that it is superfluous to emphasise it. Even admitting this distribution of talents, nothing could be less reasonable than to despise those direct and essential activities which are the measure of the real influence of peoples. But is that boasted superiority of ours in the things of the mind beyond contradiction? Does our intellectual life exercise any higher influence in art, philosophy, or science? Can we cite the works, the results, or the inventions which bear out this affirmation? The United States, "absorbed in money and figures" as the vulgar saying goes, have made world-famous the names of Poe, Walt Whitman, Whistler [Whittier?], William James, Edison, and a hundred others, who have made an original contribution to beauty, thought, and the progress of the world. Unfortunately we cannot say as much. And worst of all is the fact that the elements essential to carrying out this effort exist. Rarely has a community arisen in history so marvellously endowed with intelligence, power of assimilation, and fancy. But the eternal lack of wide vision in the direction of our minds, the lack of moral discipline, the cult of memorising, the absence of high ideals, and routine, have stood in the way of the transformation of these latent values into tangible values. On the one hand an ill-directed emulation, which means that instead of aspiring to outdo others, time is wasted in obstructing their work; on the other hand, the slight importance and consideration conceded by majorities to whatever does not involve representation or political rank, have dispersed, depressed, and debilitated our efforts, endeavours and works, condemning us to an improvised and fragmentary production which has so far not been able to succeed in realising itself on a world scale. All that has actually persisted has been an arrogant and exuberant imagination, and it is by the aid of and in the world of imagination that paradox has prospered and spread itself, taking for an accomplished fact that which might be done if the lure of discord, and the hostility of the communities for all that rises above them, had not impeded all better developments. But even supposing that we had risen superior to our surrounding atmosphere, and succeeded in carrying our aspirations into effect, even if we were to succeed one day in becoming leaders in the spheres of intellect and sensibility, we must take into account the fact that thought is the crown of a country's life, but not its basis, and that nothing is more futile than to despise the walls upon which must be raised and upheld the cupola of a civilisation.

When the Japanese found themselves obliged to open their islands to the commerce of the world, and were faced with the formidable superiority of Western civilisation, they did not for a single moment think of neglecting the essential motive forces of life in order to go on adoring legends. They came down and challenged the primacy of their rivals on their own ground, assimilated as much of the progress of the rest of the world as they could make use of, and, realising that political depends on commercial independence, set themselves to master every form of activity. If our present system of education is replaced by one adequate to the necessities of the age, Latin America can gradually initiate a similar effort. But in speaking of new methods, we have not only to keep in view the technical instruction requisite for each form of activity, but the higher aspiration, without which all knowledge is but a body without a soul. It is in those highest tendencies which turn men's minds towards initiative, free discussion, and creative energy, that the animating principle will have to be sought. For what we have to set aside, above all, is that limited conception which makes education reside in the diffusion of a body of information. Education is something higher and more important, which only acquires a beneficial and creative force, from the national point of view, when it is exercised in view of definite collective aims, in the service of an ideal growth, into which each individual composing it places his own personal good.

When there exists in Latin America a technical and moral preparation appropriate to the age, revolution will be extinguished, forces which are now sacrificed will prosper, and that unfortunate illusion will disappear which leads us to suppose that it is enough that riches are produced in our territories for them to belong to us. In many respects we are to-day virtually colonies of Europe or of the United States, and this subordination will not cease until new ideas shape our course through the centuries, and give us the instruments for their realisation.

Another problem which Latin America has to face is that of the co-existence of different races; whether we look at it from the Anglo-Saxon point of view, or whether, in accordance with our origins, we decide in favour of fusion. Obstacles of every order oppose themselves to the adoption of the former solution: facts sanctioned by custom, compact masses which it would be different to isolate, historical antecedents, etc. The United States solved the difficulty from the beginning in a harsh, but logical way, in view of the characteristics of English colonisation and the time at which the process was adopted But the America of Spanish origin, born to a certain extent of a union legitimised by the centuries, cannot go back upon its own history to rectify its effects.

The Indian has really double rights: First, as the original occupant of these lands, oppressed by the Spaniards and then subordinated to the Creoles, but the owner of an imprescriptible right; and secondly, because the new condition of affairs, the autonomy of our republics, is in great part his work. In good law, when the Spaniards supplanted the Indian, they were acting in accordance with a law of war in their day; they were the conquerors. But we, who admitted him into our armies as an equal when it was a question of achieving independence, cannot cast him out of the community after having made use of him. San Martín and Bolívar did not ask their soldiers whether they had any shoes, or from what race they sprang. It was enough that they had hearts. And the Indian formed an integral part of the armies which marched through Latin America from north to south, and contributed powerfully towards the emancipation of the old colonies; he watered those vast territories with his blood; and if his character were less downtrodden, if his enlightenment were more advanced, he could lift up his head and say to us: I have handed over the land to you, I have given you liberty, and in exchange you have only made me a slave.

Everything points to the fact that by a reaction from our tendency to follow an imitative course of action, without caring whether it responds to our needs, we shall end by taking a firm stand on realities, and deducing from them a point of view of our own in every sphere. The African only occurs by way of accident, for he only exists in considerable groups in certain regions of the Antilles. But the indisputable numerical superiority of the Indians in a large portion of our republics, constitutes a problem which cannot be put off, and will only be solved by a levelling up of culture and a brotherly spirit of equality. All that implies a distinction between the constituent elements of a nationality ends in incapacitating it for progress or defence. And since we are concerned with noble and enduring forces, whose faults are derived from the position to which they have seen themselves restricted, rather than from their own essential nature, it may be held that on the level to which the Indian is raised will depend to a great extent the level of each republic.

The greatest triumphs of imperialism have consisted in subdividing the community into numerous sections, turning the attention of the sections towards political, spiritual, or social controversies, and towards theories which divert the energy required for national consolidation. Amid the passions aroused by these struggles it is no easy task to invoke directing principles which have nothing to do with party hatred, sectarian ambitions, or those local passions which blind the eyes. Yet the atmosphere in Colombia appeared to me more propitious than most for these high aims. It is perhaps the country of Latin America in which there exists the most homogeneous and cultivated intellectual groups, and in which the soundest of thought and humane learning has lasted in the colony for a long period. To this should be added an undercurrent of memories' coming from its period of greatness, which makes it tend, like Venezuela and Ecuador, towards a broad continental conception. Great Colombia has preserved, in spite of wars, political dissensions, and dictatorships, the thrills of its great past, and it was this reflection of their original aims, magnified by time and progress, which I had seen blooming in the patriotic enthusiasm of Bogotá.

This is not to say that there were none of those unfortunate incidents and animosities which had characterised my tour from the beginning. As the number of adherents to my ideal became more marked, the intrigues against the traveller increased. To the old tactics of working on local susceptibilities by circulating false expressions of opinion, in which some republics were compared with others to their disadvantage, was added a campaign of personal depreciation. Had the attack been direct, written and tangible, I should have been able to annihilate it. But anonymous reports admit of neither chastisement nor refutation. I consider it fruitless to allude to various incidents provoked by the North American agents who observed my movements. It would be still more futile to refer to the way in which I was cut off from communications, from north to south, and to the calculated silence of the telegraphic agencies, bent upon disguising the wide-spread character and significance of demonstrations which found no echo in the remaining countries. What forces me to become my own chronicler at times is the ignorance in which they attempted to leave Latin America as to what one man accomplished, or attempted to accomplish—alone, opposed by formidable influences, deprived of all support, with no strength but that of his ideal. Perhaps a more difficult situation has rarely presented itself. Skilful and hidden emissaries caused me to appear in some places as an atheist, in others as an anarchist, in others as a secret agent of the exiled opposition parties; and by insinuating that I was in the service of veiled interests, they represented me as a literary adventurer. The hostile attitude of almost all the Argentine consuls and ministers seemed to corroborate this interpretation. The spontaneous character of my journey seemed inexplicable in certain circles, to whom it seemed incredible that a man would expose himself to so much expense and annoyance without seeking any gain. The very fact that the lectures were free, and that the offers of those authorities who desired to defray the costs of my lodging and travelling were declined, was used against me. It is obvious that if I had done the opposite, I should have given rise to accusations of venality and commercialism. It is not for me to insist upon the energy and moral courage which were needed in these circumstances to continue a tour which nothing obliged me to make but my own enthusiasm. These destructive tactics took advantage of every pretext or conjuncture of affairs to depreciate me personally, and through me, to disparage my ideals and propaganda. And it must be confessed that in the end the results were what they had hoped, as those will see who read the rest of this book. The national courage of Venezuela and Colombia was of course equal to overcoming such difficulties. But while the boat, on its way back to Panama, was going through the Canal on a southerly course, amidst the activity and whirl of the North American zone, I was prompted to ask myself whether I too was not suffering from a delusion, bound up with the destiny of our thrice romantic Latin America: romantic in its secluded *plazas* on a midsummer night, romantic in its heroic struggle for an illusory independence, and romantic in its suicidal Pan-Americanism.

CHAPTER VII

THE PROBLEMS OF THE PACIFIC

The Position of the Galápagos—Public spirit in Ecuador—Absence of interchange between the different republics—Echoes of a speech by Señor Madero—President Billinghurst—How a lecture was telegraphed to Ecuador and Chile—A fortnight at La Paz—The official world and Chilean democracy—A Latin-American point of veiw.

As soon as one leaves Panama and enters the Pacific Ocean on a southerly course, one feels the oppression of a conflict which runs, like an *idée fixe*, through every act and expression; of a problem which governs movements and forces; of an exasperated obsession which overshadows every conciliatory overture, and every attempt to survey things from a general point of view. One has to take sides in the dispute between Tacna and Arica, and one has to declare in favour of Chile or Peru.

The character of my tour and the broad conception which had defined its scope, naturally placed me in a position in which I could have no preference. For a Latin American who cultivates a broader patriotism and believes that the welfare of the fatherland, thus broadly conceived, depends upon the power of *rapprochement* or combination of the groups composing it, the disagreements of the Pacific coast can only be considered as a malady of the Continent which it is urgent to palliate or sweep away by the aid of equity, examination, and conciliation. For a temperate and skilled diplomacy inspired by higher ideals, there ought not to exist any insuperable difficulties, when it is a question of taking all rights into consideration, so as to bring into harmony the future advance of two groups which are so closely bound together by history and in the future. I am not concerned to discuss grievances. I respect the reasons which are adduced, and the legitimate sentiments aroused by local patriotism. But above and beyond all rights, ambitions, and even injuries, there rises the vision of the benefit which others may gain from the struggle, by taking advantage of our divisions to serve interests contrary to our own. This view of the matter, which may be stigmatised as lyrical, but not as partial, admits of no petty exceptions. It was with the widest sentiments of brotherhood towards Peru and Chile, with the most scrupulously balanced sympathies for both parties, and with an ardent longing that the difficulty might be solved with the goodwill of all, that I pursued my journey, which had been difficult from the outset and was every day more beset with snares as I advanced towards the south. A Japanese, a Peruvian, and a Chilean steamship company, the last two partly supported, according to what I was told, by English or North American capital, ensure the communications between the ports on the coast, from Buenaventura, the last outlet of Colombia towards the south, to the distant straits of Magellan. It is plain that both Peru and Chile endeavour to confirm their influence in the regions attached to their sphere of action by the aid of these shipping lines, the first which we had seen flying our flags since the beginning of the tour.

And so we arrived at Guayaquil, a prosperous commercial city and a vigorous centre of activity and culture, for which, owing to its geographical position, the future surely reserves the most brilliant development.

In 1913 the moderate opinion of the country which did not allow its vision to be clouded by internal politics, was preoccupied with two great national problems; the proposed measures of sanitation to be applied to the port of Guayaquil, and the rumoured sale of the Galápagos Islands. Both affairs stirred the soul of Ecuador to its depths, and a deep emotion was arousing their pride before the pressure which was making itself felt from abroad. The young men, the intellectuals, the ruling classes, the masses of the people, all understood the import of the decisions which were felt in the air; and a suppressed nervousness was surging in men's minds. We all know the arguments which are appealed to in these cases. The proposed objects were "necessary measures of health" and the "need for supporting Panama on the Pacific side." But the Ecuadorians could not fail to think of the consequences which would ensue for their young and poorly developed country, from the activities of a foreign sanitary commission on their coasts, and the more or less veiled cession of the archipelago commanding them. Thanks to their situation, the Galápagos form one of the keys of the Pacific. In an impartial view, the threat of a nation foreign to our family to occupy these islands ought by rights to have been a cause of anxiety, not only to Ecuador, which would lose in them a part of her territory, but to those republics which are ranged in a row down to the South; for the influence diffused by the neighbourhood of the new naval base would turn out to be a menace to them all.

Notwithstanding all this, thanks to the narrow local conception which gives its character to our diplomacy, nobody had a word to say about the matter, and Ecuador found itself faced by this difficulty in isolation, as our republics have always done at the crucial moment, owing to the disunion which keeps them apart.

This evil is also due to that superficiality which prevents us from observing problems until they are revealed by a sudden emergency, which shows their real character. And so, just as Spain, in letting Florida pass out of her hands, ought to have thought of the fate of Cuba, so we ought to have realised the *rôle* of the Galápagos when we heard of the opening of the Canal. This was the moment for negotiation and preventive measures. Possibly the archipelago might have come to be an indirect support against imperialism, encouraging within its sphere of influence the flourishing of those European interests desirous of developing in the neighbourhood of the Canal. Perhaps South America might have found within herself formulas equally favourable and equally satisfactory to all parties, by the aid of which the common security and sovereignty of Ecuador might have been simultaneously guaranteed. But our chancelleries have never made themselves acquainted with the terrain on which they have to give battle, and accordingly have never been able to prepare for action. In Buenos Aires we discovered the existence of the Falkland Islands at the moment of parting with them, and Mexico failed to foresee the consequences of the Spanish-American War until they were irreparable. We have always lacked that faculty of calm reasoning which enables one to measure the implications of facts before they take place and that foresight which enables one to explore in imagination the pathways of the future. It was for this reason that Ecuador was taken by surprise in the case of the Galápagos, and for this reason that the interest of the other republics failed to back her up.

The balance of the world is made up of influences which cancel one another, of divergent forces, of opposing tides. In Latin America there has never been more than one influence, one force, and one tide: that which comes from the North. It has never been checked, either by an act of our will, absorbed in internal disputes, or by an effort from Europe, obsessed by bitter rivalries. Imperialist policy has always been able to proceed in the New World, without faltering or counterpoise, as if it were really the master, multiplying strategic routes and advanced posts, without meeting any opposition or resistance. The growing domination of the United States, which has closed the epoch of Europe's world hegemony, has thus been favoured more by the dissensions of the Old World itself, which was unable to maintain its influence before the dominating advance of the Northern republic, than by the inefficacy of Latin American action.

This indifference, pregnant with catastrophes, is making itself felt equally in Asia, where the United States are carrying out their manœuvres unmindful of the Monroe Doctrine, and in Latin America, where they are intervening under cover of what it takes for granted. In former days world politics were shaped in Europe; but now it is only with difficulty that she will admit that her policy has any work to do in the world. She does not aim at enlarging her horizons. And nothing but the stationary character of her views could explain certain attitudes which she took up before the war. Since the war, the inevitable tendency of circumstances has caused Washington to hold the balance in everything. But we shall have to speak of this in another chapter.

The fate of the Galápagos is bound up with that of Panama. If Ecuador will not sell them, a disciple of Roosevelt will arise and occupy them, without discussion or explanation, in accordance with the principles of a forward policy. If Ecuador consents, this advanced sentinel of her territory will itself serve as the point of departure for new expansionist pretensions. In either case Ecuador, and Latin America with her, will have to face innumerable difficulties arising in particular from the connection between this matter and the sanitation of Guayaquil. All political hypotheses which

might have appeared valid twenty years ago, and all measures concerted on the basis of European interests, have collapsed. There
exists to-day no coalition which can check the primacy of North
American influence in the South Pacific. And since the problem of
the Galápagos, big though it is, is not sufficient to give rise to movements on this scale, all that can be hoped for is a change in the
events which work themselves out on a world scale and bring about
a new balance of affairs. The port of Guayaquil is far from being
in the sanitary condition which has been proclaimed.[1] The quaran-
tine imposed at Panama on ships coming from this port is of a
political character. Pressure is brought to bear on the country by
the aid of a boycott on their ships. The sale of the Galápagos would
immediately improve the condition of the port, whose reputation
depends upon the calculations of international policy. For when we
enter the atmosphere of the Pacific, it is necessary to rise superior
to isolated facts, and embrace the whole idea, the higher plan, the
interaction of the various movements which are going on, while the
Latin republics remain inactive, and no opposition or disagreement
shows itself on the horizon save that of distant Japan, enigmatic
and impenetrable beneath the calm of the Asiatic stars.

The attitude of Eucador was similar to that of Colombia.
Guayaquil gave a warm welcome [2] to the idea of Latin-American
solidarity, which afterwards assumed larger proportions on the occasion of the lecture which I gave in a theatre in this city.[3] Visits of

[1] In order to cope with the situation, the Government of Ecuador requested the presence of Colonel Gorgas, the North American expert, who
came as technical adviser to take part in drawing up a project of works.
The visit cost the Ecuadorian government about 20,000 *sucres*, and the
above-mentioned Colonel drew up a memorandum on the subject for the
Ministry of War of his country.

[2] "The presence of Ugarte in Latin America has drawn all sympathies
to him. His lectures have made an excellent impression and produced a
stimulating effect on the indolent minds of our peoples."
            El Grito del Pueblo Ecuatoriano, January 6, 1913.

"Ugarte is a symbolic voice which makes itself the echo of all the
aspirations and ambitions of the South American republics."
            El Guante, January 16, 1913.

[3] "More than three thousand persons filled the Teatro Eden. Outside
there was a great crowd which could not enter owing to the cramped pro-

delegations of workmen, invitations from social clubs, the support of the Press, and the telegrams which arrived from the interior of the republic,[4] with a distinguished list of signatures appended, revealed the state of the national consciousness.

At Guayaquil I made the acquaintance of representative men in politics, literature, education, and labour, such as Don Ricardo Cornejo, Don Vicente Paz Ayora, Don Manuel J. Calle, Don Luís F. Lazo, Don Virgilio Drouet, Don Aurelio Faleoni, Don Emilio

portions of the theatre, but was roused to enthusiasm by the delirious applause and felt a vehement desire to give the orator an ovation."

El Ecuatoriano, January 20, 1913.

"It was a success. Yes, a formidable, grandiose, stupendous success. Seldom, perhaps never, have we heard words so burning, so vigorous, so virile and so well reasoned as those of this great apostle of union for the salvation for the peoples of South America."

El Telegrafo, January 20, 1913.

"The enormous audience, enormous in proportion to the place in which the event took place, was swollen by another and greater body which waited at the doors, forming a long *queue,* and four or five thousand persons accompanied the orator to his lodgings."

El Guante, January 20, 1913.

[4] "Cuenca, January 18, 1913. We greet you in the name of Azuay, we congratulate you on your generous campaign in favour of the interests and ideals of the Latin race in America, and we wish you prosperity and a complete success in your mission." *Honorato Vázquez, Remigio Crespo Toral, Rafael Arizaga, Alberto Muñoz Venaza, Roberto Crespo Toral, Arcesio Pozo,* the Editor of *La Voz Obrera,* the Editor of *El Tren,* the Editor of *La Voz del Sur.*

"Quito, January 18, 1913. The Juridical Literary Society has the pleasure to greet you on your arrival at that part of the American fatherland called Ecuador, and wishes you a pleasant stay"—*Tovar Borgono,* President.

"Guaranda, January 25, 1913. The Municipal Council, in their own name and that of the city of Guaranda, greet with effusion Manuel Ugarte, the illustrious propagandist of the Latin-American cause. May his stay in Ecuador be agreeable and fortunate, since he represents the voice which shall rouse those people whose autonomy is in danger." *J. G. Camacho,* President; *V. M. Arregui, Angel M. López, Pablo R. León, G. D. Veintimilla, Luís del Pozo,* councillors; *A. P. Chavez,* municipal attorney; *P. D. Calero,* secretary.

"Babahoyo, January 20, 1913. By a resolution of the 'Luz al Obrero' Society of Artisans, we send you a cordial greeting to welcome you on your

Gallegos del Campo, Don B. Taborga, Don Carlos Alberto Flores, Don Camilo Destruge, Don José Vicente Trujillo, Don Félix Valencia, Don César Arroyo, Don M. Romero Terán, and many more whom I have in mind, but whom it is difficult to name in a rapid enumeration. I was honoured by invitations from the clubs, the higher units of the army, employees' associations, students' associations, and I met everywhere with the same atmosphere of enthusiasm.

The same thing happened at Quito, where I arrived after a marvellous voyage through rustic and picturesque regions which rise tier above tier to the summits of the Andes.

The President, General Plaza, had replied to my greetings on arriving in the country by a courteous telegram.[5] It seems useless to emphasise the point that these attentions from some of the popular representatives were formulated with the view of temporising with public opinion, and did not in the least prevent them, in the majority of cases, from doing all they could, indirectly, to diminish the effect of the propaganda which I had undertaken.

As a matter of fact I travelled, from north to south, surrounded by the hostility of all the governments and all official circles. Under pressure from the atmosphere which reigned among the people and the young men, they might at times appear to be neutral or courteous, but at heart they cursed the unwelcome visitor who came to interrupt the routine of local politics. In addition to this, I had to meet the manœuvres of imperialist agents, who stigmatised me as "the agitator" or "the adventurer" and the hostility of my own country, whose representatives, when introduced, declared that the journey was "a writer's fancy," that it was a question of "a young man representing nothing and having no significance in the life of the Argentine." Almost all of them omitted to return the call I made on them, or to attend, not the lectures (which in this respect

happy arrival at the pearl of the Pacific, and in its name and my own I pray that your labour, as disinterested as it is noble, in the cause of the Latin-American countries, may meet with success during your stay in the land of Olmedo and Rocafuerte." *J. M. Cabrera*, President.

[5] "Quito, January 15, 1913 I reciprocate the courteous greeting of the noted Argentine writer, by giving him an affectionate welcome and wishing him a happy stay in my country and every success in his high literary career." *Plaҙa*.

came within the scope of their duties) but the social festivities, banquets, soirées, balls, etc., of which numbers were given for the learned visitor. This marked estrangement of the authorities of course increased the support of the masses and the young men, and it was with the moral approval of these healthy forces that I approached the governors, not in order to seek support, but to get to know the general view of the situation in our countries.

The President of Ecuador was an energetic man, weighty and cautious, who turned the conversation in the usual direction: he had read my books; the Argentine was making great progress; and Ecuador congratulated herself upon the visit of the writer. Long years of living in Europe, and the habit of weighing the import of words, have made me sufficiently prudent in conversation to avoid discord. General Plaza could have had no fear of imprudent comments. Yet every time I tried to allude to the vital problems of Latin America, I found him desirous of quitting this ground and returning to less difficult matters. I do not know what esteem this statesman enjoyed in his own country, and I have forgotten all the remarks made to me about him by those adversaries who always abound in our republics. But in matters of international politics, if I could interpret what lay behind his silences, he seemed to me very far from grasping the most important factors. Apart from the impulse of local defence which led him to be for Chile and against Peru in the Pacific dispute, nothing attracted or engaged his attention.

This limited outlook, which means that international policy is reduced to holding in check neighbouring and sister states in a minute field lying, to all appearance, outside our planet, is to be met with in almost all the republics of the South, where local strife, frontier disputes, and the prices of local produce absorb everybody's thoughts. One might almost think that our countries consider themselves to stand outside general contingencies, isolated as by a dyke from all the currents, good or bad, which affect humanity. If they consent to admit the existence of other factors, it is merely in view of the favourable or unfavourable influence which this may exert upon the disputes which hypnotise them. If they have an army or a fleet, it is with a view to the sister and frontier state X or Z, leaving their gates unreservedly open to all aggressions from really foreign nations.

Our Latin America, which has lost much blood in the civil struggles and wars between her various subdivisions, has never dreamed
of such a contingency as having to resist the pressure which great
powers of America, Europe, or Asia may bring to bear upon those
territories. Their narrow vision makes them view as events of supreme gravity some slight disagreement between peoples which a
century ago formed part of the same viceroyalties. But it does not
trouble them that England, which defends the thesis that the Rio de
la Plata is a free sea, continues to fly her flag over the Falklands
and rules in British Honduras. Nor does it alarm them that the
United States, which occupy territories in Santo Domingo, Nicaragua,
and Panama, aspire to extend their positions towards the South.
One would almost say that in this sterile parody of a Little Europe,
nothing exists but local patriotisms, and that, beyond certain limits,
all policy and all plans are lost sight of.

Something similar takes place from the economic point of view;—
not owing to financial rivalry, for what precisely distinguishes our
republics is the almost entire lack of trade between them. The
colonial tradition of sending their produce straight to the strong
nations, for them to manufacture and distribute, is still the rule
even after a century of independence. Attempts have been made
to explain such a strange phenomenon by the specious argument
that these republics all sell the same things. In consequence of this,
it is alleged, interchange is useless. But ordinary logic tells us that
the crops cannot be exactly the same in the torrid, temperate, and
frigid zones. Moreover, it is enough to glance at the imports and
exports of the different republics to see that they can supplement one
another in many respects. Communication is hampered in some
cases by the difficulty or expense of transport; in others, by ignorance
of what is produced; and still more frequently, by the mere inertia
of the governments. And so our own produce is sent back to us
after passing through the hands of other nations, which regulate its
price and control its distribution, keeping the bulk of the profit for
themselves. Mexican sisal, Cuban sugar, Argentine frozen meat,
Colombian coffee, often return to various parts of Latin America
after paying a heavy tribute to exporters, importers, and transport
by land or sea in other countries.

Add to this the absence of industries of transformation, obliging us, in countries where leather is abundant, to import harness, travelling-bags and shoes; in regions where the best timber in the world is to be found, to have furniture brought from a great distance, etc., thus placing ourselves in the position of buying what went out of our own home lands, at the increase of price due to manufacture, insurance, customs, etc.—a paradoxical economic system which reserves to us all the burdens and deprives us of all the benefits.

During my journey I aimed at studying and arriving at clear ideas, not only about the possibility of uplifting national feeling from the moral and ideal point of view, but also, and above all, about the prospects in the sphere of economic organisation, the fundamental basis without which nothing is possible. And my experiences could not have been more painful. Gold-producing countries were importing jewelry from abroad. Peoples living on the produce of the soil had to import agricultural machinery from other countries. Nations possessing the richest mineral deposits were weighed down with debt and riddled with loans. These communities seemed to exist only to send the produce of the soil on board ships and bring back from the ships the articles necessary for their life. And even within this dependent existence of theirs, this export and import trade was almost exclusively in the hands of foreigners, who monopolised produce to sell it abroad, or brought manufactured goods into the country, collecting, so to speak, an import and export duty on production and consumption.

It is superfluous to say that in speaking thus I do not particularly refer to those republics which I was then visiting, but to all of them as a whole, with the exception, perhaps, of two or three regions, where a tendency is gaining ground to satisfy local needs by our own efforts. Latin Americans have confined themselves to the task of government, to the liberal professions, the army, administrative posts—whatever has an appearance of command; and they have forgotten to create a nationality with a tangible body—they have not taken possession of their land. They are vain of setting in motion machines which function in the void, since their motive power and the points on which they turn are subject to outside inspiration. If we go beyond the circle of our immediate interests, what we lack in the economic order is freedom of movement, because we have not assumed the management of our own wealth. In the international order we lack initiative, because we have allowed ourselves to be confined within the bounds of local dissensions. But this stage in the evolution of a people may be transitory, if we change the direction in which we are going. It is for this reason that we are drawing attention to our evils, out of a conviction that in order to remedy them we must begin by knowing them.

Quito is a pleasant and most cultured city, with a severe aspect which it preserves by the calmness of its climate and the charm of its streets, bathed in sun beneath a blue sky. During my short stay I had the opportunity of estimating the vitality, progress, and patriotism of this capital, which, aloft on its mountains, seems to recall the glorious adventures of Bolívar on the chain of the Andes. The lecture took place before an enthusiastic audience, which afterwards accompanied me back to my hotel. And as time was pressing— for my journey had already lasted for more than a year—I returned to the coast and set sail anew for the South, carrying with me the most pleasant memory of the fatherland of Montalvo.

I was further impelled to continue my tour by the news of an incident which had arisen between the Argentine and Mexico, and my well-founded supposition that it marked the beginning of a new series of devices for multiplying causes of dissension, and frustrating the work which was being carried out with such difficulty.

President Madero, in an official speech, blamed the youth of Mexico for the enthusiasm with which they had responded to my words, calling me an "adventurer, the son of a nation which had never fought a glorious war," but could only boast of having, "in company with others, oppressed defenceless Paraguay." [6] The Ar-

[6] The Mexican Press severely condemned the President's attitude. *El Tiempo*, in an article signed by Don José Antonio Rivera, said on July 8, 1912: "Señor Madero in his speech said, or gave it to be understood, in order to attack Manuel Ugarte, that the Argentine has no warlike history, and that what figures principally in its pages is the aggression which it committed against a weak people in alliance with two powerful countries —that is to say, a hateful war.

"[Such a statement is] forced and remote from all logical reasoning. We cannot see what relation can exist between the personal aims of Ugarte, speaking in Mexico in favour of the union of all the Latin-American states in order to check the policy of invasion, and the fact that the lecturer is

gentine Government did not protest against these injurious aspersions upon the traveller, but against this rash judgment passed upon a nation; and after a complicated exchange of notes, the incident was settled amicably.

But this skirmish was a symptom of that campaign of confusion and anarchy which attempts to drag down any aspiring elements in men's minds and souls. In obedience to mysterious influences, Madero was trying, at the risk of provoking yet another conflict, to sweep away, in the same phrase, not only an ideal which was flourishing vigorously among the younger generation, but the idea of harmony among our republics. There is no need to suppose that the head of a state would consciously commit these offences. Yet the same lack of foresight shows itself in another act of a completely different character. Just after the agitation which had arisen in Mexico, the young men, yielding to a most noble impulse, had organised battalions for the defence of the national territory against imperialist stratagems, should the necessity arise. The President did not shrink from precipitating these healthy forces into civil war.

Madero expiated his mistakes when he fell, abandoned by that same imperialism whose interests he served without realising it. Señor Márquez Sterling, the Cuban Minister in Mexico at that time, and an eyewitness of these events, in his book *Madero's Last Days* (*Los últimos días de Madero* *) vouches for that complicated web of subtle contrivances and calculated abstentions by the aid of which the luckless dreamer was led by imperceptible stages to his death. When we recall the incidents to which his character gave rise, we have to recognise that in this case, as in all of those which·

'the son of a country which has only had one foreign war—a war in which, in alliance with two formidable powers, it attacked a weak people, the people of Paraguay.'

"Where there is no malice there is no offence, and sure as we are that the head of the Executive had no idea of offending a friendly nation, let us hope that the good sense and culture of the Argentine Government will be able to reduce this occurrence to the modest proportions of a *lapsus linguæ*, or of a historical error such as those to which we are accustomed from our estimable democratic orator in the inevitable outpourings of his rebellious tongue and none too pure style."

* Published at Habana by "El Siglo XX," 1917. Cf. in particular, the last three chapters.

have done damage to our republics, the majority of errors are to be ascribed to the absence of a wide continental conception.

The first thing which one notices on arriving in Peru is their obsession with *revanche*. The war on the Pacific coast, the antecedents and motives of which we are not going to recall or estimate here, has left in this republic, peculiarly predisposed to extreme emotions by its fine sensibilities and its superior culture, a persistent desire and an eager intention of recovering its lost territory and its former position. This supreme aspiration, which has been the mainspring of all its movements both in internal and international affairs for several decades past, seems to hold it aloof for the time being, from all that does not tend towards the patriotic aim which it is pursuing. None the less, there were few cities in which my propaganda found such a favourable atmosphere as in Lima.[7]

The gay modern city, proud of its descent and the treasures of its past colonial splendour, connected with the harbour by a broad avenue edged by shady trees, and fringed with prosperous bathing establishments, is one of the towns of the greatest attractiveness and appeal to the imagination that I have ever had occasion to visit.

The President of Peru in 1913 was Señor Billinghurst, a simple

[7] "This is the principal merit of Manuel Ugarte's campaign—to implant an aspiration which quivers before the possible onset of an evil. He has descried the menace on the horizon, and before the tempest arises and the harm is done, he goes forth as a knight in arms, recites his profession of faith, and succeeds in putting fresh courage into the depressed, and nobility into the Sanchos." *La Cronica*, February 21, 1913.

"As we listen to Ugarte, we feel ourselves more American, more Latin, and more the masters of our own stronghold. The words of the propagandist arouse admiration and affection which in us are bound to be lasting." *Lā Prensa*, February 21, 1913.

"There were dreamers and idealists who, above the horde and the tribe, conceived of cities; above cities, of provinces; above provinces, of nations; and above nations, of those great confederations originated by the great nations which are the standard-bearers of progress in the civilised world. All these triumphs of the ideal were achieved by means of union. It is union which we must achieve in order to make our name effective. It is union which Manuel Ugarte has come to recommend to us in his tour round America." Leading article in *La Unión*, February 23, 1913.

man of independent character, who was in sympathy with the working-classes, and relied upon their support to surmount the growing difficulties of his Government. Short in stature, solidly built, and nervous—both weak and overbearing, as I was told—he defended himself vigorously in spite of his age, manœuvring in a thorny situation with rare good fortune and even with undisputed authority, in spite of that absence of any higher plan which led him to make a government out of a mosaic of improvisations. Apart from local politics and without any possible preferences, and given my ignorance of the character and antecedents of these struggles, I could not help observing, all the same, the contrast between that honest *bourgeois,* rather Louis-Philippe in nature, and the domineering harshness of some of the presidents with whom I had conversed before. I do not know what President Billinghurst stood for in Peruvian politics; but in the evolution of Latin America he came in my eyes to stand for an attempt to impose European standards upon the fevered agitation of the Continent.

Our conversation was in straightforward and unaffected language. The representative of the people did not strike an imposing attitude or try to appear a superman. He talked to me, who had arrived from a journey of ten years in Europe and two in America, with the equability of an enquiring mind seeking for information. He was interested to hear details about the democratic agitation in France, England, and Italy. He wanted to arrive at a clear idea of conditions in the northern republics. He desired anecdotes on the official personages whom I had observed *en route.* And as to what concerned the future of Latin America, he seemed to me to have a just conception of that independence which it ought to enjoy. I was particularly surprised at a certain curious turn of his mind. In his conversation questions preponderated over assertions. And this inclination was most significant of the person and the moment. This man did not aspire to command, but to direct, a notable advance in our Latin America, where an atmosphere of dictatorship emanates from most presidents.

The rise of Mr. Wilson to the presidency of the United States, which was hailed as announcing a change in the external policy of that country, and used as a soothing syrup to calm our minds, induced me, in the midst of the turmoil of my journey, to write an "open letter" which was published in the principal organs of the Latin-American press.* The events which have since taken place in Cuba, Santo Domingo, Nicaragua, etc., have proved how well-founded was the reserve which I advised, by showing what a mistake it is to put faith in promises in international affairs and emphasising the fallacy of looking to others for our welfare instead of seeking it for ourselves.

About this time I received the news that the Socialist party in the Argentine had chosen me as their candidate to represent the capital in the Senate.[8] The campaign of an international character on which I found myself engaged held me to some extent aloof from all narrowly local political action. My desire was to keep apart from internal struggles in order to continue with more authority the effort upon which I had embarked. Moreover—and I shall speak of this at greater length in the next chapter—there were certain divergencies of opinion which hindered me from accepting a representative position with a clear conscience. I am well aware that in Latin-American politics principles are more often sacrificed to office than office to principles; and the interpretations to which my renunciation gave rise may serve as an indication of the atmosphere predominating in our democracies. According to some, I declined the offer because I was not confident of success. According to others, I did so because I did not consider myself prepared for such a high responsibility. It seemed hard for them to admit that a question of conscience and the prosecution of an idealistic campaign which

* This letter was published in *Cuba Contemporanea*, June, 1913.

[8] "Buenos Aires, March 7, 1913, 10.58 P. M.: Manuel Ugarte, Lima: In the name of the Committee I inform you of your nomination as candidate for the Senatorship at the elections of March 30; your presence necessary here in order to ensure success."   *Mario Bravo.*

"Mario Bravo, Buenos Aires: Impossible accept candidature. Shall not arrive at Buenos Aires till May. I thank my comrades for the honour they have done me in remembering me."   *Manuel Ugarte.*

"Buenos Aires, March 8, 1913, 10. 57 P. M. Manuel Ugarte, Lima: Telegram received. Meeting has elected you. We beg you to accept nomination. If possible, your presence desirable."   *Mario Bravo.*

"Mario Bravo, Buenos Aires: Regret impossibility of breaking off tour prevents my accepting candidature. After Buenos Aires, proceeding to Uruguay, Brazil, Paraguay. Am with you in spirit."   *Manuel Ugarte.*

brought so many unpleasantnesses in its train might prevent me from occupying the arm-chair of a senator at the age of thirty. When, in face of this dilemma—whether to do violence to my convictions or to fail to respond to the confidence of the party which elected me—I expressed my scruples, the experts answered, in a suggestive phrase: "One develops." And it is an illuminating detail for the study of South American public life that there are many who still consider that the important moment in my career was that at which I was on the point of occupying a position in the upper chamber, namely, the incident which might give me a *rôle* in local politics, and not the impulse by which I attempted to influence the tendencies and future of Latin America.

At Lima, the point at which the two great attempts at unification had touched and amalgamated, I went one morning to lay wreaths at the foot of the statues of Bolívar and San Martín. I visited the celebrated library under the competent directorship of González Prada; and I made the acquaintance of a particularly numerous group of brilliant talents, among whom I will mention, as the names rise to my pen, Ricardo Palma, who was to die a little later full of years and renown, his son Clement, Alberto and Luís Ulloa, Mariano H. Cornejo, Augusto Durán, Abraham Valdelomar, Luís Fernán Cisneros, de la Riva Aguero, and many others whom I recalled later when reading Francisco García Calderón's study of Wilsonism, in which I came across this sentence: "Who will keep watch on this formidable protector? Must an agitated world depend on the goodwill of this elder brother, with a taste for sudden aggressions and dangerous monopolies?"

My conference went off without a hitch in the most favourable and sympathetic atmosphere.[9] These demonstrations, which ex-

---

[9] "The lecture ended with a thunderous ovation, the outcome of an overwhelming enthusiasm. The public rose to their feet and did not leave their places, and Ugarte came forward several times to give thanks in a state of visible emotion." *La Cronica*, March 5, 1913.

"When Señor Ugarte had finished his brilliant dissertation, the echo of a portentous ovation thundered through the precincts of our theatre, and there then arose what was almost a fight among the audience, struggling who should be the first to embrace and congratulate him."

La Acción Popular, March 4, 1913.

pressed something new in the life of Latin America, were only echoed over the telegraph-wires in a form cunningly devised to create difficulties. It was for this reason that my brotherly words,[10] in which the most suspicious artfulness could not have discovered the shadow of a preference—words of concord and idealism—aroused a hostile reaction in Ecuador and Chile.

It was only the fact that a steamer was late in starting that enabled me to learn of this ill-intentioned version and contradict it. The manœuvre was so calculated that I should have remained ignorant of the harsh criticism of the Ecuadorian Press and the hostile atmosphere which had arisen in Chile. I have already had occasion to repeat that there were many similar stratagems in the course of my journey. But never before had they gloried in such perfidy. Those who believed in the malevolent version were afterwards able to see, from a perusal of the text of my speech, how much they had been deceived.

The notice which had been cabled to Ecuador referred to the Galápagos affair. According to the cabled message, I had put forward the thesis that if the islands passed into other hands, Peru ought to intervene in Ecuador. It is enough to enunciate this idea, to understand the effect which was produced, in view of the

"In the presence of a crowded audience of close on four thousand persons, the famous Argentine lecturer proclaimed his message of warning and hope. The parterre, boxes, and balconies of the Teatro Municipal were occupied by university professors, distinguished representatives of our social and intellectual clubs, university students, etc." *El Comercio*, March 4, 1913.

"Once the poet Gálvez had suggested the idea of accompanying him to his lodging, everybody demanded that the return should be made on foot. It was a triumphal progress for the propagandist, a constant renewal of unmatched affection. The demonstrations were repeated, and enthusiasm reached such a pitch that in spite of the late hour many families resident in the La Unión quarter came out on to their balconies to lend their presence to the intense and sincere demonstration of sympathy which Ugarte had aroused in a few moments by his virile speech."

La Prensa, March 4. 1913.

[10] This speech, taken from the shorthand report published in *La Prensa* of Lima, appears in my book *Mi campaña hispano-americana:* Cervantes Publishing Co., Barcelona.*

* 1922.

general sensitiveness of our republics and the peculiar position of the two countries in question.   The Press believed this news, owing to the receipt of this telegram, and indignantly reproached me with my alleged attitude.   Persons were not wanting who availed themselves of this natural patriotic protest in order to distil their drop of venom.   And I am as yet unaware whether my correction [11] was sufficient to re-establish the truth in everybody's mind.

In Chile the manœuvre took a less dangerous form.   It was telegraphed that I had said as follows: "It seems as if Chile were condemned always to pit her interests against the greater interests of the Continent, to serve as a drag on the advance of civilisation on this American soil.   She had formerly the honour of inaugurating the régime of conquest on the Continent, incorporating it as a principle in her public law, as one of her talented diplomatists proclaimed not very long ago.   She has since had the felicity of being

[11] "To the Editor of *El Grito del Pueblo Ecuatoriano, Guayaquil:* Sir, I have just read the leading article published in *El Grito del Pueblo* on March 16, and although I have to continue my journey in a few hours' time, I hurriedly write these lines.

"During my tour I have been unable to correct the majority of erroneous interpretations to which my lectures have given rise.   But since it is a case of a paper of the importance of *El Grito del Pueblo,* and of a country which is so near my heart, I desire on this occasion to remove the misapprehension which shows itself in certain paragraphs of the above-mentioned article.

"The telegraphic intelligence which you have received has been far from reflecting my words and thoughts.   I have never given it to be understood that Peru either should or could intervene in Ecuadorian affairs, or in any way oppose what Ecuador resolves upon in full enjoyment of her autonomy. All my propaganda has been in favour of concord and *rapprochement,* of reaction against the political malady of disaggregation which delivers us over to foreign influence.   What I did say was, that if any nation foreign to our family of nations were to wish to make itself master of the Galápagos against the will of Ecuadorian opinion, all of us in Latin America ought to protest; adding that, in spite of temporary divergencies, Peru ought, if necessity arose, to unite her voice with that of the other republics, because deep down the matter interests us all.

"The general character of my propaganda and the respect which I have for the dignity of each of our nations prevents me from advocating actions which may in any way wound the most legitimate susceptibilities.   What I desire is that we may preserve our territories as a whole, and for this it is necessary, above all, to vanquish indifference.   Whatever hurts one of our republics hurts us all." *Manuel Ugarte.*

the only nation which did not see fit to sign the agreement for compulsory general arbitration; and she has to-day the good fortune of being also the only one which cannot benefit—nay, more, is sure to be damaged—by the opening of the inter-oceanic Canal. But doubtless the clear-sighted politicians of La Moneda have not yet taken into consideration the far-reaching consequences which this opposition of interests may have, since in no other way can it be explained why, instead of directing their interests into the path of a possible and rational reconciliation of Chilean interests with the great interests of the Continent, she has preferred to embark upon a rash campaign against them."

This unheard-of accumulation of discrepant opinions ought to have sufficed to reveal the fraud. Notwithstanding, *El Mercurio* of Chile published in its issue of March 25, 1913, a leading article entitled "Manuel Ugarte against Chile," in which, after quoting the above phrases, it invited me to give up my visit, and gravely alleged that I had expressed myself in this way at Lima, "in order to obtain box-office profits in the course of a commercial tour." It was thus I learnt that my disinterested tour of absolutely free lectures, during which I declined the lodging offered me by some cities, and went so far as to pay out of my own pocket for the hire of some halls in which I spoke, was represented by the telegraphic agencies as a vulgar speculation.

I had renounced political ambitions and the opportunities which presented themselves to me, in order to have no petty interests and to continue to be a citizen of Latin America as a whole; and an anonymous cablegram sufficed to condemn me. Quite apart from the false impression, which was bound to disappear before the evidence of my actions, the situation created by the incident affected me, because I could not anyhow give up my visit to Chile. The telegrams were conclusive. "We think you had better not come," my friends advised me. The Peruvian papers published a cablegram saying: "Our intellectual circles, commenting on Ugarte's declarations, consider them a sufficient cause for suspending his projected visit to Chile." It was, none the less, preferable to face the hostile demonstrations, rather than confirm by my absence such a monstrous supposition. My answer was, "I am coming, in spite of everything." I sent a *démenti* to the Press through the Havas

Agency. I requested the Chilean Consul-General in Peru to transmit the stenographic report of my speech to the Government of his country. And I awaited the result confidently; for in the most difficult crises, the good sense of the people and of the younger generation always triumphs.

After telegraphing to the President, I continued on my way to Bolivia.[12]

The journey by way of Mollendo to La Paz is dazzling to the eyes and soothing to the spirit. Even Nature itself wears the hues of metals and precious stones. Mountains of gold and amethyst blaze beneath the glaring light. The Andes go on from one unsuspected magnificence to another till one arrives at the great lakes on the high plateau, and the traveller feels himself overcome by stupefaction before this apotheosis of the greatness of a continent. Something superhuman exalts and calms one's being at the sight of the blue mountain-tops and the still waters, which at this elevation, thousands of feet above sea-level, give the impression of a world newly opened up beneath a sun which also appears to be new.

The impression produced by La Paz is unforgettable. This city has a strong family resemblance to Quito and Bogotá, while none the less displaying a character which distinguishes it from its sisters. A radiant light, broad, steep streets, hackney carriages drawn by four horses, clean, airy houses, great *plazas* golden in the sunshine, a sane, simple, and hardy life—all this breathes into the place a fresh, morning air which comforts the spirit.

The cordiality with which the Press received the propagandist [13]

---

[12] "To His Excellency Dr. Eliodoro Villazón, President of Bolivia, La Paz. Before starting on my journey on my way to the noble and generous sister republic, I have the pleasure to send the head of the nation the sincere expression of my deepest respect and sympathy." *Manuel Ugarte.*

"La Paz, March 1, 5.45 P. M. Via Eastern. Manuel Ugarte, Lima: I have received with pleasure the telegram in which you announce your visit to this city. Much gratified by your attention and salutations, I reciprocate them by wishing you every sort of good fortune in the course of your journey." *Villazón.*

[13] "Ugarte is fighting Yankee imperialism, and in fighting this tendency, so dangerous for the young nations, he is doing nothing but bring about the union of the South American nations, to hold back this threatening tide." *El Comercio*, April 2, 1913.

did not succeed in hiding a certain undercurrent of distrust of the nations of the South. The politicians, grasping the general problem of Latin America, admitted, with a rare independence of judgment, the necessity for resisting imperialist infiltration. But they made no mystery of the fact that they were confronted with another difficulty, less serious, perhaps, but undoubtedly more pressing, which arose out of the attitude of certain southern nations. Placed by her geographical situation and her own weakness in the position of being open to pressure and encroachment from the neighbouring republics, Bolivia understood the general danger, but could not ignore the immediate risk. This was the idea summed up by Don Alfredo Sanjines G. in an article [14] in which he said: "The great problem to be solved, then, is to extirpate root and branch those dark forces which spring up from time to time, as soon as we have managed to collect a few cannon or war-ships, and occasion the outbreak of fratricidal wars in the same household. Let the strong nations of South America cease to press upon the weak ones. Let the great nations cease to view their progress with jealousy. Let the little daughters left them by Spain and Portugal, themselves sisters, cease to rend each other. Let them cease to weaken themselves by wasting their energies in intestine wars. Let them be loyal in interpreting and carrying out their international agreements. So that, since we recognise that a single soul lives in us, a single body may arise too in the South, as great and powerful as that of the great nation of the North, and, by resisting violence, may succeed in asserting and procuring the triumph of right and justice, the great end of humanity."

This aspiration made itself felt in the conversation of politicians

"For a long time past our young intellectuals have been eagerly awaiting the arrival of that representative American figure which the person of Don Manuel Ugarte represents for the young Latin republics."

El Diario, April 2, 1913.

"Having thus summed up the significance of Ugarte's propaganda, let us listen reverently to his words, for he speaks to us in the name of our own interests, which are one and the same for all the Latin-American countries."

La Tarde, La Paz, April 2, 1913.

"The champion of a race, the representative of twenty nations, he is since yesterday the guest of ours." *El Ferrocarril* of Cochabamba, April 3.

[14] *El Norte*, of La Paz, April 7, 1913.

and intellectuals of mark, such as Señores José Carrasco, Juan T. Camacho, Alfredo Ascarrunz, Carlos Calvo, José S. Quinteros, Eduardo Díez de Medina, Néstor Jerónimo Otazo, O'Connor d'Arlach, Rosendo Villalobos, Abel Alarcón, Juan Francisco Bedregal, Franz Tamayo, Raúl Jaimes Freire, Benigno Lara, Humberto Muñoz Cornejo, Enríque Finot, José Antezana, Celso Borda, and the President himself, Dr. Villazón, a sagacious and prudent man who appeared to me to be one of the steadiest and most happily inspired politicians of our America.

There is no doubt that the principle origin of all our collective weakness has always been in the mistrust arising from that pressure which certain elements in our family of nations have taken it upon themselves to exercise upon the others.   If before Italy achieved her unity, the Austrians reached Trieste and the French reached Rome, this was by taking advantage of the strife between the elements composing the nation, and thanks to the instinct for resistance of certain national groups, which were forced to take up a resolute attitude by the excessive pre-eminence of their brethren.   In this sense it may be said that the instinct for partial domination of one subdivision over another within the same group, has always in history had as its result subjection to foreign forces.   The narrow self-seeking of certain sections has enabled them to prosper for a time, but in the long run it has infallibly resulted in a general catastrophe.

Under the impulsion of strong nations of different origin, the process of decomposition is well known.   Fear of the distant menace is sacrificed to the attraction of proximate interests, and an era is thus opened in which the necessity of the moment triumphs over the instinct for what is lasting.   The very fact of having dealings with one another and living side by side embitters the dissension.   The party victimised naturally draws a contrast between the arrogant demeanour of its brother state and the apparent simplicity of the foreigner.   And thus the way is gradually prepared for a conflict which ends in the common detriment of both.   Perhaps it was the consciousness of this that induced Señor Sanjines to add to his article: "We too have been, and still are, the victims of these violent proceedings, and that not from another race, but on the part of our own Latin brethren.   The deliberations concerning this

country, which have taken place at La Moneda, the Palacio de
Itamaraty and the Casa Rosada, have never been inspired by justice,
when it was a question of tearing from us our only port on the
Pacific, our rubber-producing regions, and the territory of Yacuiba,
in spite of outcries and protests, and that lofty spirit of justice which
ought as a condition of their race to have come first among South
Americans."

This reproach, levelled simultaneously at Chile, Brazil, and the
Argentine, does not fall within the bounds of the Pacific question,
and takes on the character of a general problem.   It is not a direct
claim advanced with regard to a given matter and within a given
sphere, but an appeal to a principle in the vast ambit of Spanish-
American policy.   And it is upon this plane that we can deal with
this tendency and its drawbacks.   We have already had occasion to
hint that in international politics there never has been, never will
be, and never can be any other guiding principle than that of serving one's own interests.   Whatever words, rules or doctrines may be
appealed to, they are no more than the showy screen which hides
real motives.   Nor is it from the point of view of ethics that we
shall condemn actions that belong to every age and every latitude.
It is in the name of practical, directing principles, applicable to the
condition of our countries; it is by an appeal to real interests, not
to theories or sentiments, that we repudiate a policy which is perhaps
more harmful to those who use it as a weapon than to those who
are forced by the logic of events to suffer from it.

Every one of our republics, however great may be the prosperity
at which it has arrived, has within its frontiers matters enough to
occupy it, in the administration of its interests.   These are often so
much neglected that foreign companies regulate, destroy piecemeal,
and even rebel against the state laws.   Our land is still exploited
by the aid of machines and tools imported from abroad.   The
minerals lying below the surface—the petroleum, coal, and innumerable products which might be the source of a splendid prosperity—
sleep in darkness as if the Continent had only just been discovered.
The exploitation in our own interest of the local means of communication—shipping, railways, tramways, telephones (upon which
we pay a heavy tribute)—would suffice for the upkeep of all our
activities entering upon futile struggles to extend the area of the

various republics. If from this range of ideas we go on to examine
the hypothesis of using our own products to start manufactures and
satisfy our local needs as far as possible, facing the task of creating
a fully developed life in these infant countries, we shall understand
the colossal magnitude of the effort which it is urgently necessary
to put forth in each country, so as really to grasp the helm of
national prosperity, and at last set our own life-blood in circulation.
All extensions of territory in the present state of affairs lead to nothing but multiplying concessions to the foreign companies which for
a century past have taken upon themselves the administration of
our economic life. We must react against the cult of appearances
and social experiments. We are not strong just because we promenade along our streets a few cannon bought at Essen or the Creusot
works. To take pride in our importations is to mistake our exhausted state for a sign of greatness. Nor ought we to confuse the
exports of the country with those of the foreign companies established in it. It is senseless to mobilise our diplomacy in order to
open markets for the manufactures of North American cold storage
companies, which are a menace to the prosperity of our own stock-
breeding industry. The problem for us is not how to make a splash,
but how to take root; it does not lie in show, but in solid construction.
Nationality does not consist in multiplying sources of energy, but in
becoming master of them. The greatness of nations is not measured
by their area on the map, but by their concentration, their solidity,
their imperviousness to the tempests of international life. And in
the flourishing, victorious stage upon which the southern republics
have entered, the important thing is to nationalise wealth and progress, making them, so far as possible, emanate from the country
itself and remain within it. The urgent problem is to reduce waste
in a machine working often by means of external force and for the
profit of others.

To these reasons, which should dissuade us from any action susceptible of being interpreted as South American imperialism, may be
added the consideration that, if we look well into the matter, our
strongest republics only enjoy a relative measure of strength, which
may appear decisive as compared with the weakness of some of their
neighbours, but which seem precarious if we raise it to a universal
plane, alongside the might of the great peoples. The encroachments

which have made themselves felt on various occasions have made use, in addition to our proverbial disunion, of precisely those particular motives of resentment and mistrust between states marching with each other, which, when faced with two risks, instinctively choose the more remote. In this way certain influences alien to the spot, influences aiming at particular ends which are not always favourable to our future, have come to have weight in local disputes which concern nobody but ourselves. In some cases we are bound to recognise that, if the weak ones have deserted the camp of racial solidarity, it has been because the strong ones had previously forgotten the consideration which this circumstance imposed upon them. But the fact that one error may justify another is not a sign that the system ought to be encouraged. In order to develop in an atmosphere of confidence, and guarantee themselves as far as possible against the contingencies of the future, the republics of the South require, above all, to surround themselves with an atmosphere of local friendships and forge a chain of common interests in matters concerning the autonomy of Latin America and its immunity from attack.

The most superficial glance at world politics will reveal to the least expert that it is a frequent practice of dominant groups to make difficulties for some peoples by means of others, which, in pursuing their immediate ends are, over and above this, serving the higher aims of those who set them in motion. France antagonises Germany, covering her action by the aid of the Little Entente; England defends her dominion of the seas by means of the Greeks, etc. The expedient is so familiar that it seems superfluous to record it. In the game of world chess we have to consider, over and above the ostensible moves, the intentions, consequences and final aim pursued by means of the partial movements of each piece. And our Latin America, to the grief of some of our politicians, is not an isolated planet. It forms part of a world eaten away by streams of conquest, which, after sharing Africa between them, have subjugated in Asia the oldest centres of civilisation and are now carrying a wave of fire across seas and continents, creating and devouring like life itself. The instinct of survival which breathes in all that lives will calm these familiar quarrels. I do not by this mean to say that at moments of crisis the more vigorous groups ought to be dependent upon unanimous resolutions. To limit the *rôle* of initiative and resolution is to arrest the progress of the world. But Prussia and Piedmont are alone able to pursue their projects of general utility in a fraternal and federal form. And it is by widening our aims, by uplifting our programmes, and by the altruism of our activities, that those predominant sentiments of friendship which aim at establishing firmly our common fortune may reveal themselves in our Latin America, destined as she is to similar vicissitudes.

In Bolivia I found a nationalist atmosphere detached from foreign influences. When the Ministers for Foreign Affairs and Public Instruction, together with various learned societies, offered me banquets and demonstrations, nobody trembled at the spectre of a protest. On the contrary, when I was attacked by the United States Minister, Mr. Knowles,[15] the very paper which had published his speech came and asked for my opinion,[16] thus asserting in peremptory fashion the independence of this country's Press. It was in this atmosphere that my promised lecture took place.[17]   A

[15] *El Diario*, of La Paz, April 6, 1913.

[16] "In connection with the phrases employed by a foreign diplomatist in a speech, we thought it opportune to go and see Manuel Ugarte. The Argentine writer received us politely.

"'The strange forgetfulness of propriety,' he said to us, 'which gave rise to the discourteous and aggressive language which you mention to me, has not failed to surprise me; but in view of my position, I am bound to be more reserved and sober. Moreover, our Latin courtesy prevents us from raising our voice in the house of another. It is timely to note once again the difference which exists between certain peoples and ourselves. We may be backward in material things; but morally, from the point of view of good breeding and tact, we take the lead; and also from the point of view of good humour, for we have a smile for every blunder."
El Diario, of La Paz, April 9, 1913.

[17] "The longing to hear the lecture by the apostle of Latin Americans had spread through the whole city, and when last night the curtains rose upon the stage of the Teatro Municipal, an ovation greeted the presence of the Argentine thinker." *El Diario*, of La Paz, April 10, 1913.

"As he finished the above phrases, the audience became delirious and uncontrollable in its ovations, producing a regular confusion."
La Tarde of La Paz, April 10, 1913.

"Ugarte's propaganda is sane and well-intentioned. It is not inspired by unconscious race-hatred, nor platonic sentimentalising. It vibrates with the

few days later I left this republic, which has as yet no port on the sea-coast. Its exportable products, rubber, timber, cocoa, tin, bismuth, wolfram, have to cross the territory of another nation to get on board ship. Without appealing to any rights or raking up the past, it is enough to state the situation to arrive at an opinion about it. One means of smoothing away the old friction between Peru and Chile might consist in preventing their frontiers from coinciding. Why not offer Bolivia, without any serious prejudice to anybody, that egress to the sea which is the first condition of her future progress? To put forward a hypothesis is not to advocate a particular solution. But by offering this country the oxygen which its vitality demands, perhaps the atmosphere of Latin America would be cleared, and we might contribute towards the solution of one of the problems of the Pacific.

As soon as I set foot upon Chilean soil I realised that the good sense of this strong, practical, inquisitive people would be bound to rise superior to the hostile state of mind artificially created by intrigues. The Peruvian press had given a correct report of my words; and although, according to the popular proverb, "if you throw enough mud, some of it is bound to stick," yet a reaction took place in my favour. Antofagasta is a new city full of active minds and great commercial activity, which does not accept ideas without examining them. A local paper led the way,[18] and others followed in a fine impulse of truth.

Notwithstanding, when I arrived at Valparaiso, this bold allegation was still lurking in the shadow. Obsessed by the old dispute with Peru, there were not many who could manage to conceive that a stranger might hold an impartial position between the two tendencies. It was in vain for the more balanced minds to argue.[19] It

reality of action and comes as a voice to arouse our indolent and shortsighted peoples." *La Verdad*, La Paz, April 10, 1913.

[18] "We have to correct the errors which have been made with regard to Ugarte, by establishing the fact that it was a calumny, or a defective piece of information, when it was said that he had spoken ill of our country."
La Prensa Ilustrada, of Antofagasta, April 16, 1913.

[19] "To speak of a just settlement between Chile and Peru, which was all that Manuel Ugarte said in the old city of the viceroys, cannot scandalise

was in vain that I availed myself of the opportunity of certain interviews,[20] to attempt to destroy the error. Their susceptibilities had been wounded, and in more than one case my frank explanations were interpreted as a convenient recantation. The reaction was not definitely established till they had listened to me in the theatre and been able, so to speak, to lay hold of the point of view which I took up. But the same national characteristics which had inspired the first movement determined the extent of the second, and seldom have I had a greater outburst of applause.

Their Basque descent, English characteristics, and dour and methodical temperament, have given the Chilean people a soul at once distrustful and enthusiastic, which passes from caution to cordiality. This smiling and hard-working city changed its tone as soon as it was thoroughly understood that I had not taken sides with Peru. The telegrams which began to come in [21] announced a favourable movement of the healthy forces of the people. Fresh from the memories of the "Baltimore" and the Alsop affair,* the pride of the people, the patriotism of the young men, and the meditations of the intellectuals rose above their care for the immediate

anybody, and might be repeated in the same words in the capital whose bounds were drawn by Don Pedro de Valdivia."
    Leading article in *El Chileno*, of Valparaiso, April 30.

[20] *El Día*, of Valparaiso, April, 23, 1913. *El Mercurio*, of Valparaiso, April 29, 1913.
    [21] "Santiago, April 25. The students have confidence in your sympathetic mission of fraternity. I request you to inform us on what day you arrive at Santiago." *Alejandro Quesada*, President of the Federation.
    "Santiago, April 24. Welcome to the poet who is struggling for the union of our Latin American." *Samuel A. Lillo.*
    "Santiago, April 22. *La Razon* greets you and places itself unreservedly at your disposal." *Carlos Rivera*, Editor.
    "Iquique, April 18. Socialists of Tarapacá congratulate you and regret they were unable to hear you"—*Recabarren.*
    "Iquique, April 17. Last night, when I mentioned your name in my lecture, the public applauded it. I have pleasure in interpreting their sentiments of sympathy for your person and ideals." *Victor Domingo Silva.*

    * See Graham Stuart, *Latin America and the United States*, pp. 350-352; *Papers Relating to the Foreign Relations of the United States* (1911), p. 38.

moment, in order to embrace a true perspective, soaring above all deceptive appearances.

In complete contrast with the resolute attitude of the Government of Bolivia, in Chile there was nothing but abstention and silence in official quarters. The President did not reply to my telegrams, and I did not succeed in making the usual call upon him. Nor did I have an opportunity of making the acquaintance of any of the politicians who then composed the Ministry. I only came in contact with the Press, the progressive parties, the popular classes, and the university. It was from the conjunction of these forces that the formidable movement arose. To it were added certain representative men in politics and intellectual life, such as Señores Roberto Huneeus, Galvarino Gallardo Nieto, Enrique Tagle Moreno, Francisco Zapata Lillo, Misael Correa, Félix Nieto del Río, Armando Donoso, Eduardo García Guerrero; the directors of the Students' Association, Alejandro Quesada, Pedro L. Loyola, Humberto Gacitua, Arturo Meza, and numerous members of the Democratic Liberal, and Socialist parties, such as Don Guillermo Bañados, Artemio Gutiérrez, Alejandro Bustamante, Manuel Hidalgo, Luis Correa, Luis M. Concha, Diego Escamilla and many others of established reputation.

The relations between Chile and the Argentine were not so cordial at that moment as they are now, and in certain circles, besides resistance to the Latin-American ideal, the traveller was met with a certain reserve on account of his nationality. In spite of this, the enthusiasm of the people and students carried all before it: [22] the

[22] "This distinguished authority on Latin-American affairs shows himself to be, if not as great as the project which he is advocating, owing to his slightly Utopian character, yet at least a worthy exponent of it, owing to his tenacity, conviction, enthusiasm, and judgment in choosing the ways by which it may suitably be achieved."

La Unión, of Santiago de Chile, May 7, 1913.

"As a man, he declines to be tempted by the flattery of fortune; as a citizen, he declines all the civil honours which his compatriots have offered him; and as a man of intellect, he prefers to go from people to people telling his story, like those troubadours of legend, infusing into the tone of his speech the archaic but human savour of the noble knight of La Mancha." *El Diario Ilustrado*, of Santiago, May 6, 1913.

"Ugarte, the apostle of the finest of causes, can be compared to those

Chilean students entered into communication with those of the Argentine; [23] the workmen's organisations sent messages to those of Buenos Aires, and for the first time the Argentine national anthem was heard in the streets of Santiago, sung by Chilean voices.

The good sense of the people rose superior to the peevish obstructiveness of some of the ruling class. For what were really, at that time, the causes of estrangement between the Argentine and Chile? Where was the origin to be found of those difficulties which had been the seed of so much disquiet on the Continent? What serious divergencies separated the two peoples? If a doctor were to propagate diseases in order to present himself afterwards to cure them, he would be less blameworthy than those politicians on both sides of the frontier who for long years kept up an artificial state of nervousness by the aid of confabulations as mysterious as they were sterile. Between the Argentine and Chile, two republics united rather than separated by the cordillera of the Andes, none but those fraternal relations can exist to which everything points. Each of these countries has its own field for development: the former the Atlantic, the latter the Pacific. And only by a subversion of all the laws of common sense would they be able to come into collision. Those short-sighted groups in the Argentine who were seeking an outlet to the Pacific, or those in Chile who looked for a port on the Atlantic, were unknowingly conspiring against the greatness of their own country. The first condition of a lasting existence for them both lies in peace and close bonds of interest between the two republics. Their products are as different as their spheres of influence. The rudimentary political sense which in the Argentine consists in flirting with Peru as opposed to Chile, and in Chile in making signs to Brazil in opposition to the Argentine, arose from

great men who held an ideal of South American patriotism. His patriotism is beyond question, his ideal is sacred, his work immense."

La Mañana, of Santiago, April 30, 1913.

[23] "Santiago, May 18, 1913. University Federation, Buenos Aires. The students of Chile offer the tribute of their homage and sympathies to the ideal of Latin-American fraternity in the person of Manuel Ugarte, and send a fraternal greeting to their Argentine comrades."

Alejandro Quesada, President of the Federation.

the narrowness and lack of experience of those who raised themselves to our chancelleries with no other source of inspiration than a tiny group in some city. The antiquated conception according to which diplomacy consists in gaining advantages over one's neighbours by indiscriminately multiplying a mechanical process of disunion between those very nations, who, if they embrace an ampler view, will perhaps in the future find themselves forced to help each other, has grievously paralysed many of our best forces. And yet we have only to open our eyes to realise that the task of watching jointly over the Straits of Magellan would suffice to destroy the alleged divergences and knit together the general will in an impulse of preservation. It was this identity of our higher interests, appearing suddenly before men's consciousness, as a reaction against the monotonous prognostications of the official augurs, which swept people away on a wave of enthusiasm. The instinct of the masses descried the green horizons beyond the traditional errors of Creole diplomacy.

The peoples of our Latin America are, in general, more clairvoyant than the groups which set up to lead them. They feel the national requirements from the international point of view, and take sides against the system of handing over everything to the foreigner, which places them, in their own land, in the position of auxiliaries at the service of other forces. What has sometimes passed itself off as a protest of barbarism against civilisation has been no more, in the majority of cases, than the anguished cry of a victimised nationality. The reaction was not in favour of backward conditions, but against that policy of abdication which leads us to direct our foreign policy or national development according to wrong principles, interpreting as a victory the deceptive brilliance of the prerogatives which we hand over to others.

The atmosphere in which the lecture took place in Santiago de Chile was more favourable, perhaps, than that of any of the capitals which I had previously visited,[24] in spite of certain opposition as

[24] "It would be impossible for us to follow Señor Ugarte in his brilliant lecture. Applause was showered upon the orator, who was interrupted at the end of every period." *El Diario Ilustrado*, of Santiago, May 20, 1913.

"When the lecture was at an end, all the students and the majority of the audience accompanied him to his hotel, where he was forced to make a speech

exaggerated as it was useless. The very rabidness with which these critics had tried to distort the truth made it appear yet more radiant when it broke through their plots and commanded belief. Every element in the Chilean Republic which was a source of activity and force, every element which had contributed to the brilliance of certain centres and the general prosperity of the country, the young men, the people, the progressive elements, united with that element which represents a healthy, primitive tradition, bound up with those forces which are the real nourishment of a nationality—not to be confused with those who merely make use of them. All of these expressed their will to raise the plane of collective action, quitting a sterile struggle between neighbours in order to throw open a wide field for development.

None the less a new attempt at misrepresentation was made. It was the moment at which the students of the National University were struggling for the recognition of certain claims. In the course of one of their demonstrations they had stopped before my lodging, but I confined myself to expressing my good wishes. ("I do not know where you are going nor what aim you are pursuing. Owing to my position as technically a foreigner, I am bound to be ignorant of it. But since youth alone can animate generous ideals, since I know the nobility and lofty views of those who have been my friends since my arrival, I make so bold as to say that my heart is with you.") Somebody distorted my words and carried a report at variance with what had gone before, and with my own convictions in the matter of religion, to the Catholic Students' Centre. What is certain is that on the following day, on returning to my hotel,

in the open street, for he was not allowed to speak from the balconies of the establishment, whose principal door was guarded by the police."
                                        El Mercurio, of Santiago, May 20, 1913.

"Long before Señor Ugarte arrived at the theatre, the auditorium at the Municipal was crammed to overflowing with a distinguished public in a state of tense expectation. *La Mañana*, of Santiago, May 20, 1913.

"At the end the crowd rose to its feet and applauded him affectionately, and then waited till he left and accompanied him back to the hotel. Here Señor Ugarte was unable to speak from the balconies and came down into the street, where he was borne upon the shoulders of the crowd and from this platform delivered a vigorous address which provoked delirious demonstration." *La Razon*, of Santiago, May 20, 1913.

I found myself faced with a demonstration hostile to the first. They were the students of the Catholic University, who shook their fists up at the windows behind which they imagined that I was concealed. When they saw me coming towards them they surged round me, and I got on a chair and explained the truth of the matter, upon which the incident was closed. But the frequency of these misunderstandings never ceased to surprise me. From the beginning of my journey, for nearly two years, misinterpretation and falsification of my words and deeds had been raised to the level of a system. The mere force of truth frequently upset these hostile calculations. But if this happened in cases when the incorrect version had been brought to my knowledge, the same could not be said when I was unaware of the intrigue. The untruthful reports which circulated with impunity cannot have been few in number. May this book, written with a calm detachment due to lapse of time, suffice to give them the lie.

The episode served to throw light upon the deep social cleavage which is one of the characteristics of Chile. This is no place to discuss the principles of internal politics, and if we note the fact, it is quite apart from any sectarian idea, and considering it solely from the point of view of the general situation. The existence of an oligarchy consisting of land-owners, old families, and foreigners related to them, is a phenomenon common to the majority of Latin-American republics, where immediately after independence was achieved, an aristocratic group was formed in which, by the irony of fate, the descendants of those who headed the movements for independence rarely appeared save by way of exception, scattered and frustrated as they were by poverty or popular connections. This group, transformed into a governing force, comes daily into more open conflict with the *bourgeoisie*, whether of immigrant or native origin, and with the masses, whose tendency is to advance extreme claims. The prevalence of certain subversive ideas in some of our great labour organisations is partly due to the reaction against these circles, which have grown up artificially owing to transitory circumstances, and have no roots in the past, as have those of Europe. They are survivals, having no appropriate functions in our present-day life, and all they are good for is to clog the evolution of the country and exasperate the tendencies which oppose them.   One of the reasons why communist ideas have not become more widely diffused in the United States, in proportion to the size of the population and the amazing intensity of their industries, lies in the fact that the place of this group, which has no logical *raison d'être* in new countries, is taken by a plutocracy, which we may admit or condemn (we are not discussing principles, but weighing facts), but which is derived from the actual local conditions and not from a tendency to the imitation of an alien idea.   Although based on monopoly and tyranny, this plutocracy does evolve in accordance with modern and elastic principles, which cause it to form a real part of the body politic, smoothing away, by a policy of continuous improvisation, the hard angles of inequality. The fortune and position of a Rockefeller, a Morgan, or a Ford have not been acquired from the possession of vast estates which they have never cultivated, nor from a marriage with some other brilliant name, but from energy, emulation, perspicacity, the excessive power of capital—which is an abuse, if you like (and the United States will certainly be forced to react against it)—but, at any rate, from a form of direct activity which has always been for the good of the community, spreading progress, giving employment to millions of men, and increasing the might of the nation.   The absorbing influence of this creative *élite* may be attacked in internal politics in the name of an ideal of equality, and feared in external politics, on account of the imperialism which inevitably arises from it; but there is no doubt that it is the efflorescence of the national life, a direct shoot of the national tree.   The same cannot be said of those parasitic forces which may, in the beginning, have discharged the function of carrying on a heritage of culture, but which to-day have outlived their original usefulness, owing to the rise of general standards, and have almost gone to the opposite extreme, owing to the fact that they remain stationary in their out-of-date ideas.

The internal problem of Chile, as of the whole of Latin America, consists in making democracy a reality, now that they have obtained independence.   By the aid of this development many external difficulties will be solved, which will find their true level when treated between people and people, as part of a broader conception of continental necessities.

It is in this sense that we can speak, not of *a* Pacific problem,

but of Pacific problems, among which the dispute between Peru
and Chile figures not as an exclusive basis, or the point upon which
things chiefly turn, but as a correlative factor contributing towards
the elucidation of something unknown;—something which is bounded
geographically by the ocean, which brings under consideration our
jurisdiction over our own coasts from Panama to the Straits of
Magellan, which calls up on the distant horizon, the formidable
vision of two great hostile squadrons, and which may decide the
fate of half Latin America in future centuries. The matter which
has to be decided in our century is not a limited question between
two conterminous republics, but the world hegemony of the vastest
of the oceans. Now that the Panama Canal is open, the imperialist
shadow is falling towards the south. Further away, like a cloud—
or like the dawn—waves the flag of Japan. All the life and wealth
of the Spanish-speaking western part of the New World has this
vast extent of ocean as its sole means of outlet. Our coasts extend
entirely undefended from Panama to Cape Horn, since our armies
and fleets have been planned in view of local quarrels, without considering for a moment the contingent possibility that we may have
to defend our territories in the midst of wider disturbances. When
we face the true facts of the situation, we see that the problem of
the Pacific is not that of knowing to which of two warring republics
certain territories are to belong, but that of safe-guarding by a united
policy the free development of our future possibilities, amid the
pressure and unexpected crises of world politics. The Canal has
marked a progress for the world; but it is a pity that this progress
has such long-range artillery. There is an old dispute between the
United States and Japan; but the Latin Americans also have a voice
in such a serious matter. From the Galápagos Islands to Cape
Horn, whether the coast be called that of Colombia, Ecuador, Peru
or Chile, we have one great unity which feels the menace equally.
And this is the essential and lasting condition which ought to inspire our movement in the future.

CHAPTER VIII

THE PRIMACY OF THE SOUTH ATLANTIC

The attraction of the great harbours—Mistakes of Argentine policy —Difference of opinion with the Socialist party—Perils and advantages of immigration—Uruguayan characteristics—The isolation of Paraguay—The diplomacy of Brazil and the dominion of the sea.

THERE has always been a hard struggle in our Latin America between the men who governed and the ideologues; between those who aimed above all at stability, and those who were more inclined to defend theories, and thought more of their ideas than of peace. Thanks to this general tendency, the anarchy of the peoples of the Southern Atlantic, now orderly and flourishing republics, took in their time the form of an ill-defined struggle between the claim to authority of the capitals and the exalted frame of mind of those regions which refused to submit, appealing to arguments which though legitimate, were at variance with real conditions. Both parties were right. The great centres were in communication with Europe, and understood the risks of a prolonged agitation. The states in the interior had arrived at a consciousness of their destiny and desired to moderate the influence of the oligarchy on the coasts. The two tendencies fulfilled a useful function: the provincial tendency in claiming rights, and the seaboard in keeping alight the lamp of culture and civilisation during such difficult years and in such remote latitudes. These antecedents explain certain phenomena of our day which will have to be solved by reference to them.

In every age the point of departure for the prosperity and progress of peoples has been a small group, a bolder or more fortunate city, which has led the progress of the collective forces. Civilisation, like a fire, begins to burn on a hearth before it spreads. Thus arose the great towns of the South Atlantic, Buenos Aires, Montevideo, Rio de Janeiro, whose creative greatness was to end by becoming the expression and collective image of the enormous regions over whose development they preside.   In nations whose essential activity is the exportation of the produce of the soil, the advantage of capitals on the sea over capitals in the interior need not be insisted upon. Capitals in the interior are the centralising source of energy for self-sufficing peoples.   But in regions which send their raw materials abroad and receive from abroad manufactured products, the directing organisation, if it is to be really efficacious, must be on the coast, avoiding the anomaly of a flourishing port and a parasitic capital.   Buenos Aires, Montevideo and Rio de Janeiro stand for this conception.   A rivalry between these great centres of progress would not be in accordance with logic.   If it has sometimes existed, it has been a matter of imagination and *amour propre* rather than of a conflict of real interests.   The greatness of these different centres, at the stage through which our republics are passing to-day, is by no means incompatible, and it is going too far to suppose that any of them may be an obstacle to the others.

It was in this sense that I felt in all Latin America an ardent sympathy, an effort of will going out towards the triumphant and prosperous far South.   But even while one was receiving this impression, one became aware that susceptibilities had been wounded by neglect. Owing to the historical pre-eminence of the great port, the ideas of Buenos Aires on the continental ideal have always predominated in the Argentine.   There is no doubt that the egoism and pride of which we are accused in the rest of Latin America are more apparent than real.   But it is also certain that a prolonged course of divergent development and certain imprudent expressions of opinion on the distant republics, artfully disseminated by those who foment ill feeling, justify a state of mind in which an instinctive affection is veiled by resentment.   In the course of my journey I had often to struggle against this atmosphere, exasperated by the futile quarrels about Bolívar and San Martín.

I have not undertaken this book with a view to flattering the governments, but rather in order to censure them when necessary; but I do not write it to flatter the peoples either,—only to state, at a critical moment in the history of our Latin America, what in my judgment I consider to be the truth.   If I could find the necessary energy to go to the United States and speak in opposition to prevailing opinion, how much more ought I to have enough to point out those tendencies in my own country which appear to me harmful. The Government of the Argentine has neglected its higher mission by disparaging the ideals of 1810, by shutting itself in and confining itself to purely local tendencies, by refusing to play that general *rôle* on the Continent which fate offers it. Without prejudicing its friendly attitude to any people, and without in any way compromising its stability, our country could extend an open hand to the North, and hint to those born of the same revolution that, though others sow troubles—for their national symbol is the stars of the night—we cultivate fraternity, for our ensign is the sun. This does not mean that I would advise rash action. Political prudence often consists, not in provoking events, but in turning them into a certain direction; not in moving oneself but in taking advantage of the movements of others. And in this sense the activity of imperialism has offered us abundant opportunities for putting forth in Latin America—while observing all respect, and impartiality—a point of view favourable to a calm solidarity, and making this attitude the centre of our evolution in world politics.

Far from obeying this logical tendency, the Argentine has developed in Latin America a policy of frontier strife; sometimes inclined to wrangle with Chile, sometimes directed towards prolonging an absurd rivalry with Brazil, and always ready to dispute boundaries with Bolivia, or to quarrel over jurisdiction with Uruguay; frittering away her strength in secondary activities, which, whether they were reasonable or not, were to diminish her prestige in treating with the United States and Europe. In so acting they forget that in diplomatic, as in military action, there are strategic fatalities. One position may have a decisive influence on the defence of another. An antagonistic attitude or an abstention may lead to grave damage. Two great streams of water control the life of Latin America on the Atlantic watershed. The Amazon, which by its affluents goes back to Colombia, Venezuela, Ecuador, Peru, and Bolivia; and the Río de la Plata, by which the riches of the Argentine, Uruguay, and Paraguay reach the sea. One of the first conditions of common vitality is that these means of communication should be entirely dominated and controlled by those peoples whose coasts they bathe, without excluding or favouring anybody, but with the vital guaranty that none of them shall favour, directly or indirectly, at any moment, the movements of maritime powers outside this family of nations. By definitively excluding any hypothesis by which the foreigner might ever find a favourable opportunity permitting him to extend his influence in this region, the three republics will have gained the best of battles. And this security in the future, equally favourable to each and all, can only be achieved by the aid of a policy of fraternity.

I will not say that in 1913 Argentine policy was directed in a sense contrary to the ideals which inspired my tour. But there is no doubt that the Government roundly declined to recognise my journey. If the attitude of the official representatives in the various countries through which I passed, and the ignorance in which public opinion was kept with regard to my progress, are not sufficient to establish this, I will recall the refusal returned to my request for an audience. Dr. Sáenz Peña had defended in his youth a thesis opposed to Pan-Americanism, supporting it by the well-known formula "Latin America for Humanity." Before becoming President, he had on several occasions given proof of his friendly feeling for me in connection with my books. His patriotism does not admit of a shadow of doubt. Moreover, there were no convictions, weaknesses, or personal motives which prevented him from granting ten minutes' conversation, which are granted to all who ask for it, to a fellow-countrymen returning to his native land after winning applause for the Argentine flag from north to south of the Continent. The fact that he arrived at a resolution which was not in harmony either with his courteous character or the esteem of which he had given me proofs years before in Paris, shows that more important reasons must have weighed with him, arising out of the constant protests on the part of the North American Government to which my tour had given rise.

The Ministry for Foreign Affairs had been occupied by distinguished men, worthy of all respect, but wedded to narrow local ideas and little fitted by their own calibre to conceive vast courses of action or embrace new horizons. Brand-new diplomatists are characterised by an excessive reserve. Veterans have discovered how to be discreet with a smiling negligence. They [i. e., the Argentine diplomats] appealed to that one-sided friendship "which has always bound us to the United States,"—a friendship in which, since everything cannot be equal, we have provided all the devotion, and that country has obtained all the benefits,—and, considering my attitude dangerously lacking in respect, they put obstacles in my way even in the slightest details. They even went so far as to take the unusual step of making representations to a Spanish-American Minister, who had taken it upon himself to invite me to an official banquet. I did not see in this any hostility for the "dreamer" with "no previous knowledge of politics" who was "ignorant of American problems." Personally they were courteous and correct; but, whether from conviction or tactics, it remained an established principle that I was to be kept aloof from all governmental or international action, as if my very presence at a party, or the letters of my name in a list, might be the cause of dangerous complications. It was not precisely a boycott—the boycott came later, seizing the opportunity of the War—but a growing estrangement, which spread quietly, in silent circles, till it had produced the immobility of the void.

Suggestion is exercised by the United States on Latin America in two forms: first, that obsequiousness which leads to submission; second, that prudence which takes the form of inaction.

In opposition to the tendencies of the two great internationalists whom she has produced, Doctors Calvo and Drago, the Argentine was not willing to listen to anything about any Latin-American problems but those which affect her own frontiers, and any propaganda contrary to these ideas was considered imprudent and harmful. From the continental point of view, my tour had been a move towards conciliation and the knitting together of our hostilities in view of a higher course of action directed towards our common preservation. From the national point of view, it could not have been more favourable to Argentine prestige; since, for the first time, our flag had been cheered even in the far north by peoples who had previously been unacquainted with us. But apart from these considerations, the chief sentiment in official circles was annoyance that, by the mouth of an Argentino, attention had been drawn to that imperialist activity which everybody desired to ignore, though they all felt its effect; an imperialist activity which, according to the prevailing opinion, could not harm us, since it had not reached our frontiers. It was this point of view, supported by those forces which direct national tendencies, that one man alone had to resist.

Notwithstanding, public opinion was favourable to my campaign, especially that of the young men at the universities, who, knowing my difficulties, organised a lecture [1] and seconded me enthusiastically in the plan of action which I tried to carry out.

I could have wished that the Socialist Party in the Argentine, which I had joined some years ago, and which I represented at the International Congresses of Amsterdam and Stuttgart, and also on the Permanent Committee at Brussels, might, without departing from its general theories and principles, have shown itself a great force of immediate justice in the foreign policy of Latin America, like a heart yearning toward the weak.

It has proved a grave error to start from politics in order to create nationality. It will always be more logical to base ourselves on nationality in order to shape politics. The necessities of the moment are the basis and origin of general ideas. They therefore rise superior to these general ideas, which it may be inopportune to apply at any given moment. Such, at least, was the opportunist point of view which I had defended in Europe, supporting the

---

[1] More than ten thousand persons, mostly students, crowded together, eager to hear the words of the fervent propagandist of Latin-American fraternity." *El Diario* of Buenos Aires, February 3, 1913.

"At a very few hours' interval, Mr. Roosevelt in New York, and Manuel Ugarte in Buenos Aires, were speaking on subjects having obvious affinities . . . The words of the Argentine orator were greeted with thunderous applause, and so, according to the telegram, were those of the North American. Which means that a continental problem really exists, and that a conflict of two races is appearing which we shall shortly have to study at some length." *La Gaceta*, of Buenos Aires, February 3, 1913.

"Señor Ugarte was enthusiastically applauded by his audience."
La Prensa, of Buenos Aires, February 3, 1913.

"The enthusiasm with which the enormous audience in the amphitheatre received our fellow-countryman's lecture is a proof of the deep sympathy aroused by his cause." *La Prensa*, of Buenos Aires, February 3, 1913.

"To sum up, the interest aroused by Ugarte's dissertion did not flag, and last night's meeting was a great success both for him and for the University Federation." *La Argentina*, of Buenos Aires, February 3, 1913.

"A large section of the public accompanied Señor Ugarte to his house. Here he again began to speak, taking leave of his escort, and advising them to set up a Centre of propaganda for Latin-American ideals."
La Nación, of Buenos Aires, February 3, 1913.

thesis of Jaurès in the various debates to which the first entry of M. Millerand into a ministry gave rise. As regards our Latin America, my idea was that, grouped round a just aspiration, the popular parties ought to defend it, not only within our frontiers, in matters concerning internal organisation, but in world policy.

I do not wish to recall the dispute which separated me from this organisation almost immediately after my arrival in the Argentine except for the purpose of expressing my regret.[2] In spite of the blows sustained by my feelings, not a trace of animosity remains in my mind against the leaders, or against the group whose tendencies I have defended for more than fifteen years, and whose popular and democratic aspiration has not ceased to be my own. The future can be trusted to re-establish the truth.

Setting aside sentiment, the difference of opinion can be reduced to very simple lines. Certain remarks published by the official paper of the Party on the occasion of the national anniversary of Columbia prompted me to publish a correction[3] and from this

---

[2] *Manuel Ugarte y el Partido Socialista*, documents edited by an Argentino. Union Editorial Hispanoamericana, Buenos Aires, 1914. *La Campaña de Manuel Ugarte y las opinones socialistas.* Casaretto y Lozano, publishers, Buenos Aires, 1913.

[3] Buenos Aires, July 21, 1913. To the Editor of *La Vanguardia.* "In your Sunday issue I have read with surprise a paragraph on the anniversary of Colombian independence which ends as follows: "Like all the South American republics, this country was for a long time convulsed with civil wars; Panama will probably contribute towards its progress by entering fully [*sic* for 'and Colombia will enter' (?)] into the concert of prosperous and civilised nations. I protest against these words, hardly fraternal in tone, and against the implied insult to this republic, which deserves our respect, not only because of its misfortunes, but also because of its glorious past and that pride to which it has never played false. In saying that Colombia will enter 'the concert of prosperous and civilised nations' it is implied that she has not yet done so, and a grievous wrong is done to this country, which is one of the most cultivated and high-minded that I visited during my tour. To allege that Panama will 'contribute to its progress' is to mock the grief of a people, the victims of imperialism, which has lost, in circumstances well known to all, one of its most important provinces,—and so has, forsooth, been 'civilised' by those bad citizens who acted as the instrument by which their national territory was mutilated.

"As this note on Colombia was published in the same number of *La*

arose a controversy on the question of patriotism. The inspiration which had led me to travel through the Continent certainly bore within it a vigorous national tendency, not in the sense of expansion, but of defence. My Latin-American preoccupations were not, in my opinion, irreconcilable with the new doctrines and democratic principles. The opposition lay rather in procedure. While I tended to set general ideas in relief against the background of our own needs, those who opposed me were inclined to force our necessities into the mould of general ideas. No disagreement would have existed, if account had been taken of the action of internal affairs upon international politics, and of international politics upon internal affairs. Owing to causes arising, some out of the social conditions of the Continent, and others out of its situation as regards the world, Socialism cannot long postpone the stage of reform among us, and even if it adopts the Marxist point of view, we cannot see in any of the possible reforms the slightest obstacle to the maintenance of collective autonomy. On the contrary, so long as its theory and principles avoid coming into collision with the vital necessities arising out of our surroundings, the national vigour will redound to the benefit of democracy, just as social progress will contribute towards strengthening the muscles of nationality.

In standing up against imperialism, and checking the activity of the conquering oligarchies, Socialism was sacrificing no principle. Another aspect of the disagreement arose from my opinion of all those dark forces which might injure the future of the country, and from my conviction that, if Socialism became national, it ought to spread from the capital to the provinces, ceasing to be a minority in the Chambers, in order to gain in volume and arrive at power. Perhaps the evolution of the world has since confirmed some of these arguments. This is not the moment to dilate upon a theme which

Vanguardia in which an editorial of mine appeared, and as this coincidence might cause some to believe that I share these opinions, I find myself obliged to write this letter, and to declare that I am completely at variance with the article in question, which strikes me as unnecessarily offensive; moreover I will add that, if the standpoint of this paper leads it to speak disrespectfully of the Latin-American republics, I, who have devoted my energies to defending the fraternity of our peoples, shall find myself regretfully forced to abstain from collaborating with it." *Manuel Ugarte.*

I set forth at the right time in an open letter.[4] In these pages, written in retirement by a man who does not wish to go back and play an active part in the internal politics of his country, only such observations are appropriate as refer to the general situation of our Latin America and its destiny within the limits of continental policy.

One of the reasons of the indifference with which some speak of nationality is the almost universal absence in cosmopolitan communities of any roots in the past. Spain did not bring to America a spirit of innovation, a flexible character capable of adapting itself to new horizons or new needs in such a way as to develop from them a new life. She brought her customs, her traditions, her set forms, and applied them with a narrow-minded assurance which led her to build dwellings like those of Alicante or Málaga in regions which, owing to their latitude and altitude, had a cold climate. In regions where all wealth came from the soil, she developed urban at the expense of rural activity; and, while struggling with a lack of communications, she preserved all that constituted an impediment, down to her inconvenient costume. This is the reason why, since the transformation effected by elements coming from the four quarters of the world, respect for origins has grown pale. A flood of immigrants, only partly absorbed, has since diluted the nascent sentiment. It is to a large extent from it that that progress springs which is gaining ground; and nothing can be farther from my mind than to oppose, however, indirectly, such a fertile inrush of force and vitality. The more copious the supplies, the richer and more bountiful the annual tide, the greater will be the factors making for victory in the process of raising collective standards. But immigration is a food which can only be assimilated according to the capacity of the stomach which absorbs it. There are substances which are assimilated immediately, slowly, or with difficulty, according to circumstances; and the organism must fix the quality and character of the doses which it has to transform. In the United States the number of subjects who may enter the country from each nation is settled annually, taking into account the number who have previously entered, their kinship with the original body, and special conditions affecting the ease with which they are assimilated. In the Argentine the factor of immigration, perhaps the

[4] *La Patria Grande* (in press).

most important in its independent life, has up to now been regulated by chance alone. Our naturalisation laws, based, like most of our laws, on theory, demand the same facilities for all comers, thus giving their sanction to the illogical position that elements of similar nationality, like the Uruguayans, are dealt with under the same forms, and placed on the same level, as elements so different from ourselves as the Chinese. Thanks to this lack of foresight and these experimental methods, there is going on in the Argentine an amalgamation of peoples which has already built a magnificent city and raised immense tracts of land to a state of prosperity, astonishing the world by the rapidity of its improvisations; but which has not yet succeeded, in the midst of its prosperity and wealth, in creating a body politic adapted to its needs, or giving to the community its final form.

Besides its value as an agent of progress, European immigration has the peculiar merit for all Latin America that it does not involve any idea of predominance. Even the technical experts engaged by the governments to discharge certain difficult tasks, keep to the work which they have to carry out, without pursuing other aims. Peru has had its army organised by French officers, Chile has developed under the influence of German leaders, the Argentine has borrowed from various nations educators, men of science, lecturers; but their influence has never gone beyond the limits laid down for it. This is what marks the difference between European action, which respects sovereignty, and the action of North American imperialism, which makes use of commercial or intellectual expansion as a political weapon.

On the other hand, this immigration which is so profitable to us, has never been administered in such a way as to make it yield its full benefits to the country. Spain, Italy, and other nations have sent thousands of high-spirited men, ready to work; and the theory is to a certain extent justified by which this exodus constitutes a source of weakness. Even if we reckon up the considerable sums sent annually to their home country by the emigrants, we must understand that this drawback is largely compensated for by the entry of capital. And there is no doubt that it may be necessary to examine at some time the results of this constant drain which— if we add together that which results from the coming and going of seasonal immigration and that which arises from immigrants who have enriched themselves from our soil, and go to spend the proceeds of their fortune abroad—causes a part of our prosperity to be fictitious, owing to the systematic exodus of salaries, interest, or capital.

But the essential thing is the maintenance of a guiding principle of culture, the development of a genius all our own, of a personality in which the new elements become fused. And this can only be achieved if we continue to draw attention, with ever increasing fervour, to our antecedents and origins. I do not believe in the ultimate splendour, the complete triumph, of an Argentine nationality unconnected with the sister nations of Latin America and having no interest in the fate of kindred nations. However great their progress may be, it will lack solidity in the present, and depth in the past. Our force, our future, and our victory depend, on the contrary, on a free association and collaboration of the renovated Latin America of the extreme South with the indigenous Latin America of the North; and it is this vast conception which, in my opinion, must inspire our policy of to-morrow.

The stupendous driving force of our victorious nationality must be firmly based upon foundations solidly Argentine and broadly continental in character, taking as a model the systems which prevail in the United States. And at this point we must make a distinction between two ideas forming part of the same concept. It is right that our countries should defend themselves from all that implies interference or predominance, by opposing their activity and vigilance to all imperialist manœuvres; but even in order to carry out this plan, it is indispensable to adapt to our own life the underlying principles whence that greatness arises which we at once admire and fear.

And it is not in what concerns outward forms, but in what concerns the essence and efficacy of things. There was a time when we believed that all that was needed in order to acquire Anglo-Saxon qualities was to learn English, and that one acquired military science by adopting the uniform of the army in vogue. Our apprenticeship must not take the form of imitation. Let us stamp upon all our activities our own personal impress, but let us observe all the nations which have most recently achieved a brilliant position, in order to be able to counteract those cunning moves which are inevitable in the rivalry of peoples. The Japanese assimilated the whole of Western progress in four decades, not in order to join the train of other natïons, but precisely so as to compete with them, so as to avoid subjugation, so as to defend their own personality. This example, of which we can never be too mindful, may induce us to develop our competence in every order of activity, and to set our own hands to the levers of our national life. An old precept of social economy says: "If I own a business, and allow somebody else to install himself in my office, receive the profits, and give orders as master, what does it matter to me whether the enterprise prospers and triumphs, since it is not mine?" Banks, insurances, railways, cold-storage plants, enterprises of every order, must in the end be set in motion by our efforts, our own intelligence, and our own capital, in order that we may one day pride ourselves without reserve upon the flourishing condition of our country.

The factor which has determined the general submissiveness of our Latin America has been our disposition to oppose all those who have desired to accomplish something new. The failure of so many undertakings has ended by creating in our political and economic life generations of ironical lookers-on who hope to obtain by routine, luck, or inaction what they cannot achieve by their own actions. Thus those who have reflected the least coolly, or done the least work, have often risen to the highest office. Thus vast fortunes have been made by leaving immense landed estates to acquire value by lapse of time and the work of others. One of the peculiarities most surprising to foreign observers is the fact that no inventions are made in our lands, that existing ones are not modified, that we contribute no new industries, no peculiar forms of life, or new ideas, to the onward march of the world. Progress is always achieved by the means which we find at hand. We are not inspired, like the Anglo-Saxon peoples, by that spirit, for ever wide-awake and creative, which makes every function, knowledge, or activity part of a constant advance towards an ideal of infinite progress and incessant evolution. The Argentine has reacted vigorously in this sense; but it is only by emphasising this guiding principle, opposed to all immobility or lethargy, that it will succeed in fully realising its imposing future.

But this future, which would be a source of energy to us, even
if it were not a test of realities from now onwards, this prodigious
raising of the national position, which opens a field for the most
daring hopes, and fills us all with legitimate pride, cannot be attained in all its fulness if, led by an excessive prudence or an unpardonable vanity, we isolate ourselves from the family of nations
with which we are bound up, geographically and morally. A nation of eight million inhabitants, lacking in industrial developments,
with immense territories and heavy debts, does not represent a
force strong enough to be able to develop and maintain itself in the
world without intermingling its activities with those of kindred
nations. And this is perhaps the point in Argentine policy which
stands in most urgent need of correction. We shall have to develop
in harmony, not only with the republics lying upon our frontiers,
but with the spiritual atmosphere of Latin America as a whole.
And this, far from involving a sacrifice, constitutes the greatest
benefit which could be offered to the good fortune of a people.

The figure of San Martín, as great as that of Bolívar, if we reckon
generosity and renunciation in the scale of values, dominates the
whole horizon of the Argentine, and, beyond the Andes, the national
antecedents of Chile and Peru, recalling amid their dispersion their
common points of departure. A statue and a tomb in the Cathe-
dral perpetuate his memory. And owing to his inspiration, the cult
of a glorious past, recalling grievous injustices and a tardy recognition, is reaching gigantic proportions among the young men.
Sparing of his utterances and confidences, San Martín is great above
all by his silence. In exile he contemplated the sea in which his
hopes were drowned and waited in resignation for his death. Few
examples of energy and patriotism can be compared with that of
the victorious captain who sacrificed even the spread of his own glory
on the altar of austere principles and heroic abnegation. But there
can be few such examples of a blind confidence in the future. For
there are some sacrifices which are only possible when faith exists
in the resurrection of an ideal.

Continuing my journey, I embarked for Uruguay. In crossing
the Río de la Plata from shore to shore in a few hours, and in
passing from the capital of one state to the capital of another, without any change in the language, aspect of the country, or customs,

one again proves the artificiality of our divisions, founded on the fortunes of civil war. The divergent points of view and personal antagonisms which, after the achievement of independence, determined how a viceroyalty was to be split up, have given rise to a state of affairs in which two different flags are reflected in the same waters. But there were no facts, ways of life, or tangible characteristics upon which to base a difference which did not exist. It is so difficult to see any difference between an Uruguayan and an Argentino that, even after long experience and dealings with both, it still proves a difficult task to classify them. Only certain terms enables us to do so. For this is all that the distinction between "Orientales" and "Porteños" amounts to. These very terms reveal a significant limitation of sense. "Porteños" are literally the inhabitants of all ports, and so those of Montevideo and Buenos Aires fall equally into this class. And as for the term "Orientales," the slight difference of longitude between the two neighbouring towns does not justify a term which recalls that used by Europeans in speaking of remote Asiatic peoples. The period at which "Banda Oriental" and "Porteñismo" were spoken of, is reflected in the very formulas which they employed, revealing a self-absorption and a narrow local conception which is to-day as unjustifiable as it is meaningless.

Montevideo is a great, smiling city, modern and particularly prosperous, which arrests the traveller by the serenity of its climate, the beauty of its women, and the noble and sociable character of its inhabitants. In proportion to its population it is, perhaps with Bogotá, the most intellectual capital in Latin America. And what surprises one in Uruguay is not only the culture of a ruling group; in very few republics is public institution so well organised and so widely diffused. The relatively small area of the country has favoured a rise in general standards, and, as a consequence, a hardy modern tendency which is reflected in its customs, laws and institutions.

I laid a wreath upon the tomb of Artigas with the sincerest devotion. Far from being due to any opportunist idea of gaining the sympathies of the country, my action arose from a calm conviction and the desire, as an Argentino, to react against obsolete mistakes. The significance of Artigas in the movement for independence goes beyond the frontiers of the republic which he founded. It would be a grave mistake to continue, at the distance of a century, to regard him as no more than a schismatic *caudillo*. The instructions which he gave his representatives before the Constituent Assembly reveal the high ideals of a statesman. He demanded for his province autonomy within a confederation which he accepted as indispensable. On the wide stage filled by the revolution which was disturbing the Spanish colonies from Mexico to the South, his attitude in no way clashes with the general movement of the whole. In this sphere of ideas I am much inclined to share the views of the Uruguayan historian Don Hugo D. Barbagelata,* who is, in my opinion, the person who has made the most important study of this great figure, disowned, misunderstood, and yet, in spite of all, imperturbable. The very fact of Artigas's exile and long years of ostracism in Paraguay gives the measure of his ideals, for our peoples have only been hard on those who have really served them. Perhaps the time is not far distant when we shall cease to prolong controversies, and examine in a brotherly spirit, without violence or recrimination, the somewhat confused activity of our countries in the years following the effort for independence. It is certain that the figure of him who, far from limiting his consideration to the sphere in which he was operating, raised his head above the smoke of battle to try to link up his activities with those of Bolívar and San Martín, will not emerge impaired from a calm investigation.

At the time of my arrival Uruguay was governed by Señor Batle y Ordóñez, one of the advance guard of politicians, vigorous and tenacious, who aroused at once violent resistance and clamorous enthusiasm. As I had had relations with him in Paris, where he had lived for some time, he received me with fine courtesy. But he avoided any allusion to the matter which had led to my journey round Latin America. From his prudent and suggestive conversation, beneath his declarations of amity and brotherhood for all peoples, could be gathered an admission that Uruguay was not in a state to consider any course of action on a fully continental scale. Placed between two strong nations, Brazil and the Argentine, his policy had to be one of constant self-preservation, by the aid of the former or the latter, or of some remoter state. His thesis, given

* *Artigās y la revolución americana.* Paris, P. Ollendorff, 1914.

the actual conditions of place and time, might appear reasonable, and it confirmed once more the grievous dislocation of our politics. Señor Batle y Ordóñez was certainly right at the moment at which he was speaking. But this very reasoning, fragmentary and partial, carried with it a most severe censure on those tendencies which have the force of law in Latin America, and revealed a general error to which Señor Batle was contributing in common with the other Presidents.

In spite of its reserved attitude the Government of Uruguay put no impediments in the way of the development of my propaganda, and the lecture took place in the theatre on July 18 without difficulty.[5]

The students offered me their premises, the writers organised a banquet, Eduardo Vaz Ferreira devoted one of his lectures at the University to me, and all that surrounded the traveller was propitious. But beyond the tides which rose and fell, I could not fail to perceive, in a general review of my journey, something of the symbolic Sisyphus who kept painfully raising the rock only to see it fall down again, in an eternal labour frustrated by superior forces. When the first flush of enthusiasm was over, which formed a mere parenthesis among local interests, the old round of the forces of confusion would start once again. What had happened everywhere else, was bound to happen in Montevideo as well.

Had not a newspaper arrived during the last few days from Ecuador, in which I was harshly attacked (I quote its very words), for "having spoken against this country in Chile" calling her "in-

[5] "Señor Ugarte spoke for more than an hour, and at the end he received the tribute of an impressive demonstration of sympathy."
   La Democracia, of Montevideo, August 19, 1913.
"The public, which had applauded the orator frequently in the course of his lecture, hailed his final words with a fresh and sustained ovation."
   El Diario de La Plata, of Montevideo, August 19, 1913.
"At the end we heard some sincere words, truly sincere, coming to us without any eagerness for facile applause, with no pose, and no hidden spirit of gain." *La Tribuna Popular,* of Montevideo, August 19, 1913.
"The immense multitude which filled the vast hall, as a tribute to the mighty champion of the Latin-American cause, accompanied him on foot to his house in a numerous body."
   La Razón, of Montevideo, August 19, 1913.

firm and weak," and for having proclaimed in another speech "the necessity for placing her under the tutelage of another nation, saner and more capable of administering her finances, without doing serious damage to her neighbours?"

A deep discouragement weighed upon my spirits. What was the good of sacrificing my time, my health, and my fortune in championing a *rapprochement* between our republics, loving them all equally, within the bounds of a higher patriotism, if an anonymous cablegram was enough to make them all give credit to a calumny? Memory and logic should have sufficed to make the imposture impossible. None the less, I wrote the letter demanded by the situation to the principal papers, in which I once more denounced the campaign which had been organised for playing upon their susceptibilities.[6] Did these lines ever reach the Ecuador papers, and through them, public opinion? The distances are so great and the lack of communication so complete, that it is always difficult to correct these things effectively. But even if the *démenti* finds its way there, and counteracts the malicious version, the unpleasant feeling aroused by the false statement always persists; and in this fact precisely lies the power of those who make use of the system.

The calumny would be harmless if the calumniator did not reckon upon the credulity or support of numerous groups of people who, in good or bad faith, make themselves the accessories of his act. Owing to the vicissitudes of my fortunes, I began to understand this; and in the succeeding years I had painful cause to test its truth. Opinion is always inclined, more out of *naïveté* than malice, to accept tendencious reports. It is thus that international conflicts have been inflamed, it is thus that the value of those riches has been depreciated, which, once they have passed out of our hands, have brought fabulous wealth to foreign companies; it is thus that a sort of super-government has come to weigh constantly upon our Latin America. The impressionable soul of these new lands accepted without sufficient reflection the guiding principles which were imposed upon it, and more than once took sides against its own interests, led astray by a carefully calculated inaccuracy, aroused by an apparent injustice, discouraged by an imaginary treachery, and

[6] *La Razón*, of Montevideo, August 23, 1913.

dazzled at every turn by specious inspirations. By the aid of the cable and the telegraph, all the threads of our collective life were gathered into the hands of those interested in perpetuating disorder, of those who desired to induce us, by the bait of general ideas or generous passions, to favour their interests and second their plans. It was perhaps due to these conditions that we were such obstinate free traders, that we were passionately enthusiastic for the "independence" of Cuba, that we ranged ourselves in the war in the train of the United States, and that we allow the ferment of anarchism, which the great republic of the North repressed so severely within her own borders, to spread among us as a factor of disintegration.

More than once in the course of my journey, I heard the arguments of "internationalists"' and "the future of humanity" appealed to, to calm our anxiety in face of the aggressions of the North. "What does it matter" some people would argue, "that another people dominates us, if frontiers are to disappear, and if we are advancing straight towards a fusion of humanity?" This tendency to appeal to general ideas in justification of our abdication is particularly dangerous in countries where immigration is abundant, and where the national element is sometimes diluted by others, which, owing to their recent arrival and heterogeneous antecedents, have no interest in the durability of the group within which they are for the moment developing. While nourishing a more liberal spirit, and accepting whatever progressive ideas are compatible with the actual conditions of the moment, we have to keep on the defensive against philosophic inductions which may be made use of to serve ends contrary to the very ideal which they proclaim. All of which does not prevent us from opposing the law of residence, which is contrary to the spirit of the age.

It is necessary, while still using legal means, to aim at higher ends by a careful regulation of immigration. It is not stifling thought to prevent foreigners from coming in to break up our nationality. This is written in no spirit of hatred for foreigners. The real foreign danger for our Latin America has never lain in the political idealism of the masses of working-class immigrants, but in the ambitious selfishness of international capitalists. By controlling the entrance of certain elements into the country, we shall more easily prevent the destructive propaganda which is coming from abroad. By directing education on more just lines, that which may arise from within will be more easily frustrated. Besides their direct action in themselves, theories acquire a certain reflex action in the struggle between nations. But it is not enough to stifle the germs of dissolution. In the heart of these new communities, in which a certain bewilderment and lack of homogeneity sometimes shows itself, we have to encourage the growth of a moral atmosphere which may amalgamate, sustain, and harmonise the activities of the group. Nowhere is the welding power of nationalism so necessary as in those groups which are in course of forging themselves on individual character. But this nationalism has to contain in its essence the whole extent of the Spanish-speaking continent. In the schools, in the streets, on the platform, in every incident of daily life must arise a movement towards the uplifting of the community, without being deterred by a vain fear that our national symbols may become vulgar and insignificant if they are seen on every side. They represent an aspiration, a general will, and its efficacy lies, on the contrary, in its democratic intermingling with all the conditions of our life. In the United States we come across the flag on houses, shop fronts, tramways, cigarette boxes, and the most familiar objects. It is the first toy given to the child, the mascot carried with him by the traveller, that which every man has always before his eyes and near to his heart. The colours seem to form part of every life, and it is in the exaltation of this sentiment, which unites in itself memories and ambitions higher than the individual, that we have perhaps to look for the secret of national greatness.

These and other reflections, equally applicable to Uruguay, the Argentine, and the majority of our republics, were what occupied my mind as the train ran across the plains sown with grain which stretch away in the direction of Paraguay, one of the most prosperous and fertile regions of our Latin America.

Paraguay is a hospitable country, where we find a social and intellectual *élite* comparable with that of any other Latin-American capital; and where, as regards the masses, the effects of the simple, kindly teaching of the old Jesuit missions still persist. At Asunción, the highest comfort and the artificial allurements of great cities are of course not to be found. But the culture of the upper classes and the patriarchal flavour which life retains there, arrest the visitor's attention and give him a peculiar sympathy with this valiant and long-suffering people.

What surprises one beyond anything is the scanty communication which exists between Paraguay and the regions surrounding it. The ramparts standing in the way of intercourse and commerce between republics lying on each other's frontiers, perhaps arise from an ignorance of our resources and the high rates of transport fixed by the foreign companies.

The peculiar conditions of our Latin-American life tend to make those most capable of observing and judging conditions crowd into the capitals, which they quit to go to Europe. But the traveller who thinks, however superficially, has no difficulty in noticing that in Paraguay there exists a favourable field for enterprises of every order. Yet in spite of this, the Trapiche wine from the Argentine province of Mendoza is sold in Asunción at a higher price than French wine of a superior quality; and the cheap tobacco produced in Paraguay can only reach Buenos Aires in quite insufficient quantities. The disorders which prevail there, perhaps sometimes encouraged by the fluctuating influences of international policy; and the economic pressure weighing upon this nation without a coast-line, have placed obstacles in the way of its progress. But such a rich country as this only needs peace and light to raise itself. The republics on its frontiers could contribute considerably towards this future greatness if they would set aside outworn ideas and encourage a general interchange of local products in conditions favourable to all.

The President of the Republic at that time was Señor Schaerer, a Paraguayan citizen of German origin, and the functions of Minister for Foreign Affairs were discharged by Dr. Manuel Gondra, who was afterwards drawn into some revolutionary adventure. Neither of the two seemed to command wide views in matters concerning the future of Latin America. Anxiety about a military coup, in internal politics, and, in external matters, a perennial anxiety caused by the neighbouring countries, were obviously the points on which the action of the government turned. It is understandable that the fundamental problems should present themselves in this form, in a republic torn by frequent insurrections and aggrieved at the memory of a hostile coalition. But even given this local character of their anxieties, the tactics with which they chose to face them betrayed a more limited view. Like some illnesses which can only be cured by the open air, certain evils can only be counteracted by widening our horizons and raising our ideals. Confinement only perpetuates the evil. Prudence merely aggravates the risk. And the very eagerness of the desire to live is often an obstacle to the healthy reactions of life. When it is only a question of remaining in power, a programme may be more useful than resistance. And besides the caution which leads them to dissimulate, this course of action serves in certain cases to preserve for the fatherland a higher conception, or a doctrine. I do not wish to imply by these words a criticism which only applies to Paraguay. The tendencies which we have emphasised are common to the majority of our republics. But in view of her situation in every aspect of life, Paraguay would profit more than any of them by widening her moral orbit. By universal suffrage, in order to make internal peace secure; and by Latin-American idealism, in order to consolidate her external position. A policy of egoism frequently only brings renunciation in its train, and it has been whispered that a counterpoise to weakness can only be found in rising to greater heights.

The Paraguayans are traditionally a hospitable people, and received the traveller with favour.[7]

The Press and the young men at the University took the opportunity to manifest sentiments in contrast with the cautiousness of

[7] "Our illustrious guest is one of those exponents of the energy, firmness, nobility, and high breeding of that stock to which we ought openly to prove that we belong, and for whose ideals we ought all to work."
El Diario, of La Asunción, October 6, 1913.

"Welcome to him! To him who with no petty interests comes to bring us to the fraternal embrace of other Americans, of other young peoples who like us aspire towards the ideal that the master is inculcating in our minds by word and pen. Welcome to him!"
El Liberal, of La Asunción, September 30, 1913.

"Seeing that he was accompanied by the mass of the students, he got out of his carriage, responding by this sympathetic act to the attentions of the young men. He went off towards his hotel surrounded by a dense crowd, and during this whole time enthusiastic cheers continued for Ugarte and the Argentine." *El Tiempo*, of La Asunción, October 1st 1913.

the Government. This implies no 'censure, but emphasises the fervent hope and patriotic instinct which leads the masses, from north to south, in all the sister republics, to long for a bolder policy than that practised by their rulers. A proof of this was the goodwill with which my lecture was received . . .[8]

The unanimous attitude of silence adopted by the authorities, and the unanimity of the masses in favour of action is a phenomenon as curious as it is inexplicable. The mass of the nations everywhere desires to depart from its inaction and begin to advance towards its destined end. The rulers persist in remaining mute and maintain a complete reserve. In the former movement we meet with a spontaneous instinct. In the latter, with a route based on prejudice. But if no clear reason exists for advocating such an attitude in the extreme north of Latin America, subject to the influence of neighbours and weighed down by past errors, still less ought we to find it in the extreme South where the influence of Europe and the interests of several nations offer an incomparable support to free evolution. However timid their inclinations may be, however cautious their presence—and it is not an indisputable axiom that fear is always the best quality for a statesman—it is obvious that no difficulty, friction, or conflict can ever arise from a policy which takes all factors into consideration, and by respecting all rights, tries to obtain the greatest benefits for the country.

I have never advocated carrying the din of controversy into

[8]"The theatre was too small to hold the enormous audience which thronged it, without finding room enough."
      El Nacional, of La Asunción, October 7, 1913.

"An immense audience which completely filled the premises, overflowed into the aisles and stood in a group at the entry to the hall. It listened to the words, at times calm and cold, steeped in irony and sympathy, at times vehement and warm, full of virility and fire, of this orator who has already won the devotion of Latin-America."
      El Diario, of La Asunción, October 7, 1913.

"He received an ovation at various points and at the end, which was more than deserved, for, apart from his facile and attractive words, he spoke the truth." *El Colorado*, of La Asunción, October 7, 1913.

"The trace which events of this sort left in the national soul, ought to serve as our guiding principle for ever."
      El Tiempo, of La Asunción, October 7, 1913.

ministerial quarters. In speaking before popular assemblies in my own name, I have simply underlined with red ink what diplomacy would naturally be compelled to present in a different form. But calm need not exclude firmness, and civility is no obstacle to forethought. The surprising and disconcerting thing about our diplomacy is not its immovable and courtier-like façade, but the absence of all considered plan, of all preliminary guiding principles; which means that this façade is at once the façade and what lies behind it. There is no line of conduct laid down either secretly or ostensibly, no graduated scale of aims, no way marked out for the nation to pursue through the contingencies of daily life.

Our international programme, like our financial one, is a continual improvisation. Just as, in the economic sphere, new debts are contracted in order to pay the interest on the old ones, and our views fail to embrace a general vision or a coherent plan for overcoming our difficulties one day; so, in the diplomatic sphere, little conflicts with our neighbours crowd upon one another, the activities of the great powers are repeatedly met with silence, and no guiding principle for the future ever appears. We live from hand to mouth, drifting at the mercy of the current, and do not perceive in the far distant years any light towards which we may guide the prows of our distracted ships. It is from this that the difference arises between the attitude of the peoples and that of the chancelleries. The masses, with their primitive instincts, are aware of a dynamic aim which contrasts with the uncertainty of suspense. It is for this reason that the divergency between the people and the rulers breaks out on every occasion, and for this reason I endeavour, as a member of this same public, to give a concrete expression to the general aspiration in this paragraph. Aloof from politics, on a plane superior to the heartburnings of city life, let us draw up a remonstrance from the continental point of view. What we need is a policy. A discrepancy of ideas which inclines some in one direction and some in another would be comprehensible. However mistaken it may be, the thesis is always the result of reflection. But what we cannot explain is indifference. Whither are the rulers of our countries leading us? What line of continuity are they pursuing? To what ideal do they aspire? These questions alone arise, before the confusion of a Latin America which does not put forth, either as a whole or piecemeal, any expression of will, or any plan of action in the diplomatic sphere.

If a coherent policy were announced to-morrow in the South, freed from narrow views and with an eye to the future, there is no doubt that Paraguay, like Bolivia, would second it with enthusiasm. I have always believed that this might be the *rôle* of the Argentine; and it was in this sense that I directed my propaganda on returning to my country. The less exclusive and direct are our actions, the greater will be our prestige and strength. The more we identify ourselves with the political doctrines of the revolution of 1810, the easier and the surer will be our action. We shall never be able to initiate any movement on a world scale if we have not previously developed an American plan of action. And to continue to ignore the favourable atmosphere which surrounds us in Latin America is an error which may have fatal consequences.

My journey had to end with a visit to Brazil. Although by its origin and history this republic has been continuously detached from the countries of Spanish origin; although it did not bow before the colonial rebellion of a century ago and although it has since organised itself on the basis of different political institutions, it must be considered as an integral part of our family of nations, as part of an ideal emanating from the Spanish peninsula, which rises superior to the influence of theory and is converted by geographical and international causes into a vital necessity. It is not a question of race, but of situation; it is not in the past, but in the realities of the moment, that we find, in the last resort, that supreme necessity which ought to make us include Brazil within the higher moral combination which we compose. It would be a still greater mistake to believe in the possibility of a partial Latin Americanism, which would drive the country isolated by it into developing a hostile policy, giving a handle to every intrigue. Brazil, a people of different origin and language, lying on the frontiers of all the South American republics, ought to be kept within the bounds of our grasp and treated like a brother within one great family.

Perhaps it is this peculiar position which has brought about its superior diplomatic capacity, or has given it a keener sense of what this activity ought to be. In the school of Rio Branco capable minds have been formed which handle without difficulty the complicated threads of a manifold, invisible, and sure activity, in matters concerning the relations of Brazil with the republics on its frontier. But its superior ability and foresight are less clear if we embrace a wider orbit and consider its policy from a world point of view.

Yielding to subtle suggestions, which perhaps went so far as to dangle before her the hegemony of the South Atlantic and vain of the preference shown her, for interested motives, which was directed towards perpetuating a chronic struggle between her and the Argentine—Brazil has frequently appeared to forget the higher problem of common stability in a policy of localising her activity and limiting her preoccupations to those territories which stretch to the south of the line of the Equator. Perhaps this attitude is due to those errors which we have pointed out. One reserve springs from another. But if we take a long view of the lasting interests of the Continent, Brazil has contributed to the confusion by fomenting a maritime rivalry, based on chimerical fleets, which are splendidly adapted to the destruction of each other in fratricidal conflict and the swelling of the revenues of the countries which build them, but are completely useless for defending the sovereignty, integrity, and destiny of South America against the strong powers. In the Atlantic, as in the Pacific, all thoughts of war have been governed by vanity and local considerations, with no appeal to patriotism in the wide sense. Brazil and the Argentine watch each other, vie with each other in the tonnage of their ships, calculate and cultivate whatever support they may obtain in case of a conflict. But while waiting for a clash which could not be justified by an opposition of interests, and while obsessed by a rivalry which is based on nothing but *amour propre*, they forget that their immensely lo.ig coasts lie at the mercy of powerful nations—who can with impunity at any moment, bring naval pressure to bear upon either of these two republics, or upon both at the same time, and that the cruisers bought in view of local conflicts could hardly put up any resistance worth speaking of. The vast maritime frontier extending on the ocean from Pernambuco to the southern ice-fields, comprising the coasts of Brazil, Uruguay, and the Argentine is absolutely undefended. The capitals lie open. There are no national railways which permit of transporting troops to regions which may be threatened. There are no munition-factories. And in case of a powerful attack, our sole resistance would have to be sustained, as in primitive times, by trusting to the factor of distance in the forests of the interior.

All our conceptions are based upon the idea of partial conflicts among ourselves, counting, in case of need, upon mercenary sources of supply from which to obtain ships, artillery, projectiles, all that maintains or feeds an armed struggle. We have never considered the hypothesis of a disagreement with those very nations which supply us, and would naturally begin by denying us everything necessary for defence. And this is a point which must make us anxious.

If we consider the position of these republics with regard to the great nations of the world, the situation is suggestive.

These vast, almost unpopulated territories are a temptation to peoples overflowing their boundaries. Our capacity for consumption, unsatisfied by local industries, may perhaps lay us open to foreign exactions. Our deposits of petroleum, mines, etc., even our wealth in stock and agriculture, have no protection against coercion in the rush to control the vital sources of power in the world. Our financial situation, which makes us debtors for considerable sums, gives a handle for interference and intervention. And the innumerable foreign enterprises established in our lands may at any given moment come to be a point of departure for insolent demands.

None of the southern republics has reached a stage of development which can impel it to widen its territories; force its products on others, or take possession of its neighbours' source of wealth. Their population is sparse, their industries have not yet begun to satisfy their own needs, and they lack the economic vigour which leads to expansion. Nor does that factor of dissension exist which may be created by debts or financial companies. There have been no loans or migrations of capital between them. So there are no causes which might reasonably give rise to conflicts among ourselves; and there are numerous considerations which should lead us to reconcile our interests in view of our common preservation.

On entering the marvellous bay of Rio de Janeiro, where Nature and the initiative of man have achieved an apotheosis of colour and beauty; on passing through the broad avenues and sumptuous gardens of the capital, the flourishing centre of the vastest country in Latin America, I was at once struck by the differences which separate Brazil from the Spanish-speaking republics—localised forms of culture, racial composition, a particularist conception. But over and above all these discrepancies there is a racial kinship, an identical type of mind, an atmosphere of past and future solidarity which insists on recognition. Nowhere did I notice that antagonism imagined by some elements. From the workmen's organisations to the highest classes I met with marks of sympathy, not only as the mouthpiece of a continental cause, but as an Argentino, a son of that country which is in some people's minds a probable enemy. The students received me at the university—the President of which was then Count Celsio—with cordial courtesy; a group of deputies, among whom I recall the names of Señores Nicanor Nascimento, Floriano de Brito and Raphael Pinheiro, offered me the banquet which is *de rigeur*. The intellectuals and noted journalists, such as José Verissimo and Luis Gómez played their part. And the whole Press found words of welcome for their guest.[9] The lecture organised by the University Federation took place in an atmosphere of approbation,[10] and there was no trace of aversion or reti-

[9] "Señor Manuel Ugarte is a mind of subtle keenness. As a man of letters his works command respect naturally, or rather by right; as a politician, his prestige is of a kind which establishes calm; as a propagandist, he has the fire of conviction and the high courage of a visionary."
                                        A Tribuna, September 10, 1913.

"The Socialist party desired lately to put forward his candidature as a Senator. It would be a triumphant candidature. But Señor Manuel Ugarte refused this offer, because as a patriot, he could not ask for the votes of a party which is trying to lower the Argentine cause. It was a fine gesture."
                                        Jornal do Comercio, August 27, 1913.

"Don Manuel Ugarte, who is at present our guest, is a figure of incontestable prominence in the political and intellectual world of the Argentine Republic. His literary capacity has been brilliantly displayed in books of great artistic merit and strongly-coloured style. As a politician he enjoys rare prestige for the vigour of his pen, which is always prepared to treat the most serious social questions, and by his incontrovertible gifts as an orator." *A Epoca*, August 29, 1913.

[10] "The great hall of the Palacio Monroe was completely crowded and the audience, largely composed of a great number of students of our upper schools, contained representatives of the highest classes in the country. There were also present diplomatic corps, lawyers, politicians, journalists,

cence. The Government offered official premises for the purpose, and Dr. Lauro Müller, the monosyllabic Chancellor, received me with courtesy.

Notwithstanding, the nation, as a whole, showed itself faithful to its traditions of friendship with the United States. This was emphasised by one of the papers on the day of my departure, and confirmed by a certain politician in commenting upon my declarations to a newspaper.[11] Pedro [sic for Eduardo] Prado, the author of *A Iluçao Americana,** who was to see his book confiscated and was himself persecuted for his hostility to the policy in favour, would perhaps meet with more tolerance to-day, but not with more support. It was Brazil who first raised the cry of "Qui vive?" in Latin America, by the mouth of this writer, but the public was afterwards less inclined to listen to it.

The chimerical dream of a hegemony of the Atlantic distorts their vision. And seldom has the general will been mobilised in view of a more illusory end. It is a mercantile marine, with its constant voyagings to and fro, which is the guaranty of the possession or

industrialists, bankers, etc., and all were carried away at times to applaud warmly the words of the orator, who, with the most perfect dialectics, the most harmonious tones of voice, and a deep historical knowledge of the matter he was treating, continued for two hours to engage the general attention." *Jornal do Brasil,* September 19, 1913.

"Several times Señor Manuel Ugarte was interrupted by enthusiastic applause, receiving a prolonged round of applause when he left the platform."
O Paiz, September 9, 1913.

[11] "Señor Ugarte, by his talent and qualities as a perfect gentleman, leaves in Brazilian society an agreeable memory, but his efforts as a propagandist against the United States were completely useless, for in Brazil we continue to think that Latin America, or non-Latin, is not for the peoples of this origin or that, but for all those who, by their work and collaboration, desire to contribute to the amazing prosperity and grandeur of the New World." *O Paiz,* of Rio de Janeiro, September 12, 1913.

"Brazil lives by exporting coffee and rubber, and North America buys two-thirds of both these products from us; while we only import from the United States 20 per cent of what we sell them. Let Señor Ugarte realise this. We ought to be able to make this request to a guest like Señor Ugarte, who is one of the most brilliant men of letters of America."
A Imprensa, of Rio de Janeiro, September 11, 1913.

*See Editor's introduction.

primacy of the ocean. When the case arises, this domination is asserted by means of cruisers. But the starting point lies in commercial routes and economic interests. Trade between Brazil and the Argentine is limited, and in the greater number of cases is carried on by means of ships foreign to both nations. As for the commerce between Europe and North America, we are all acquainted with the anomaly which lies in the fact that our republics, though essentially exporting countries, find themselves supplanted in transport by other peoples, and pay a heavy tribute in order to enable their produce to reach the consumer. The sea, like the earth, belongs to those who make it fruitful. And nothing can be more futile than to sigh for an outward show when we have not yet succeeded in achieving the essential effort of taking possession of the sea and assuring out of our own resources the means of communication in areas subject to our jurisdiction.

The Argentine, Brazil, and Uruguay will have in the future to become maritime powers. The length of their coast line, the dimensions of their ports and that tendency of their commercial life which directs their produce towards the sea—there being as yet not the slightest serious attempt at commerce on their land-frontier—will lead us to devote special attention to the problem of navigation. But we must start, in accordance with logic, at the beginning, by creating dockyards, founding a fishing industry, building up shipping-lines of our own between the different ports—trying, in fact, to compete with foreign shipping companies in order to lead our export trade to its destined end under our own flag.

Our local products actually pay, in addition to the heavy tithe taken by the international monopolists, or the intermediate enterprises such as the cold-storage companies, a ruinous tax to foreign fleets, and in the form of maritime insurance. As the standard of our life is gradually raised, and the evolution of these new countries gradually produces a real and lasting effect, we shall undoubtedly have to face reducing this expense and substituting mechanism of our own. Thus our future commercial fleets will have to be built up slowly, as part of a flourishing naval activity which has not yet occupied the attention of the younger peoples.

For the moment, the hegemony of the South Atlantic cannot belong either to the Argentine or Brazil. To achieve this end a few dozen cruisers or transports are quite insufficient. Even admitting that everything comes second to military strength, these elements, powerful as they may be in view of South American conditions, will always be inconsiderable in comparison with the formidable forces of the great powers. The South Atlantic virtually belongs to-day to England and the United States. It would be the greatest mistake for our republics to become unconscious pawns in the rivalry between powerful nations. All that foments antagonisms in South America ends by weakening us all, and producing a fundamental incapacity for facing the problems of the future as a harmonious whole. Since colonial times England has exercised considerable influence in these regions by means of her commercial fleet, backed up in certain cases by landing troops, by blockades, and even by lasting occupations of territory, as in the case of the Falklands. The strategic importance of these islands, which was brought into prominence during the late war, has apparently given rise to international negotiations directed towards a possible cession to the United States, in return for compensations which have not yet been fixed. The question is of such supreme importance, and touches such a valuable source of strength, that it must undoubtedly be considered with the greatest care.

Thus the existence of problems of a higher order, rising beyond the rivalries of prosperous and triumphant capitals, stands fully established. The hegemony of the South Atlantic cannot be ours for the present. But if the Argentine, Brazil, and Uruguay will interpret, in preference to the sentiments of their ports, the thought of the nations at the head of which these ports stand; and will then frame a well-thought-out policy of preservation, they will be able to exercise the most fruitful influence which has ever made itself felt in Latin America up to the present.

CHAPTER IX

THE TEST OF WAR

Roosevelt's "gesture"—Mexico Invaded—Exalted Effusions of the South—Fresh Invasion of Mexico—Carrizal—The Invasion of Santo Domingo—Suggestion by Cable—General Carranza—Philosophy of the Conflagration.

MR. THEODORE ROOSEVELT'S journey in November, 1913, once more drew attention to the mistakes of South American policy. The events in Panama, emphasised by the peremptory utterances of the impetuous statesman, were still fresh in men's memories. The invasion of Nicaragua and the subjection of this country, after a struggle in which the best patriots perished, had left the stain of blood upon men's consciences. Notwithstanding all this, no visitor to Buenos Aires had ever been met with such acclamations. He was received in solemn session by the Chamber of Senators. The forms of official etiquette were revolutionised in his honour. It is superfluous to recall the terms in which the cable announced this intelligence to the rest of the Continent, and the effect which they produced in the sister republics, confirming the uneasiness which one of the most important daily papers of Mexico expressed in indignant language.[1]

I am far from having any vain desire to draw attention to the political blunders which were made, still more from the petty vanity

[1] "Yes. Sadly it must be said. The three sister republics, three great Latin peoples which think as we do, which live by the same ideal, which nourish the same hopes, are ranging themselves beside the sworn enemies of our race on the American continent, abruptly breaking with old traditions of kinship and civilisation. The Argentine, Brazil, and Chile, in their *entente* with the United States, do not yet recognise the Government of Mexico. Let us not blame the people of these nations for this, but their governments, which undoubtedly distort and run counter to the wishes of public opinion. What will Manuel Ugarte say now?" *El País*, of Mexico, September 10, 1913.

which might lead the writer to lay claim to the merit of having seen what was coming. My desire is that if, to-morrow, those proceedings are examined which have jeopardised the future of a continent, the responsibility may not be thrown upon our peoples, whose intentions have always been excellent. It was not sterile protests and a hostile outcry that the situation demanded, but a coherent line of action, a well-concerted attitude towards events, a policy. Above and beyond those sporadic demonstrations which might appear amid the general action like strident echoes of the struggle, there floated a conception which was susceptible of various interpretations, but which formed an organic whole, arose from a logical point of view, and was crystallising at that moment into a possible course of action.

The war had not yet upset the balance of the world. France, England, and Germany were mighty powers which, at the height of their triumphant prosperity, and with no immediate anxieties of a political or economic order, were endeavouring to diffuse throughout the world their commerce, influence, and future. Economic conditions were far from being then what they are now. Gold and influence had not yet emigrated from the Old World to the New by way of New York. The United States had to reckon with the formidable counterbalancing weight of an organised Europe, productive of life. In these conditions a calm process of drawing together and mingling the kindred peoples of the Continent was perfectly feasible, using as the fulcrum of their lever the interests of the leading European nations. Those same local anxieties which provoked remonstrances, against Brazil in the Argentine and against Chile in Peru, would have become less serious as part of a higher system which should remove these problems from the sphere of immediate and local interests into an atmosphere universal and lasting. European commercial interests dominated the South so entirely that, quite apart from all theories, the vital instinct of their nation's traditions might be used as an instrument, not for acting in hostility to any people, but for restoring the balance between the races and the future destinies of this new section of humanity. The spirit of Latin Europe tended to find its continuation and spread itself more widely in those regions which drew their inspiration from its traditions. Moreover, its interest lay in creating a counterpoise to the power of the United States in the south.   The political views which in 1806 brought England to the Río de la Plata and in 1864 brought France and Austria into Mexico, were obviously mistaken ones.   But certain aspects of them might be turned to use in the field of commerce and diplomacy.   All that was necessary was to embrace a wider horizon, taking into account the whole age rather than the present hour, collective rather than partial interests.   The inmost tendencies of all the nations of our Latin America were in harmony with this aspiration, the economic advantage of the great industrial peoples would have found satisfaction in it, and all seemed propitious for starting on a new path and asserting a personal point of view, directed by an intelligent volition.   What I said in 1913 [2] is equally appropriate in 1923.   The activities of great masses of people are like a game of chess; they seem to be governed by certain regular laws; and, thanks to the inevitable march of history, we have lost our move.

The diplomacy of the A B C was agreed upon playing in Mexico the *rôle* which Mexico had played some years before in Central America.   In order to inspire confidence, and give an appearance of collective meditation to what was in reality nothing more nor less than a direct intervention, the United States had induced Mexico to associate herself with them [1907 ff.] in various Central American conflicts, and she was then proud of the active *rôle* which was granted her.   But the great Aztec nation knows how her good faith was rewarded, and what she lost in the adventure.   A similar procedure was afterwards adopted in Mexico.   The A B C took upon itself to minimise friction, to pave the way for action, and to act before the world as a shield for these manœuvres, without obtaining in exchange anything but the natural resentment of those who had been victimised.   For the distinguishing quality of this policy— for which imperialism, widening its scope of action, is now trying to find a prosperous sphere in Spain, so as to use the prestige of the parent nation to mask its general activities—is the vacillating loyalty of its attitudes, and, more than this, the painful nullity of its re-

[2] "Time will show that our duty and our interests counselled a policy absolutely opposed to that which we are following.   By the time everybody has realised this, it will perhaps be too late in the day."
—Interview in *La Tarde*, Buenos Aires, October 28, 1913.

sults. Neither Mexico in Central America, nor the A B C in Mexico, nor Spain to-morrow in Latin America, will obtain any advantage of a commercial, political or spiritual order. Any calculations of this sort that they may have made will simply be turned to derision, and will merely serve to make more sure the fate of those peoples or races which, instead of raising themselves by solidarity, are falling apart out of selfishness.

After Mr. Roosevelt's tour, as if to show just how far the general complaisance and disunion could go, a southward advance was set in motion.

On April 22, 1913 [sic for 1914] Rear-Admiral Fletcher's squadron appeared off Vera Cruz and took possession of the city, overcoming an improvised resistance in the course of which more than four hundred men, cadets of the Naval School, soldiers of the regular army, ordinary patriotic civilians, paid with their lives the price of an improvident, misdirected, and incapable policy. The country was surprised in the midst of its internal disorders, weakened by its long struggles, and thrown into anarchy by the time-honoured declaration that the landing of troops was directed against the Government and not against the people; but it none the less found the necessary strength for preparing that insurrection in the interior which modified the plans of the invader.

The impression produced in Buenos Aires by these events was a mixed one. The semi-official organs maintained an impassive front. Public opinion, on the other hand, broke out instinctively into a burst of condemnation. This unamimous impulse gave birth on that self-same day to the Pro-Mexico Committee, supported by the University Federation, and with a membership of close on ten thousand. Those who were present at the first meeting have surely not forgotten how significant it was. Many of those on the Committee have since held political office, such as Dr. Diego Luís Molinari, Under-secretary for Foreign Affairs in Señor Irigoyén's Government. Obdulio Siri, Minister for the Administration of the Provinces, etc. The generous impulse of the younger generations provoked in every quarter of Buenos Aires, and every city in the Argentine, a tumultuous movement which placed the government in a very difficult position. As President of the Committee, I was its spokesman to the government. The newspapers of the time give reports of the interviews and conferences to which the matter gave rise [3] and of the official resolution prohibiting all demonstrations. [4] It is just to give credit for the protest made by a part of the Press, *El Diario Español* among others, which, after recalling the complaisance with which demonstrations in favour of a Free Cuba were tolerated in the Argentine, thus wounding the sentiments of Spain, envisaged the problem in its general aspect. [5]

Congratulations arrived from Mexico. [6]

[3] "In the morning Manuel Ugarte was summoned by the Chief of the Police and waited on him at the Central Department, where he took part in a short conference with Señor Ugarte. This functionary hinted to Señor Ugarte, in the name of the Minister of the Interior, the advisability of suspending the demonstration.

"In the evening, at the request of the Minister of Foreign Affairs, Señor Ugarte paid a visit to the Chancellery, where he took part in a conference with Doctor Murature. The Minister requested him to give up the idea of holding the demonstration, since it would be inopportune at the present moment, when negotiations are being opened by the mediators."

La Prensa, of Buenos Aires, April 29, 1914.

[4] "The Minister of the Interior, through the agency of the department of the Chief of the Police, has communicated with the Pro-Mexico Committee, the President of which is Don Manuel Ugarte, who has decided not to authorise the demonstration projected as a tribute to the sister nation.

"The Minister of the Interior reserves the reasons which have induced him to take these prohibitive measures, reasons which belong to the sphere of public affairs, within the terms of reference of the conference held yesterday between Don Manuel Ugarte and the Minister of Foreign Affairs."

La Razón, of Buenos Aires, April 29, 1914.

[5] "Recently, when Ugarte returned from his continental tour, he desired to give a lecture in the Teatro Municipal. His application was refused and we are assured that powerful influences intervened to bring about the refusal. The people of Buenos Aires are now being denied the right to demonstrate to a sister country the sympathies which its attitude merits, by applauding it in the name of Latin-American fraternity. Undoubtedly the gentlemen who form the Argentine government, cajoled by the applause of the latest Yankee visitors, who have lavished such eulogies on them, are inclining towards the stronger side. This is a date which the people should take into consideration against the time when danger comes nearer."

Leading article in *El Diario Español*, of Buenos Aires, April 29, 1914.

[6] "*La Prensa*, Buenos Aires. The Association of Metropolitan Journalists of Mexico City fraternally begs you to convey to Manuel Ugarte our deep gratitude for his timely and courageous pro-Mexico campaign."

Mariano Cetallos, President, *Juan Seauterey*, Secretary.

The mediation which had been announced as an event which ought to check the protests, confined itself to discussing how far the invader was to be justified. I do not wish to multiply quotations, nor burden my phrase by uselessly citing authorities, but nothing would be easier than to find in the Mexican Press in 1914 and following years a hundred articles in which the action taken by the A B C is condemned and the bitterest irony poured out upon the subject of Latin-American fraternity. Instead of encouraging the injured country, the southern nations ended by sanctioning foreign intervention, as the author of this work had foretold in various interviews.[7]

I cast no doubt on the good faith of those who intervened in the negotiations, directly or indirectly. I bring no accusation either against individuals or governments. Though the vilest aims have been attributed to me, and even to my ideal, I take pride in recognising good intentions even in the midst of errors. I will even go further. The break-down which took place at this time was not one of conscience or capacity, but of system and policy. The sole manner of finding a solution of our difficulties lies in facing them. And the initial error lay in appearing unconscious of them, in feigning blindness, in refusing to take into consideration a general situation, a process of expansion, a historical phenomenon, in which the Mexican conflict was merely a sign, an accident, or a stage. The doctors considered the symptom without studying the illness which had caused it, and the remedy was so temporary that the scar reopened a year later.

The Pro-Mexico Committee, converted into a permanent Latin-American Association,[8] whose extensive programme embraced the

[7] *La Argentina*, of Buenos Aires, April 22, 1914; *La Mañana*, of Buenos Aires, April 23, 1914; *La Tarde*, of Buenos Aires, April 20, 1914; *La Argentina*, of Buenos Aires, April 23, 1914; *Giornale d'Italia*, of Buenos Aires, April 27, 1914.

[8] "The Pro-Mexico Committee, founded with the immediate aim of giving expression to that impulse of sympathy which binds us together with the sister republic, and drawing close the bonds which her painful situation only strengthens, cannot look upon its task as ended while foreign troops occupy the port of Vera Cruz, and while the international situation hangs upon the settlement of internal conflicts. But, in view of the fact that the Mexican conflagration has contributed towards drawing attention to the

problem in its ultimate essence, next undertook a work of patriotic propaganda, of *rapprochement*, of going back to our origins. Accordingly, we celebrated the anniversity of the founders of our nationality; we protested against an attempt of Commodore Rivadavia to hand over the petroleum to the Standard Oil Company; and thus, too, we celebrated the memory of Christopher Columbus for the first time in Buenos Aires on October 12, 1914.

In the midst of this activity, which aimed at creating a lofty sentiment, and should be at the same time Argentine and continental, we were surprised by the war.

While the conflagration was judged from a point of view all our own, without those peremptory influences which made themselves felt later, the general impression was merely one of stupour, of humanitarian feeling, perhaps even of pride that we should find peace all round us, while the great nations, which had so often reproached us with our chronic state of convulsion, were rending each other in a wholesale slaughter without precedent. But in this first impression, as yet untouched by propagandists, by telegrams, by the action of alien interests, and by the international pressure which became so frequent later, there already appeared the germ of that exalted fervour which led us to test events of this transcendental importance by a literary standard, a moral consciousness, and an appeal to the memory of what we had read. To judge the war in itself, as a social phenomenon, and glory in the fortuitous circumstance that seemed to place us out of reach of the scourge, was to give proof of an incomplete conception of the world import of a disturbance of

aims and methods of imperialist policy, in view of the visible connection between the events at present developing and those which some time ago had as their theatre Cuba, Porto Rico, Colombia, and Nicaragua, and in view of the inadmissible ambition which prompts the United States to pursue a plan of predominance and hegemony in the Gulf of Mexico and in the rest of Latin America, the Committee, without losing sight of the Mexican question, resolves to take measures for envisaging the problem in its widest bearings, by transforming itself into a permanent organisation, under the name of the Latin-American Association, able to make its activity felt at every place and time, so often as this is demanded by their sentiments of Latin-American fraternity, which are ever growing in strength." (From the Declaration of Principles.)

such vast magnitude, and of how imperative may be the necessities of the hour for a country. The scholastic spirit, the humanities, systems of philosophy, have never had any connection with international politics. And the naïve outlook which induced us to condemn proceedings independent of our will was as misleading as our idea that distance and abstention would keep us entirely protected from the cataclysm. What we really saw before us was a subversion of the whole order of things. It was a clash of forces which had broken out, and ethical principles—or an appearance of them—could only be used as auxiliary values at the service of these forces, in accord with what has happened in all the upheavals of history.

Forgetting that in international upheavals sentiment has no place, our point of view was from the beginning more literary than political. In harmony with our literary education, we gave a free rein to the most noble aspirations towards human perfectibility. Unfortunately, cataclysms do not take place in accordance with the ten commandments, nor are they weighed in the scale of justice. Belgium was the first victim. And the Latin-American Association summoned a meeting of protest at Prince George's Hall,[9] because it understood that in defending the rights of a small nation it was defending a principle to which the nations of Latin America will perhaps have to appeal to-morrow. It is enough to read the speech which I made on this occasion,[10] to measure the error of those who afterwards slandered me during the war by considering me pro-German. And if we wish to understand the undercurrents of diplomatic tendencies, it is enough to observe the contradiction between the facility with which permission to hold this assembly was obtained, and the absolute prohibition with which we had been met a few months before, when we wished to give expression to

[9] "In the hall was an enormous, enthusiastic crowd, thrilling with generous sentiments, which responded sympathetically to all the emotions which were transmitted to it, and even reflected them with double intensity. So great was the crowd that the police found themselves unavoidably compelled to close the doors leading to the theatre."

La Argentina, of Buenos Aires, June 20, 1915.

[10] *Mi campaña hispano-americana* (Cervantes Publishing Co., Barcelona, 1922), p. 183.

the same protest in favour of Mexico. If the principle of abstention in face of belligerent powers was to be defended in principle, it
would have been more reasonable to do so in a fearful world-
conflagration, which was gaining ground every minute, than in a
collision confined to two neighbouring countries. But, according to
the political conception of our rulers (and everything that is possible is "political"; the only discrepancy lies in the opinion as to what
these possibilities are worth), it was what was nearest at hand that
had to be sacrificed.

It was in this atmosphere that the second invasion of Mexico was
set in motion in August, 1915.* The pacific Wilson of the fourteen points and universal agreements judged the moment in which
the attention of the world was concentrated on Europe propitious
for pursuing in Mexico the same hypothetical bandits as Roosevelt
had pursued in Panama. Under the command of General Pershing,
who was afterwards to win fame in the Great War, the North
American troops advanced towards the south. Without giving any
notice to the authorities this time, I called a meeting on the Plaza
del Congreso, and before a gathering of more than 10,000 persons
I told the whole truth about the situation,[11] condemning, above
all, the fresh tendency to mediation which was beginning to be
talked about in the papers. The meeting was signalised by the

* Pershing did not actually invade Mexico until March, 1916.

[11] "The Latin-American Association recently organised of its own
accord a demonstration in honour of Belgium, on the simple report of a
possible annexation. How can we do otherwise now, when Mexico expresses
to us her anxiety and suffering, in the name of those sentiments of fraternity
which we share so intensely. A few days ago it was the letter of General
Carranza, head of the Constitutional armies, which revealed to our Government the invader's intentions, and begged the Argentine not to encourage
them by her support. Yesterday it was the impressive telegram of the
workmen's associations to the Socialists of the Argentine, in which they
accused imperialism of plotting the most blameworthy of intrigues. To-
day it is the young men up there who are addressing the young men here.
Authorities, working classes, university bodies,—it seems that all Mexico
has risen to her feet, to call to us from one end of the Continent to the
other: 'You must not take part in what is being prepared.' With what
justice can we support another intervention in Mexico, if she expresses her
will in such a definite manner?"
Fragment of a speech published in *La Argentina*, of Buenos Aires, August
23, 1915.

inevitable conflict [12] with the forces of authority, which brought me on the following day a police summons. [13]

As the movement was meeting with ever-increasing difficulties, we resolved to possess an organ of the Press. The funds with which we started our venture did not amount to 20,000 pesos, subscribed by half a dozen persons. *La Patria*, a daily evening paper, was to be neutral as regards the European War (we published nothing but the official *communiqués* of the opposing armies), but proposed to defend all that tended to give vigour to our nationality, develop our industrial advance, or create a consciousness of our own; and aimed at a union of the Latin republics of the Continent in the face of imperialism. Our desire was, in internal matters, a nationalist democracy, and in external matters an autonomous policy.

The moment was propitious for developing this programme. As the restriction of maritime communications had made our imports dwindle considerably, a movement was started for manufacturing inside the country the articles most in demand. With regard to external activities, the concentration of the forces of the world round

[12] "Once the speeches were over and the demonstration declared to be at an end, the audience, as a pacific demonstration, desired to accompany Don Manuel Ugarte to his house, not far from the Plaza del Congreso. When the demonstration reached the corner of the Plaza at the Calle de Rivadavia, it was stopped by the forces of the police corps, who ordered the column to disperse at once.

"As the head of the demonstration was trying to advance forward, in spite of the orders of the police, a detachment of mounted police began to back their horses into the crowd. This provoked cries of protest, rushes, and a greater insistence, on the part of the demonstrators, on accompanying Señor Ugarte. Violence was not long delayed. The police charged the crowd, pursuing them even on to the pavements.

"A numerous crowd, which had also assembled in the Calle Pozos between the Calles Victoria and Rivadavia, before Señor Ugarte's house, was also dispersed by force. Raúl Regueira, a student at the Colegio Nacional Avellaneda, was arrested and taken to the sixth police station, being afterwards set free at the petition of Señor Ugarte. Many persons visited our offices later on, to protest against the action taken by the police."
La Nación of Buenos Aires, August 23, 1915.

[13] "Police of the capital. Urgent. Be it known to Señor Ugarte, Calle Corrientes 2038, that he must present himself to-morrow at 10 A. M. at the office of the Chief of Police for reasons which will be made known to him."
F. Correas.

a single problem left us greater freedom of initiative within our own sphere.   In my judgment the Argentine might obtain more advantages than disadvantages from the strife, if she manœuvred in the same way as the United States, profiting by the opportunity to serve her own interests and raise her voice with more energy.   The warring nations required food, they desired to conciliate the sympathies of the neutrals, they avoided all unpleasantness with them. The opportunity could not be more favourable for reducing our external debt and opening up an era of diplomatic initiative.   The propaganda of our newspaper was in such harmony with the popular instinct, that a few days after its appearance, the police again dispersed demonstrators beneath our balconies.   *La Patria* protested against the capture of an Argentine ship by the English fleet, and the young men seconded it in its claim with the enthusiasm which the younger generation always brings to the defence of a patriotic ideal.   The inexplicable severity of the authorities gave greater backbone to the resistance.   But in reality, what could a group of University students do, amidst the conflicting currents of such great interests as were represented in Buenos Aires by the foreign colonies and the groups connected with them by material or spiritual bonds?   Was an effort of real, responsive Argentine feeling possible, in an atmosphere harassed by such powerful influences? The persistently colonial character of Latin America rose up still stronger under the influence of war.   Where were our conceptions, our interests, our ideals, our own life?   The nation was really divided into two parties, corresponding to two streams of European interest.   Men's consciousness was hypnotised by the full cablegrams of the Allied Powers, or by the mysterious wireless messages of the Central Empires; their hearts were torn between two enthusiasms, and no room was left for any conception of our own which might interpret the disquiet, the advantages, the pride, and the destiny of the nation.   The price to which paper rose at that time, and a combination of hostile interests, which went so far as to obstruct the sale of the paper, put an end to this attempt at a higher nationalism in four months' time.

This was the precise moment at which, as a result of the inexperience of an Argentine diplomatist accredited to La Paz, the endemic conflict with the Republic of Bolivia broke out afresh.

Dr. Dardo Rocha, founder of the city of La Plata, and the only Argentine minister who stated this question in its true terms in the years of 1895 and 1911, had laid down such clear guiding principles that the matter offered no difficulty except the limited capacity for understanding of those who had to transact it.   As I had commented on the incident in an article, inspired by the fraternal sentiment which ought to guide our activities in South America,[14] somebody mentioned my name to take the place of our representative, Señor Acuña, who had just left La Paz.   The idea met with a favourable reception.[15]   The semi-official organ of the Bolivian government spontaneously expressed its goodwill [16] and Dr. Dardo Rocha himself entered into negotiations with the Government in favour of my candidature.   But all this only gave occasion for once more making manifest the uncertainty of South American politics.

I had never sought public office.   On the contrary, I had refused to stand either as a deputy or a senator.   The tendency of my mind was never in the direction of discipline, but rather toward opposition, based on sincerity.   But it was a question of doing away with an

[14] "By her character and destiny the Argentine is obliged to show herself before the great nations to be as imperturbable and as sound as in the early ages of her history, and, before the nations who are less strong, to be as courteous and disinterested as when our ancestors went about the Continent striking blows for liberty."

—Leading article in *La Patria*, January 25, 1916.

[15] "La Paz, February 5: The rumour as to the probable nominating of Señor Manuel Ugarte for a special mission has been received with joy in Bolivia."—*La Razón*, Buenos Aires, February 3, 1916.

[16] "A telegram which we have just received from Buenos Aires brings us the pleasant intelligence that it is probable that the distinguished man of letters and world-famous writer, Manuel Ugarte, may be nominated as Envoy Extraordinary and Minister Plenipotentiary to Bolivia.

"The Argentine Government could not make a fitter choice, in view of the great prestige which this noted personage enjoys here, and the deep sympathy and affection which are professed for him in Bolivia, and very particularly in La Paz, where he is personally known and sincerely esteemed.

"His honourable nomination as representative of the Argentine would be received with pleasure and true sympathy by the Government and people of Bolivia, and would be all the more opportune, if we consider that Manuel Ugarte is the most genuine representative of the lofty ideals of peace, justice and American fraternity, to which we all aspire in this Continent."

—Leading article in *El Diario*, of La Paz, February 2, 1916.

archaic phantasm, which for half a century has broken the harmony between the two peoples. Profiting by a suitable opportunity, I had demonstrated my agreement with the atmosphere which had been created. But the Minister of Foreign Affairs, while observing the sincerest courtesy, recalled my Latin campaigns and declared to me that the nomination was impossible. Hence arose an exchange of letters which have not been published, and some vexatious echoes in the Press of the Continent.[17]   The Bolivian papers held forth on the incident, a minister was appointed who, as usual, could not stand the climate of La Paz after a few weeks, and the original conflict, in spite of the lapse of so many years, is still likely to cause further convulsions.

The tragic episodes of the European War exercised such an absorbing fascination, that almost everybody had forgotten the presence of an invading army on Mexican soil. The slightest fluctuations of the line of trenches separating the European belligerents were followed on the map with little flags, but nobody in Buenos Aires knew how affairs went in the State of Chihuahua, still less at Carrizal, where on June 21, 1916, the engagement between the Mexican patriots and the North American troops of occupation took place.[18]   When the latter began to retreat, our Association held an-

---

[17] "Buenos Aires, March 12. I have learnt from a perfectly trustworthy source that the Argentine Government abstained from nominating Manuel Ugarte as its Minister Plenipotentiary in Bolivia, for the reason that he is an open enemy of the external policy pursued by the Government of the United States with regard to the countries of Latin America."
La Tribuna Popular, Montevideo, March 12, 1916.

[18] The North American troops had reached the immediate neighbourhood of Naquimipa, and as they were contemplating a further advance, General Treviño, leader of the operations in Chihuahua, consulted President Carranza. The order was categorical. If they attempt to continue the advance, it must be stopped. On the morning of June 21, General Félix Gómez received intelligence that a strong detachment commanded by Captain J. Moore was trying to seize the line of the Central railway. He went out to meet the invaders, made his dispositions for defence, and, in order to avoid shedding blood unnecessarily, advanced followed only by his Texan orderly and interpreter, H. L. Spilliburg. He proposed that the advance should be checked. Moore answered that he would continue his march in spite of all. General Gómez and his orderly fell dead. But the second in

other public meeting [19] and new telegrams of gratitude arrived from Mexico.[20]

But the significance of Carrizal goes beyond that of a little skirmish in the War. The battle, which lasted two hours and engaged only a few hundred men, had only a relative importance from the military point of view, but it marked the first time since 1848 that our Latin America had spoken out effectively against that gradual

command of the Mexican column, Colonel Rivas, gave the signal for an attack, and routed the North American troops, killing a large number, and taking seventeen prisoners, fifteen of them men of colour. They also seized all the stores and munitions. General Obregón, now President, and at that time Minister of War, sent the following message in reply to General Treviño's report:

"I congratulate you on your success in carrying out the orders you had received not to allow the North American forces to make further incursions into the south, east, and west of the place where they are at present. I learn with grief, and almost with envy, of the death of General Félix Gómez, to whom fell the glory of forming the vanguard of those whom we are ready to sacrifice in the defence of our national dignity. The prisoners must be sent to Chihuahua. I have communicated your report to our citizen president"—*Obregón*.

[19] "The meeting was announced for nine o'clock, but half an hour before this time the capacious hall, and the vestibule and corridors of the same were completely filled by the public." *La Prensa*, Buenos Aires, June 27, 1916.

"Señor Ugarte was warmly applauded by the public, which listened with obvious interest and visible emotion to his long speech. At the end the meeting approved by acclamation the sending of the following telegram to the people of Mexico: 'Enthusiastic public meeting is at one with the cause of the valiant Mexican people.'" *La Nación*, Buenos Aires, June 27, 1916.

[20] "Washington, June 21, 1916. Two representatives of the organised labour movement of Mexico, we are going to the Argentine to second your campaign against the North American imperialist policy now displayed with effrontery." —*C. Loveira* and *B. Pagués*.

"Mexico, June 30, 1916. Your cable gives me satisfaction. The Mexican people in defending its sovereignty is also defending that of the Latin-American peoples. Greeting." *Venustiano Carranza*, President of the Republic.

"Mexico, July 11, 1916. Have sent you two cablegrams. Yesterday was celebrated with pomp the Centenary of Argentine Independence. Sumptuous procession combining intellectual and labour elements. Speeches before the Argentine and Venezuelan Consulates. I will send you by post the

invasion which was crushing her resistance little by little. It was the first shot fired at that uniform which seemed to have the privilege of going about in neighbouring countries as if frontiers and autonomy had been abolished. It was not a handful of soldiers who fell at Carrizal, but the superstitious respect surrounding the agents of imperialism. What all the presidents of Latin America had not dared to attempt by means of peaceful diplomacy was effected, rifle in hand, by a mere colonel, and those tragic penalties which our governments allude to whenever they are opposed, did not make themselves felt in any form. The invading army gathered up its dead and retired from the country. But does this mean that one bloody fray is enough to change our destiny? Must we deduce as a conclusion, that a military effort can save us?

Nothing would be more puerile than to suppose that imperialism timidly gave up the struggle. It would have been easy for the United States to pour 200,000 men over the frontier, and reach the capital in a fortnight. Why did they not do so? To Latin-American ideas it would have been by no means a brilliant feat. We should have gone on, appealing to military honour and all our principles. The psychology of the great nation in the North is different. Faced with the resistance which seemed probable, involving a series of ambushes and interminable guerilla warfare in the mountains, it calculated the advantages and disadvantages, stated the problem in practical terms, taking into account the circumstances of the moment, the sacrifices demanded by the enterprise, the benefits which it might bring them, and the possibility of achieving the same end by other means. With regard to its timeliness, the events which were revolutionising Europe obliged the United States to reserve all their strength for a decisive intervention, which was already appearing before the mind's eye of their clear-sighted rulers. As regards the cost of the enterprise and the effort which it would be necessary to put forth, an expert general drew up a statement of the subject with figures. As to the possible benefits, they appeared insufficient compared to the risks.

address of General Candido Aquilar, Minister of Foreign Affairs, which he pronounced at the Argentine Consulate. Fraternal salutations."

Juan B. Delgado, Head of Information.

The mental balance, the sense of reality, the most obvious characteristics of this people, declined the adventure. The favourite plan of Germany was to immobilise the United States by means of Mexico. A reflected light from Europe played upon the frontier. And besides, given the mentality of the age, was the effort useful or necessary? From the economic point of view, did not the United States hold the future of the country in their hands?

For the same formidable conflagration as was devastating the world was proving axiomatically that coal, petroleum, food-stuffs, capital, the organisation of the forces of peace, were stronger than artillery, even in battle. Even the final outcome of the war has since come to prove to us that military victory is a formula superseded by the evolution of humanity. What used formerly to be a conclusive fact is to-day only a relative fact, dependent upon supplementary phenomena of industrial and commercial activity, upon diplomatic schemes, upon forces derived neither from strategy nor strength. A new imperialism, based on firm premises, could not let itself be frustrated by impetuous actions contrary to its very principles. Hence the retreat from which the Mexicans could not really draw any ulterior advantage, however noble and convincing might be their action. It was only by making their effort general and extending it equally into every department; it was only by mobilising, step by step with their warlike impulse, the country's potentialities in production and thought; it was only by making the spirit of resistance wide enough to include the field of commerce and ideas, that their passing advantage might have borne fruit. To sum up in a phrase, we may say that Carrizal was an effort, but not a realisation; by which we do not of course undervalue either the personal heroism of those who fought, or the still greater moral heroism of those who took responsibility for action.

All this naturally passed unnoticed amid the din which deafened men's consciousness. The attention of our cities was absorbed so entirely by the European tragedy, that all things seemed futile which did not reflect the anxiety of the crowds, which ran through the streets, hoarse with shouting for one side or against the other, carried away by the whirl of other interests. The conviction that this war was to make an end of violence in the world robbed the

real conflict of its significance. It was only a question of time. If
we waited a few months, everything on this planet would fall into
harmony with the strictest standard of equity. Why trouble
about what was going on in Mexico, if the mere solution of the
conflict between the Allies and the Central Empires was bound
automatically to remove all difficulties? I can still see the smile
of pity with which some people listened to my objections. "You
have no broad vision," they said; "the little injustices of Latin
America are part of the universal injustice which is being liquidated."

No case of collective hypnotism has been known in history such as
that brought about in our republic by the propaganda of the
agencies. Those few of us who refused to swallow whole the guiding principles which were transmitted to us, and tried to focus events
from the point of view of Latin-American interests, were heaped
with insults. I cast no doubts upon the sincerity of those who were
the servants of these passions, though there were not wanting those
who took advantage of the turmoil to exert an ephemeral influence.
It was so easy to let oneself be carried away by the stream! But
the immense majority was influenced by a saner impulse. And it
is precisely this which strengthens our objection. If the enthusiasm
and combative spirit which found expression in favour of general
ideas or the claims of countries alien to our group had been placed
at the service of our Latin-American cause, at a moment when all
the forces of reaction were absorbed by anxiety for their own interests, our republics would be in a very different position to-day.
Seizing the opportunity offered by the crisis, our Spanish continent
could have balanced its finances, created industries, and recovered
its free will in international movements. Timidity and routine
were opposed to this. We were consistent in our dependence, even
at the moment in which, owing to the force of circumstances, our
dependence was ceasing to exist. Formerly, when a galley sank,
the galley-slaves profited by it to escape. To-day, when a prison is
on fire, the prisoners escape by the windows. We behaved like a
dog tied to a weak branch. We were held by the superstition that
we were bound to be obedient, rather than by our chain. And so
thousands and thousands of Latin Americans left Cuba, Panama,
and Porto Rico to go and be killed anonymously under the flag of

the United States,[21] for the greater glory of that country, while imperialism was landing its troops in Santo Domingo and establishing the domination which has lasted till to-day. Was not this contradiction the greatest proof of the confusion and anarchy of the continent?

On May 14, 1916, the pacific President Wilson, acclaimed by the world for his declarations in favour of the right of peoples to self-determination, sent a squadron to Santo Domingo, with the task of establishing order in the little republic. The antecedents of this operation are explained in an article by Tulio M. Cestero,[22] in the Memorial of Protest addressed to the Ambassadors of the Argentine, Brazil, and Chile by the members of the Academia Colombina,[23] and in the book, quoted above, by Isidro Fabela.[24] This is not the moment to pass judgment again on this new imperialist adventure. The important thing to emphasise, within the limits of the present chapter, is the silence maintained by Latin America. With the exception of a few Cuban papers, in which the Minister for Santo Domingo, Don Manuel Morillo, succeeded in giving expression to his wounded patriotism, not a voice was raised against this violence. And yet the official newspaper of the weak republic [25] was filled with the echoes of the nominations and dismissals of civil servants decreed by Mr. H. S. Knapp, "Captain U. S. Navy, Commanding Cruiser *Force*, U. S. Atlantic Fleet, Commanding Forces in Occupation in Santo Domingo," as he was called, in accordance with the Anglo-Saxon cult of brevity.

Even the questions asked in the United States Congress as a result of outrages committed in the island by the troops of occupation, found no echo in Latin America. In the Memoirs which I am writing tranquilly in my retirement I shall have details to give about these and other incidents, conscious of the contribution which they may make towards a knowledge of the true situation; and I shall be able to include letters and photographs of documents which will throw

[21] The island of Porto Rico alone gave the United States 14,000 soldiers according to *L'Action Française* (June 6, 1922) and the *Revue de L'Amerique Latine* (July, 1922).
[22] *Reforma Social*, of New York, December 1916.
[23] *Listin Diario* Printing Co., Santo Domingo, 1916.
[24] *Los Estados Unidos contra la libertad*, p. 220 ff.
[25] *Gaceta Oficial*, Santo Domingo, January 17 and February 21, 1917.

a flood of light upon some things which seem inexplicable. The patriotic and popular character of my campaign brought me, not only hatred, but at the same time the silent collaboration of some of the very persons who were concerned in these doings; and all this must come to light, when, going beyond our own lives, we can think of establishing lasting truths.

The *Protest* of the Latin-American Association on this occasion, as well as the message which we sent to the Chancellor of Brazil,[26] and the study which I published on the philosophy of the war,[27]

---

[26] "The University Federation, the central organisation of the Students' Societies of the Argentine, an institution founded with the aim of drawing close the bonds between the kindred republics of Latin America, have the honour to present their best greetings of welcome to the honourable representative of the Brazilian people.

"The profound satisfaction with which we were present at that interview between the Chancellors which marks a date memorable in our campaign of *rapprochement*, induces us to request your Excellency to take advantage of the healthy atmosphere of brotherhood, and at the same time make manifest the noble aims of the A. B. C. so as to devise, in company of H. E. the Minister of Foreign Relations of the Argentine, to whom we are making the same petition, the best means of effecting the remission of the debt and the return of the trophies of war to the Republic of Paraguay.

"This friendly act, which will not need to be initiated, since it is an old aspiration of the Argentine and Brazilian peoples, after a war of such peculiar character that it left no rancour behind it, will contribute towards strengthening the mutual confidence between all the Republics of our America." *Manuel Ugarte*, President of the Latin American Association, *Osvaldo Loudet*, President of the University Federation, *Luis Curutchet*, Secretary of the University Federation, *Bartolomé Zaneta*, Secretary of the Latin American Association.

[27] In this study, published in *La Nación* of Buenos Aires. May 16 and 20, 1916, and entitled "The Decline of Socialism and the European War," I said: "Just as the 16th century was the age of religious controversies, and the 18th century that of political controversies, the age in which we live will be that of international controversies. All other preoccupations will be unlistened to and sacrificed, because the new dominating influences and the displacements produced by the modifications of the map since the end of the war, will keep the nations in a constant state of disquiet and disturbance. The repeated annexations, reconstructions, and federations which will reduce the number of existing autonomous entities will confer greater comprehensiveness and tenacity upon indestructible rivalries. With this will coincide an alarming economic expansion; and as it is a well-known thing that in order virtually to dominate a country it is sufficient to gain control of

were so far removed from the prevailing interests that they appeared the result of an unseasonable persistence. An attempt to form a popular committee, with the aim of taking advantage of the circumstances to create a strong national atmosphere,[28] met with the same fate. The only horizon was that of the war, and everything moving in any other orbit was outside human interests.

The impressive argument of defending France and preserving certain financial mechanism, there will begin a silent and desperate resistance by the weak, bent upon preventing the seizure of their forces, in order that their real autonomy may not disappear, leaving nothing standing but a paltry paste-board nationality. Amid the conflicts provoked by this essential activity, directed towards avoiding vassalage and maintaining the integrity of groups, a new conception of politics will arise; and it is superfluous to say that of the above-mentioned ideals of youth, nothing will remain but the tendency to the entire democratisation of life; not in the name of remote ideals, but in the name of immediate interests; not only to show a respect for justice, but to arrive at one of the conditions of general greatness."

[28] Its programme contained the following "Proportional representation of minorities. Protection and fostering of national industries to prepare for the economic emancipation of the country. Reforms in education, directed towards shortening the period of elementary studies. extending professional instruction, creating schools for all children and drawing up a comprehensive scheme of Argentine education, in accordance with our character and needs. Cheapening of railway services, and resolute action of the state to make its influence felt on the Companies. To cultivate especially relations with neighbouring republics, development and protection of the mineral and forest wealth of the country, especially fuel, and their exploitation by the state. Regulation of relations between farmers and land-owners and the establishment of agricultural colonies with the object of combating the system of large estates and bringing about a dividing-up of the land. Tax on the full value of landed property, simplification of the system of taxation, progressive imposition of taxes on consumption. Elimination of the obstacles which hinder the growth of a national mercantile marine. Progressive conversion of foreign debt by means of internal loans. Extension of the benefits of the laws on pensions and retiring allowances already voted, to those bodies not already enjoying this privilege. Law of security of tenure for public officials. To combat monopolies and strive by all means to cheapen articles of consumption, especially those native to the country and abundant in it. To study the problem of unemployment and take measures so that every able-bodied man may have the opportunity of earning a living. To foment in every way patriotism, a feeling of national responsibility, political purity and the reforming and creative impulse which ought to make the greatness of the Argentine."

Latin civilisation was put forward with such great success, that the true lines of the conflict disappeared, and everything was reduced to a struggle between idealism and darkness. We were all in favour of France. Every fibre of our being thrilled unanimously with the cult of a tradition and thought which have had such a powerful influence in the development of Latin-American life. I was and am passionately attached to the great fatherland, where I spent a large part of my youth, and where I acquired precisely that knowledge which enabled me to develop my anti-imperialist campaign. But the terms of the problem were different.

Although France was the theatre of the war, the opposing interests were of a more general order, and France herself, in defending her immediate interests, was drawn into the orbit of more complicated plans, as has been proved by the painful liquidation of the war. The wars of antiquity were limited to a shock of battle; modern wars take on the form of a game of chess. The attack on a sector is not a final aim: it marks an episode in the action. And just as Belgium was a stage on the way to France, so the latter might turn out to be the victim in a war between the German and Anglo-Saxon world. It is obvious that France, like Belgium, was defending her invaded territory, and could not do otherwise. But it is in the sum of its consequences that we have to seek the foundations of a policy, which, as it developed, gradually disclosed its strategems and revealed its objectives. England fooled Europe; and the United States, by coming in at the last moment, fooled England. The two branches of the Anglo-Saxon race divided the ultimate pre-eminence, and Latin America, by romantically supporting the Allies, was really serving, not France, whose sufferings were advertised in order to gain proselytes, but the ultimate hegemony of those very forces which had always been a menace to her. The present situation proclaims this aloud. And so our enthusiasm was due to suggestion by cable, which dazzled us like a blaze.

In view of the prospects which were opening out, and that necessity which has at all times caused politics to be regulated by interests and not by sympathies, some of us thought that the important thing was to adopt a line of action devoted exclusively to preserving the development and survival of our republics in the midst of the tempest. Had not the moment arrived to take advantage of our breathing-space, and recover the free disposal of our movements in the sphere of diplomacy? Peóples have ·always drawn near to or away from each other in history according to the identity or the opposition between their interests. And it was in the name of the latter that we had to adopt a fighting attitude during the hurricane.

During those days I received from the Mexican Minister accredited to Buenos Aires a note of thanks,[29] and soon afterwards an invitation from the University of Mexico to go and hold a series of lectures at that centre of studies.

In the circumstances, this visit was bound to give rise to the usual manœüvres. It was semi-officially communicated to the Mexican Minister that the Argentine viewed this overture with satisfaction, but that the present writer was not a suitable person to go to that country. There were intellectuals of higher merit who would play a far more brilliant rôle. The Mexican Minister maintained his position, and emphasised it by offering a farewell banquet to the recipient of the invitation, at which were present the Spanish Ambassador, the Portuguese Minister, and all the Latin-American Ministers accredited to the country, but which the Argentine Secretary and Under-Secretary for Foreign Affairs excused themselves from attending. Once placed on this footing my departure was sure to bristle with difficulties. Owing to the insecurity of communications on the Atlantic, I adopted the route by Chile and Panama, touching at Havana. But the chief obstacles were not in the matter of transport, but in the obstacles of a moral order which were placed in the way of carrying out the plan. Before leaving, I made a call upon the Rector of the University of Buenos Aires, who de-

[29] "Mexican Legation, Buenos Aires, December 11, 1916: General C. Aguilar, Secretary for Foreign Affairs to the Government of my country, has sent me the note which I have the great pleasure of copying as follows: 'By your favour dated August 15 last, No. 6, Register 6, I am informed of what you are so good as to make known to me with regard to the fact that the distinguished Argentine writer Don Manuel Ugarte, owing to the difficulties which had arisen between our Government and the United States of America, organised a popular demonstration in favour of Mexico. Kindly express to Señor Ugarte the sincere thanks and personal sympathy of the Constitutionist government for his labours in favour of the union of the race.'

" 'To the thanks of the Mexican Government I beg you to be so good as to add the expression of my own gratitude,' etc."

clined my offer to carry a message from one University to the other, adding that in his opinion, imperialism need not trouble the Argentine. The President of the Republic, whom I asked for an audience, could not receive me. And all was prudence around the free lance who, in the general operations of Latin America, was going to risk himself in a position that had been abandoned.

On arriving in Chile I was questioned by journalists, and explained in various interviews [30] the causes of my journey. We formed a distant entity and ought to have a policy of our own. At a time when the war was modifying world views and unfamiliar problems were emerging, it was more urgent than ever to draw close the bonds between the kindred nations of the New World. We should have to set aside those ideological tendencies which had hitherto predominated, in order to contemplate the possible course of our diplomacy with a true sense of realities, disentangling it from prevailing influences, and giving it a motive force of its own. Such was the general tone of the declarations for which I was afterwards blamed by some people. As regards the war itself, I did not hide the fact that the intervention of the United States involved a special problem for our republics, which could not be solved by our sympathies for this or that European country, but by a direct examination of what suited us, from the point of view of our Continent.

General Carranza's government was at that time making a special epoch in Latin-American policy. For the first time one of our republics was confronting imperialism and addressing it on equal terms. Still soaked with the blood of the last encounter, with the vision of the retreat fresh in her memory, the weaker country met all insinuations with a calm tone, full of energy and at times of good humour. Some of their answers had their moment of celebrity, such as that in which General Aguilar, on the occasion of a protest made by England through the agency of the United States, deplored the fact that owing to the lack of a sufficient naval force on the Mexican coast he could not give satisfaction to the request formulated, that he would check the operations of German submarines; and sug-

[30] *El Mercurio*, of Santiago, February 14, 1917.
La Nación, of Santiago, February 14, 1917.
La Opinión, of Santiago, February 16, 1917.
La Unión, of Santiago, February 17, 1917.

gested the idea that it might perhaps be better to avoid further unfortunate incidents, by preventing these submarines from issuing from their naval bases in Europe.

Carranza was the classic type of the South American General of the good old days; frank, calm, and paternal. Possessed by a fanatical instinct of patriotism, and an innate courage, he exercised a steady influence over those around him. He received me without any elaborate etiquette, and during the audience, which lasted for an hour and a half, he spoke of joint resistance, and of wide ideals, as no other president had ever done before me.

"In view of the general circumstances, and given the peculiar position of Mexico," I asked him, "would a full expression of the truth be harmful to the policy of this country?"

"Explain whatever you consider necessary," he answered after a moment's reflection, "and be sure that nothing you can ever say against imperialism will go beyond what I think."

Afterwards, in speaking of the steps which were taken to prevent my departure, he referred to his conversation with the United States Minister. The diplomatist had appealed to the relations which were beginning to be re-established between the two nations since the retirement of the troops of occupation, and complained of the slight implied in the attentions shown a man known to be hostile to the Minister's country.

"It is an invitation from the University," answered Carranza— "and in Mexico, as in the United States, the Universities are self-governing. I cannot take any measures for preventing the writer who is visiting us from landing on our coasts. But if the United States are interested in preventing his arrival, it is within their power to stop his passing through Panama."

And the old patriot smiled, stroking his long white beard.

"I further pointed out to the Minister," he added, "that supposing I had been able to prevent a man from entering the country for having spoken against the policy of the neighbouring nation, I should have had to request reciprocal action; since there are many who speak against Mexico and its Government in the United States."

A few days later I was received by the Minister of Foreign Affairs.

"You cannot imagine," confessed General Aguilar, "the difficulties we have had to conquer in order that you could come to Mexico. To complete what the President has told you, I will say that the representative of the Argentine called on me in person to hint to me that you had no official standing, so that if you were expelled from the country, he, as a diplomatist, would not formulate the slightest protest."

The burst of feeling with which the traveller was received on landing at Vera Cruz,[31] as he passed through Orizaba,[32] and on his arrival at the capital,[33] accentuated by the fêtes organised by the students, for whom he was the bearer of messages from the universities of the Argentine and Chile, did not prevent the fact that, owing to influences which had nothing to do with the Government, the first lecture took place in too small a hall, and had consequently to be postponed [34] till it could be held a few days later in a theatre.[35]

[31] "The Confederation of Labour Syndicates invites generally all the working classes, especially the syndicated groups, to make a demonstration of affection and sympathy towards the protagonist of the ideals of Latin-American union." *El Dictamen*, of Vera Cruz, April 8, 1917.

[32] "The poet came forth amid five thousand persons, eager to welcome the representative of the sister nation. From the station to the Hotel Diligencias, he walked through a numerous crowd, who never ceased applauding and cheering our nation and our race."

El Pueblo, of Mexico, April 16, 1917.

[33] "When the whistle of the engine was heard in the distance a general thrill was felt going through this flood of humanity, as if it desired to overflow with enthusiasm in order to express its intense sympathy for the traveller." *Excelsior*, of Mexico, April 12, 1917.

[34] "Ugarte's lecture, announced for last night, could not take place, owing to the great crowd which rushed the hall of the School of Engineers, the place set apart for this event. The hall was so crowded by half past six that they thought of holding it in the courtyard, but this had also to be given up." *El Democrata*, of Mexico, May 10, 1917.

[35] "Ugarte spoke for an hour and a half, and though most of his lecture was spoken calmly, there were sentences in which his words were marked by a deep and sincere exaltation, producing a profound sensation which at the end expressed itself in thunderous and vehement applause."

Excelsior of Mexico, May 13, 1917.

"When the lecturer concluded, prolonged and vibrant applause broke out from the audience, carrying on the former thunderous acclamations, applause which was repeated when he left the theatre, accompanied by the members of the National University who were present."

El Universal, of Mexico, May 13, 1917.

A short review of the evolution of our diplomacy and of the exigencies of the moment was of course in no way likely to annoy any country. I have since included this lecture in my book, *Mi campaña hispano-americana*, and published it broadcast without meeting with any objection. Notwithstanding, a sharp protest was uttered at that time by those who were obsessed by the European problem. The second lecture accentuated the impression of the first, and the rector of the University, Señor Macias, had to issue a statement that these functions, which took place in a theatre, had no official character. A similar incident occurred with regard to a Mexican flag which the University Federation of Mexico desired to send to that of Buenos Aires. The women students of the colleges had embroidered it, and ceremony of presentation took place;[36] but on the pretext of one detail which was missing, the flag remained at the University, and was never handed over to me. The noble intention of the young people was frustrated by underhand manœuvres, and the symbol of an honourable trust offered by the younger generations at one end of the Continent to those at the other was reduced to a bold attempt, which was checked in its course of petty timidity.

The pressure brought to bear upon Mexico at that time was so formidable that only the iron will of that people could have withstood it. But what weighed particularly heavily on this republic was, not only the insistence of her all-powerful neighbour, but the general exigencies of Europe, which in obedience to its interests, was trying to heap every inflammable element on to the fire. Particular advantage of this was taken by imperialism. But the resistance was stubborn; and the tripod of Latin America, whose apex was in Mexico, while its base lay in the parallel attitude of the Argentine and Chile, was maintained upright.

[36] "It was a sentiment of solid Latin-American fraternity which led our students to place our national ensign in the hands of Manuel Ugarte. The students desired to remain closely united with the youth of the Argentine by the bond which holds the greatest symbolic force and has the greatest significance, namely our nationality. And it was a sight worth seeing to see the apostle of the doctrine of union between the Latin peoples of America raise our flag reverently after kissing it with respect. The students, electrified by this action, broke out into cheers for the Argentine and the youth of the sister country." *El Democrata*, June 6, 1917.

When I set sail southwards again from Salina Cruz, after visiting the cities of Puebla and Guadalajara, I felt more oppressively than ever the atmosphere of watchfulness and intrigue surrounding me. I was the victim of two robberies in the course of five days, between my departure from the capital and my arrival on board. The thieves had made a specialty of papers. The first time they took my writing case, and the second time, a big packet of letters which I carried in my overcoat. I had, of course, no secrets to hide. Nothing could have been more transparently open than the campaign I had undertaken. But the Mexican invitation, added to the persistence of my efforts, made them perhaps suppose that an invisible hand was pulling the wires. When I arrived in Chile, a third theft confirmed my view that they were part of a system. But this time it was cunningly carried out, in such a way as to make me appear the victim of a pretended theft when I reported the matter to the authorities. The reality of the offence was afterwards proved beyond all doubt. But some effect is always made by such an accusation, even when it is withdrawn.

A North American squadron was at this moment cruising in the South Atlantic, and was received with great pomp in all the ports. Brazil and Uruguay, as belligerent nations—for they had declared war on Germany—were performing a natural action in fêting an ally. But the position of the Argentine was different. As a neutral, it had the right to refuse to receive in its waters, or on its coasts, any of the forces engaged in the struggle. It is not necessary to be a specialist in international law to know that neutrality is equivalent to abstention and impartiality. In accordance with this theory, the Argentine Government declined the honour of the proffered visit. But the visitor insisted, and after a few days of vacillation and hushed consultations, the capitulation took place. The seriousness of the act does not consist in the attitude taken up, but in changing this attitude under pressure. I am not ignorant of the reasons of a local nature which may have intervened. On the battle-ground of diplomacy we may say that Admiral Caperton had taken Montevideo by using Rio de Janeiro as a base and next took Buenos Aires by using Montevideo as a base. This influence placed us in the painful position of emphasising the futility of our resistance by a gesture of obsequiousness. It was the moment at which the maximum of pressure was being brought to bear, in order to force us to take sides. The Argentine Chancellor was on the point of yielding, and in his turn abandoning neutrality, which, by the mere force of equilibrium, would have meant handing over Mexico to foreign influences. It was on this occasion that I sent a telegram from Chile to the Argentine Chancellor, which remained unanswered.[37]

For we have to take into account that the difficulties of Latin America only began at the moment when the United States entered the war. The Allies, in the original sense of this term, never brought pressure to bear upon us. They carried on their propaganda, they published their arguments abroad, they sought commercial advantages, they tried to win adherents; but all this in accordance with the most rigid respect for regional autonomy. The best proof of this is that the problem of our intervention in the war never cropped up at this stage. It was only forced on us later, when North America intervened in the conflict.

What the United States counted upon was simply a policy of aggravating conditions until a favourable field had been prepared for intervention, graduated according to their requirements, keeping in view their original aim of confirming their hegemony over Latin America, and the wider end of counteracting the world influence of Europe, or substituting their own for it. On entering the war, they naturally tried to draw after them the greatest possible number of

[37] "An Argentine citizen who has never aspired to public office, who has never followed the path leading to honours, but only that of duty, takes it upon himself respectfully to call the attention of this Government to the necessity of calmly weighing the acts which may carry us away from the neutrality and peace which are favourable to our future development. Recent events, sad and blameworthy as they may be—and I am the first to condemn them—cannot make us wish Latin America to forget old grievances in new enthusiasms, and to fall to-morrow under the influence of England, whose procedure in the case of the Falklands we deplore, and of the United States, which revealed their programme at Panama. It is from the continental point of view, apart from the impressions of the moment, and with the desire that we may maintain a higher creed of patriotism within a policy of abstention, that I take it upon myself to formulate this petition, braving immediate unpopularity, and assuming responsibility before the future. Events have a value proportionate to their after-effects, and we have to measure what would accrue from a rupture in view of the future of Latin America."

satellite nations, and it was thus that in the course of a few hours Panama, Cuba, and other republics hastened to imitate their action, with no more urgent motive than their dependence upon other spheres of influence. But from this moment an incessant stream of suggestion was directed upon the remaining countries. By the aid of the cable, attempts were made to influence the decision of some of them by inaccurate and premature statements as to the decision of others, in an ever-renewed circle of cunning wiles. It is for this reason that we may say that the neutrality of the few republics which stood firm was in no way a sign of indifference to France. France never reproached us with that. It only began to be alleged when others began to make use of the prestige of France. And the great Latin republic, beneath the ægis of whose generous hospitality we are writing this book, understood our attitude perfectly.

How could Spanish Americans be on the side of the United States, in a war which was bound to give the United States an exclusive influence over all our republics, and the hegemony of the world?

About this time there arrived at Buenos Aires the Cabrera-Montes Mission. General Carranza, whose person and nation were hemmed in on all sides, was sending his emissaries to the far South to attempt at least to communicate with the other republics. For fear of making this chapter too long, I do not wish to speak of the difficulties which had to be surmounted by Doctor Cabrera and General Montes, who were molested and searched during their voyage to Buenos Aires; nor do I intend to refer to the sharp protest of Señor Fabela, the Mexican Minister at Buenos Aires, whose diplomatic valises were stolen on his arrival in Cuba. Nothing has been told us in Latin America about the object of this mission, nor about the projected wireless communication between Mexico and Buenos Aires, nor about the possible foundation of a direct steamship line between Progreso and Bahía Blanca, the existence of which would be ensured by the transport of sisal from the north to the south, and of wheat from the south to the north. Perhaps there was a moment at which the dream of a direct interchange of these products might have been carried into effect, which at present pass through foreign ports and foreign hands; and this precedent will be utilised in the future.

When the confusion is past, and true views re-emerge, it will seem astonishing that in order to combat an idea they should have tried to crush a man. I never thought that the fact of working in my country's cause could have brought me such odium. In the desire to justify their hostile attacks, they went so far as to ascribe ignoble actions to me. And the evil of calumny does not lie in the calumny itself, but in the docility with which it is repeated. There are insinuations which only soil him who stoops to take them up. I waited for someone to step forth from among the masses and say: "A man who has devoted his whole life to the defence of a doctrine cannot be vile. A man who has sacrificed all he possesses to truth, cannot be venal." But no voice was raised in my favour. I found myself alone, poor, discredited, defeated in my ideal, since I had been deprived of the prestige which would have enabled me to defend it. If it had not been for the conviction which sustained me, I should have given up the struggle. But there are circumstances in which the supreme form of courage lies in waiting. And I was confident,—I am still confident,—that in the end these errors will be understood. As a man and as a Latin American, there is no stain upon me but that of having persisted in my ideal. And if I say so, it is not in the hope that my country will make reparation for its injustice, but that it may understand it, and place me in such a position that I may be useful in the evolution of its destinies.

As soon as the war had come to an end, in the unsatisfactory way which has since given rise to so many difficulties, I went to the Ministry to ask for a passport to Europe, mentioning the invitation which I had just received from the Centro de Cultura Hispanoamericana, of Madrid.

Owing to the resignation of a colleague, the Minister of Foreign Affairs had temporarily assumed the functions of Minister of Public Instruction. While I was waiting in the Secretariate, a delegation of students arrived from the province of Córdoba. They were in conflict with the university authorities; they had declared a strike, and were in search of a mediator.

"Will you not allow us to propose your name?" they said to me, with the healthy enthusiasm of youth.

The Minister's Secretary looked at me, and we both smiled. Perhaps the delegates interpreted this attitude as one of contempt. But be it known to them now, if these lines reach their eyes, that my skepticism arose from the contrast between their assumption and the reality. I was leaving the country precisely because it was so obvious that I could hope to do nothing within it; and there was an involuntary irony in their proposition which emphasised the situation.

What had the war meant to us in the last analysis? We had not sold our produce at a higher price, we had not redeemed our debts, we had not vindicated our national position. Most of the republics which had taken sides in the conflict confined their war-like operations to seizing two or three boats at anchor in their harbours; and this questionable benefit was outweighed by so many obligations that it can hardly be taken into consideration. As for the Porto Ricans and the Nicaraguans who fell beneath the folds of the North American flag, they will never have any monument, nor will they be mentioned on that which will perpetuate the glories of the northern republic. They shed their blood in defence of general ideas, when they had not given a drop of it for the reconquest of their territories. Suggestion, which had absorbed the strength of India, the existence of Africa, the life-blood of all the subject peoples who sacrificed themselves, carried them away like a torrent. With the high aim of defending France? With the great aim of saving the future of Europe? If it had been so, their death would not have been in vain. The result would have been noble and favourable to our republics. But the only effective conqueror was to be the rival whose power was to be nourished with all the blood and gold which were consumed in the conflagration of the Marne and of Verdun. They only helped to shift the centre of world politics. And in face of a Europe dislocated by implacable conflicts, amid the ruin of the cataclysm whose consequences we were unable to foresee, all that can be done to-day, from our point of view, is to send up our prayers and lamentations, which are only met by silence and confusion.

CHAPTER X

IN THE PRESENCE OF ANGLO-SAXON VICTORY

Evolution ...of Hispano-Americanism—The European Situation—World Primacy of the United States—Break-down of Pan-Americanism—Towards the Future.

THOSE peoples which are destined to survive, group themselves together on a basis of racial kinship around the golden thread of an ideal of civilisation. Our America, Spanish in its origin, is essentially Latin in its tendencies and inspirations. If it does not take a firm stand on its antecedents and its memories, whence is it to draw the necessary strength to preserve its personality, in spite of its disintegration and cosmopolitan character? A people which in developing is false to its race, is a lost people. In accordance with this principle, all the fibres of our being should draw us towards Spain, France, and Italy, who uphold the cupola of an age-old civilisation. The richer the stream of fertilising idealism that we draw from our origins, the stronger will be our national personality and our roots in the soil.

By leaving Buenos Aires, I thought I should be able to carry on the work I had undertaken with greater success. The Centres founded in various countries of Latin America were gradually melting away. What was left of that wonderful impulse which had roused the young men to enthusiasm? Some withdrew, discouraged by injustices, others lost their way during the conflagration, others were shipwrecked in the strife of parties. There was no lack of those impatient spirits who look for any pretext for getting rid of their illusions, and shed their convictions during the ups and downs of their career, in order to succeed more quickly. To this was added a literary controversy, for the same instinct of rivalry which caused our political anarchy makes itself felt in intellectual life. But over and above these minor considerations, which only apply to a limited

271

number of men, among a healthy community full of generous life, we must look for the causes which made my effort miscarry in that exasperated confusion which was born of the war. Among these frantic avalanches an ideal could be no more than a fragile scrap of paper disappearing in the turmoil. Convinced that the ship which I was steering was a mere phantom, it became my dream to start another line of action from Europe, by founding a publication of a continental character, which should gather up the scattered threads and serve as a rallying-point for our hopes. Need I say that these illusions, too, vanished, and that Mæcenas who could make this new campaign possible has not yet appeared? For he who had begun the struggle fifteen years before, relying upon his economic independence, left Buenos Aires with no other means of subsistence than his contributions to the papers.

I arrived in Spain in 1919. It will be difficult for some to reconcile my admiration for the mother country with the criticisms which I have made on more than one occasion upon some of her characteristics. They are all due to a desire to see her great. The "fine pages" of Anglo-Saxon history have always resulted in profit; the "fine pages" of ours have brought us nothing but sacrifices. And it is my anxiety for a change of heart that shall add to her recognised excellences a practical consciousness, which has sometimes lent my pen an involuntary harshness.

The old simile of rocks exposed to the fury of the elements may be applied to those peoples who develop a preponderant action in history. They are sometimes weighed down by their faults, and have to resign themselves to being responsible even for those crimes which they endeavour to avoid. By making herself mistress of a world and an age, Spain provoked the humanitarian denunciations of her rivals. And history cannot be founded upon a diatribe. In so far as this opinion is fully justified, her administrative delays and the inconsistency of her policy of colonisation are to be blamed. But this state of affairs is subsequent to the conquest. The mistress of the New World fell, as a consequence of her arrogant self-sufficiency, and of her conviction that the effort which she had achieved had won for her a lasting domination. She forgot that, whether we are dealing with people or aeroplanes, when the propeller pauses and the motor stops, the descent begins, in the form of a gentle glide or of a catastrophe, according to the skill of the pilot. The traditionalism which was reflected in the treatment of the colonies was nothing but confusion translated into immobility. This is what distinguishes it from the traditionalism of England. The cult of the past has a different character in the two peoples. What has preserved England are her forms; what is eternal in Spain are her inspirations. The best proof of this is that the causes owing to which she lost her colonies still persist essentially, and produce their effect in the regions subject to the present aggregate of nations. Centralisation appeals to principles, which are used for their own purposes by particular interest [1] and sometimes by foreign influences, thus carrying on throughout the ages those guiding principles which had already proved a failure.

With this is combined a new mistake, which belongs not only to Spain, but also to our Latin America. I refer to the tendency to shape international policy out of the fragments of internal policy, allowing the controversies between citizens to exert an influence in our relations with other peoples. And so it has happened that these tendencies have sometimes controlled the attitude of parties towards the national interests, much to the detriment of common interests and of the prestige of the flag; for internal politics are petty in themselves, and become even more paltry when they pass the frontier in the form of a collective attitude.

From the material point of view Spain had undoubtedly taken an enormous step forward during the war. Never had the *peseta* stood so high. Her ports seemed to dominate the trade routes. Whole new quarters had sprung up in the cities, transformed by a growing prosperity. Great modern hotels were put up. And all things spoke of strength, vitality, and overflowing life. Notwithstanding, when one probed matters to the core, it was not difficult to satisfy oneself that Spain had only obtained temporary and fleeting advantages from the unique situation in which she had been placed

---

[1] "A ton of coal taken on board at Barcelona for Palma, Majorca, and carried in a boat with a state subsidy (ten hours' crossing) pays a charge of 30 *pesetas*. The same ton of coal taken on board in England in non-subsidised boats (twenty days on the sea) pays a charge of 22 *pesetas*." Report of the Municipality of Palma to the Minister of Commerce, January 24, 1921.

by the force of events, and that these would vanish as soon as the world resumed its normal activity.

Like our southern republics, she is devoid of that practical sense which can get the last ounce out of opportunities; and so she had not managed to retain, even in part, what chance had offered her. What the tide had brought, the tide was to sweep away, in accordance with a fatality which has nothing to do with the will of man.

As regards politics, I found ancient Spain bled white by the ever-lasting Moroccan war. No estimate can ever be made of the treasure and energy which have been thrown away in Africa without any hope of profit. Such a persistent illusion, such proud endurance, are painful to see, yet arouse one's admiration. The upshot was that I found myself in the presence of a preoccupied nation, which could only spare an indulgent smile for such a remote subject as Hispano-Americanism. Even on the occasion of our Racial Festival, the exalted expression of our common aspiration, incredulous notes were written in the papers. I was surprised by a certain tendency in some to temporise with imperialism. They were few. But politicians were not wanting who were inclined to repeat what Mexico had done in Central America, or to repeat the action of the A B C in Mexico, without heeding the fact that, on the day when this policy finds a concrete expression, the last abdication of the Empire of Charles V will be consummated, recalling other catastrophes of history, the collapse of other influences and powers, which by depriving moral influence of its worth, confirmed for ever the ruin of military defeat.

I did not come to Madrid, like other Spanish Americans, to repeat a sham lecture intended to find an echo in the official paper of my home-country. I was led by a central idea. After travelling through the New World urging a union of men's wills, I desired to give an acount in Madrid of the result of my struggle against the sweeping away of the remains of the Spanish Empire. For this reason my disappointment was all the greater when, for the first time since the beginning of my activities, I found myself faced by an almost empty hall. The courtesy of the audience of three or four dozen, who attentively followed my exposition, the words of Don Miguel Moya, then President of the Press Association, one of the few representative Spaniards who were present, and the froth which was lavished by the Press upon the event, though they were most valuable manifestations, did not succeed in making up for this impression. Quite apart from petty vanity, I was surprised at such indifference before this most transcendental of problems.

I afterwards learnt that the progressive parties, who had heard an incorrect version of my dispute with the Socialists of the Argentine, intended to punish a disagreement which, in their eyes, amounted to a defection. Intellectual circles and the young men—who during the war had embraced the allied cause, led away by all that ennobles and uplifts the mind, even if it cannot always be safely applied to the dispute for the leadership of the world—were ready, on their part, to see in the new arrival a dissident element. Thus a political question, and the preferences of a spectator of world controversies, relegated to the background the essential interest of watching over a historical tendency which is at the root of our peoples. To this was united the suspicious abstention of certain conservative elements, who continued to judge the traveller as a pugnacious controversialist,[2] in spite of his respect for all kinds of principles, and the legends put about by the old propaganda which had attacked me. If we add to this the well-deserved discredit attaching to a certain empirical kind of Hispano-Americanism, which made a noise without any further aim than to cause a momentary thrill, this reserve on the part of public opinion is comprehensible.

There are venerable names among the Hispano-Americanists of Spain, and I am the first to respect them. But there reigns in certain spheres an over-conciliatory spirit which impels some to pass over realities and continue to be ignorant of the existence of imperialism. There is no lack of orators who, in dealing with this theme, forget that there are foreign soldiers in Cuba, Panama, Santo Domingo, and Nicaragua; and, what is more serious, they are ignorant that this blindness is favourable to the invader. Their ideal reaches no further than the applause of an audience, the eulogies of the newspapers, and the approving smile of the King. And one is terrified by the insignificance to which brotherhood between a hundred million men is reduced, when everything is subordinate to an

2 *Razón y Fé*, of Madrid, June, 1921.

interest in music. This phenomenon has its equivalent in the New World. Many exist, even in our cities, who after these landings of troops, these invasions, and this unremitting pressure, ask in a surprised tone: "Do you really think that imperialism may be a danger to us?"

Speech is the motive force of all effective action, the soul which animates and vivifies all human movements. But among peoples of facile oratory and sumptuous imagination sounding metaphors have been so much abused, that anything which appears inclined to renew vain speculations is looked upon with mistrust. Of course my propaganda was directed towards quite different aims. Side by side with that Hispano-Americanism which recalls the "floral games," or rather, apart from it, there exists a political tendency which can be really and beneficially applied, a diplomatic formula of world-wide importance, which will be to-morrow the very antithesis, as we may say, of that antiquated melody which has lulled us to sleep. Every idea has its positive value and its militant value, thought and muscle. To separate these component parts is to kill it. And the forgetfulness of those who have not taken into account the activity which must be displayed in view of the ambitions of other peoples, has always seemed to me particularly dangerous. There can be no effective Hispano-Americanism apart from an instinct of legitimate defence, a protest against all that is harmful to kindred bodies, and a conception of the problem as a whole.

Few things have been written about with such persistent acrimony as the task of "drawing close our bonds." If half the cleverness and ink which have been lavished on ridiculing this tendency had been devoted to placing it in a position to develop advantageously, the situation of our family of nations would be different. There are some who consider it a sign of mental superiority to talk against what is habitually expressed as a commonplace, without realising that its opposite, by lapse of time, comes to be an equally lamentable commonplace.

The important thing is not to prove that things have been badly done, but to do them well, without seeking in the errors of yesterday an excuse for present inaction. It is necessary to state the problem in its true terms. Spanish-Americanism must not look to the past, but to the future. It must be militant, or it will disappear.

The cordial hospitality [3] and innumerable courtesies which were offered me at the beginning of my stay did not prevent me from noticing a certain reserve, which we shall try to explain. When I made speeches at La Rabida, at the Academy of Cádiz, before the statue of Columbus, or at the Ayuntamiento in the presence of the King,[4] I met with courteous approval and sympathy. But by putting together my impression of these moments and the observations which I was able to make during the speeches of other orators, I realised that, even though the ill feeling arising from the separatist movement has faded away, there persists a certain uneasiness, the fruit, in the first place, of the parting of the ways, and in the second place, and on both sides, of the same reserved and stubborn pride.

Though the Spaniard fraternises on the whole with Spanish Americans, in whom he merely sees his brothers by race, in certain circles we come upon a more hesitating attitude; for in reality it was not the nation which was dispossessed by the revolution of 1810, but an oligarchy, and it is in its descendants and successors that this unavowed opposition is most clearly to be seen. The Latin American, on his side, has, perhaps unintentionally, accentuated the division by uttering criticisms which have not always been just, by ascribing to himself a questionable superiority and cultivating an irony as unoriginal as it is lacking in political sense. For this reason it is as well to ask ourselves, in the atmosphere free from reticence in which this book is written, whether there really exists any intimate and complete fraternity between Spain and the republics to which she gave birth, either in facts or in states of mind. The question may seem harsh, but it is better to formulate it, allowing room for all and sundry to answer it according to their consciences, than to prolong a silence which encourages every sort of confusion.

My proved devotion removes me from all suspicion. Few Spanish Americans love Spain as I do. But I must declare in all sincerity that in my opinion there is not that intimate response to each other's every movement which is indispensable if we are to make an

---

[3] "The illustrious Argentine writer is once more among us. We do not say he is our guest, for his love for Spain makes him an adopted son of our country." *A B C* of Madrid, April 12, 1919.

[4] Some of these speeches are to be found in *Mi campaña hispano-americana*, Cervantes Publishing House, Barcelona.

effective future. We do not refer to Utopian enterprises, which can only be born of a delirium of words in assemblies of ideologues. Nor is it possible to imagine a united action of Spain and the overseas countries, even on the diplomatic plane. The peoples of Latin America have their own sphere, while Spain moves in the orbit of European interests. But while respecting these courses of action which are imposed by circumstances, there is a certain region within which a higher union of ultimate aims would be possible. Without appealing to the past, but to the realities of the moment, by interpreting our identity of language rather as a facility offered for mutual understanding than as a traditional bond, by advancing the practical argument of our common weakness, rather than any sentimental reasons as a motive for a *rapprochement*, we can lay the foundations of a serious and fruitful activity. None the less, these experimental principles themselves require the moral basis of a free and effective fraternity. And it is this sentiment which does not, perhaps, yet exist with due intensity between our peoples.

Sometimes because the habit of appealing to the past prevails over the instinct of foreseeing the future; at other times because thin-skinned sensitiveness is more powerful than pride, there is no clear impulse towards defining the situation by the test of reality. Spain, as the mother country, recalls her disillusionment. Latin America remembers her colonial subjection. Each continues to accuse the other in silence, in the secret depths of its consciousness. And the chief obstacle is their persistence in turning their eyes towards yesterday, when all windows are opened on to-morrow.

Perhaps the new generations have not yet really faced the difficulty. They ought to recall history in order to seek for its lessons, one and all correcting their past inexperience. We have worshipped phantasms long enough. And there are questions which we can unite in asking. Whither did the gold of Latin America find its way? Where is the treasure of the famous galleys? It is enough to look around us in order to understand that the riches of a continent did no more than pass through Spain on their way to those countries who knew how to gain control of them without an effort, and that the blood drawn from the new land, like the sacrifices of the *Conquistadores*, ended by benefiting other races.

Sentimentality, pride, dynastic preoccupations, petty ambitions, rendered the effort abortive, and caused a certain lack of interest in the affairs of Spain to arise among the new nations, because she had so disastrously squandered the future. Anglo-Saxon influence, represented by England or the United States, according to the region concerned, threw into relief those contrasts which open up a horizon to the ancient colonies, but which entail a grave risk of denationalisation. The legitimate desire for prosperity impelled men to seek new inspirations from these flourishing sources. But the nourishment which strengthens and uplifts them dilutes their own personality. It is evident that their increasing greatness is derived from the modernising of their sources of energy. But lasting strength can only come from life-giving roots. And all would be reconciled if in these new ways, this intense activity, this mental renovation, some of us did not see an obstacle to the glorification of our antecedents, if we could raise ourselves to a conception grasping ultimate aims truly in accord with history.

During my stay in Spain the drama of Latin America continued to develop itself. The fall of General Carranza took place, swept away by one of those annihilating storms which are borne on the winds from the north. The delegates of the Republic of Santo Domingo, Señores Henríquez y Carbajal and Henríquez Urena, who undertook a journey to the republics of the South in order to solicit moral support in favour of their country, oppressed by foreign occupation, were coldly received and returned disappointed. An attempt at a partial federation, favoured by the public opinion of Central America, came to nothing in the hands of those whose principal aim was to raise their own position or make terms for themselves. It is superfluous to say that the telegram which I sent to the Minister of Foreign Affairs of Salvador [5] remained unanswered. On the other hand, *La Prensa*, of Buenos Aires, on June 1, 1920, published a long telegram from New York, in which, *à propos* of the tour of a Porto Rican senator, it said that his lectures "would counteract the harm done by Manuel Ugarte, one of the speakers most bitterly opposed to the United States, who accepted pay from

[5] "Madrid, June 6, 1920. Minister of Foreign Affairs, San Salvador. I place myself disinterestedly at the disposal of this Government for the grandiose plan of a Central American union. Enthusiastic congratulations on the courageous, patriotic attitude of Salvador." *Manuel Ugarte.*

a German bank which was making every sort of effort to establish relations with South America before the war." The same paper, *La Prensa*, gave me complete satisfaction a few days later,[6] but something remained of the slander, as we have already said. And this is the end which has been persistently pursued. The letter which I wrote on this account[7] was not published by any paper and the malicious version did its work.

[6] "The Argentine writer so abominably treated is known both within and without our country for the independence of his judgment and his honourable point of view. In his political propaganda throughout the continent, he might be opposed to the policy of the United States, which he considered pernicious and aggressive. But he was never suspected of serving the cause of any European nation or commercial imperialism for money. We do not make this comment, it will be understood, for our own country, where Ugarte is known, and needs no more light thrown upon his life than what comes from its honourable conduct and his literary talent. We do it for the writer of the article, to whom we thus give an opportunity for correcting himself with a clear conscience, and for the public of other parts, which might accept the same version. We owe this action and these words to the absent writer, who is our friend, and we have no hesitation in adopting the one and pronouncing the other."

La Prensa, of Buenos Aires, June 5, 1920.

[7] After summing up the dispute, I said: "Who can find in this persevering activity, in this persistent unity of a life, any argument against my honour or sincerity? If I were the servant of Germany, I should now be with the United States, the only country which now defends the conquered empire. If I had been a commercially-minded person I should have made a handsome fortune simply by abstaining from giving lectures, since so many governments tried every means to stop them. If I had been led astray by *arrivisme*, I should have taken precisely the opposite course to the one which I have followed; for to rise up against the northern colossus in Latin America has at all times been synonymous with poverty, ostracism, and sometimes dishonour and death. Examples abound, from Bolívar and San' Martín* to the last presidents who were overthrown. It is nothing but an attempt to disparage the moral authority of a man which has succeeded in giving rise to this absurd slander. My efforts have never aimed at obtaining a position, but at defending truths, even when I knew that they would close the way to the most legitimate ambitions. I may not manage to be anybody in my own country, I shall perhaps never be anything on the Continent. But when our republics, fettered by imperialism from the political. diplomatic, or economic point of view, find themselves obliged, in a few decades' time, to bow in some form or another to a continental Platt Amendment, somebody will recall the fact that there was a writer who, amid mockery, silence, and insults, preached from the beginning a joint resistance

In continuing my journey from Spain to France and in leaving this friendly atmosphere which enjoys my most disinterested attachment—disinterested because I have never received from it any honours, decorations or support of any kind—I was thinking of the necessity of widening my horizons.

Without a vast coalition of hopes and interests, Latin-Americanism will always keep marking time round a shadow. Rising above those exclusive tendencies and limitations which have brought us to our present situation, it is necessary for us to create an accumulation of forces capable of neutralising the invading or dissolving winds of international policy.

Before the varying prospects of events nothing is more futile than to take one's stand upon an assertion. What was easy in 1850 was impossible in 1900; and what appeared capable of realisation on the threshold of the century is seen to be absurd since the war. One has to live at the pace of one's age. The weakness of Spain and of Spanish America—may I be allowed to join them in this statement of opinion—has always been to try and force realities within the limits of axioms, instead of deducing axioms from realities. There is no doubt that, rising above an empirical policy, the practical conception is beginning to take shape of a constructive and experimental action, which accepts, respects, and admires all that was done by our predecessors, but which, in accordance with the spirit of the age, desires above all to obtain results. Latin-Americanism will gain health if it opens its windows, and at the same time its eyes, to the realities of the age.

We must not allow words to obscure our ideas. When we are told of the spread of the Spanish language among the Anglo-Saxon peoples, far from interpreting this fact as a victory or a tribute, we meditate upon the contradiction which leads them to propagate our

of the South, the only policy which can save us. And then will come to light the intrigues, the conspiracies, the painful trials which have been borne by this isolated individual on his way from city to city, in the name not only of a racial inspiration, but also of his own land; for what I have caused to be applauded from north to south—it is necessary that my country should know it once for all—has been at once a continental ideal and the Argentine flag."

* What did the United States have to do with the exile or downfall of San Martín and Bolívar?

language in Pennsylvania, and to combat it in Porto Rico and the Philippines. Setting aside isolated symptoms, we have to embrace the motives, programme, and logic of great movements. It is obvious that the real victors in the war have been the United States, whose economic power and political influence have to-day no possible rival. As the inevitable expansionist policy of this country is bound to be carried out chiefly to the detriment of the remains of the Spanish empire, the magnitude of the problem is clearly to be seen, and therefore the inconsistency of any exalted plans of spiritual reconquest. Fifty years ago it was perhaps possible to balance its imperialist force by the moral influence of Spain. Fifteen years ago this result could only be achieved by mobilising the whole Latin world. But to reach this end to-day the united influence of Europe would hardly be sufficient. So that we must not see in a broadening of the process any disparagement of the tendency, but on the contrary, an effort to draw it out of its debilitated state and give it at last a motive force.

In order to understand the possible evolution of our Latin America, we must take into consideration the general state of the world since its radical upheaval. Let us consider above all the state of France but let us consider it from our point of view, which approaches as closely as possible to that of France, but of course keeps in the foreground its care for the interests of the Latin-American group of nations. In defending its territory, France, in accordance with her rôle throughout the ages, was defending lofty general principles applicable to the whole human race. But this great nation, the victim of diplomatic duplicity, has in the final reckoning seen her generous instincts exploited by more utilitarian peoples, who carry their cleverness so far as to make her to-day, in the midst of her arduous difficulties, appear to be the element which disturbs the peace. One feels a deadly disillusionment when one discovers what appetites were hidden behind the fine words which led so many millions of men to their death. And there is a cry of mingled irritation and discouragement, a shattering of idols and principles, an indignant and painful consciousness of fraud.

The mere rate of the exchanges marks the proportions in which the benefits of victory have been shared. And there can be no greater contradiction than to accuse of greed the very nation which has gained nothing.

It was part of the Anglo-Saxon programme to eliminate Germany, whose commercial competition was ruinous. But it is superfluous to say that the idea of encouraging French prosperity was never part of it. On the contrary, once victory was attained, its greatest interest lay in making this prosperity impossible. And so to-day we see the victorious nation, with its hopes frustrated, forced by the exigencies of the game of European politics to foment a lasting hostility with her neighbour, which must necessarily hamper her freedom of action and limit her intervention in world controversies.

To these conclusions of a general order must be added those which arise from our own surroundings. One of the most significant of the post-war phenomena is the haste with which some of the Franco-phils of yesterday have pronounced against their former friendships. They cannot admit that what they were pursuing, beyond France, was the shadow of England or the United States. But the eternal insinuation of the cable prepares new passions, just as yesterday it imposed the old ones, in accordance with certain interests, which do not always agree with ours. Diplomacy, like warfare, has its camouflage, which serves to hide movements, and it is through all these cunning devices that we have to see a general view of the tormented age in which it is our lot to live.

It is the real situation, in its political complication and economic confusion, that it is urgent to consider carefully if we wish to gain an idea of what we may expect or aim at in the new state of affairs. The war has exhausted the financial potentiality of some nations. Behind the dictatorial appearance of France, the Cæsarism of Italy, and the nervous activity of many peoples, there is a vital depression arising from the formidable loss of gold and blood caused by the crisis. This uneasiness is completed by the anxiety arising out of disagreements which grow constantly more embittered, the covert rivalry, the constant struggle, which are going on within a peace which is favourable to nobody outside the Anglo-Saxon group. The prevailing anarchy impels Russia to devote all her energies to diffusing the principles of her revolution; impels Germany to concentrate her energies on avoiding annihilation; Italy to develop the strength of her muscles and the work of internal consolidation; France to struggle against the greatest difficulties in order to balance her budget. Faced with the possibilities of enormous zones of production and consumption, which amount to eighty million men in Latin America, fifty million in Africa, eight hundred million in Asia, there only appear two forces of world activity which continue to diffuse their full influence: Great Britain in Europe and the United States in America. But does this mean that in the universal Anglo-Saxon victory nothing is left to us Latin Americans but the option of choosing between the two branches which are disputing the predominance?

It is impossible not to see that during the last few years there has been a remarkable change in the distribution of strength, and that we are faced with a new world-map of interests. Our republics cannot remain indifferent to the new political geography. The idea of a Latin-American system, drawing its support from Europe in order to maintain the balance between two civilisations in the New World, seems hard to carry out when we measure the violence of the conflicts, and urgent immediate needs which absorb the activity of all the great powers, and the final result of the conflagration.

Notwithstanding, all these nations feel the need for seeking to balance their commercial budget by finding markets beyond the seas. And it is on this urgent common need that we may base our hopes for the future. It is not Spain that will be able to exercise a decisive influence; it is not France, absorbed in her anxieties of the moment, that will succeed in developing that activity which we all desire. But it is from a combined group of nations, without exceptions, that we may hope for that influence which shall balance or regulate events in the New World, provided that we succeed in shaking off those errors which weaken us.

Commercial concessions are for certain peoples of Latin America what revolutions are for others. It is not the official agent who stoops to whisper in the ambitious ear of the *caudillo:* "I have rifles and money; you too may be a president"; but the man of business who is all the while preparing to control the vital energies of the country, though he so arranges things that even those whose interests he threatens exclaim: "We have never sold our steers for such a good price!" Brazilian coffee and Argentine stock-breeding may suffer the same fate as Cuban sugar. And in mentioning these products, we are referring to them all in general. The evil arises from the fact that the real owners of this wealth do not think of making it productive, and so increasing the common vitality by their efforts; but let it pass into other hands, making a much lower profit, but one sufficient to exempt them from trouble or work. How many railroad concessions, how many businesses of every sort have been acquired with the sole aim of reselling them! And as it is always foreign companies who acquire them, it is our own property, our own country, our very flag which we are handing over to others. Before taking up arms in civil conflicts or sterile warfare, we ought to learn to manufacture them in times of peace. And it is not only in this sphere that we have got to begin at the beginning, but in every activity and the whole upkeep of our collective life. From the economic point of view, every one of our republics is a badly-organised business, till such time as we are ready to show ourselves capable of hard work and foresight. Our representatives in Europe have made efforts to introduce frozen meat which is prepared, trans-ported, and sold by English or North American companies, forget-ting that they leave all the profits in London or New York, and that nobody has the remotest idea from which republic comes "X & Company's Cold-Storage Produce, South America."

In international politics there is not one truth, but as many truths as there are opposing international interests. And it would be child-ish to blame imperialism for profiting by the opportunities which offer themselves. On the contrary, it may be said that the United States have always been supremely idealistic. Not in the sense of ideal systems which have nothing to do with the government of peoples. But from the point of view of a higher and broader conception, a conception which, far above those very sacrifices they impose upon others, they pursue in view of the future greatness of their community. As a Spanish American, I revolt against this policy, I fling all I possess into the sea, and I make my life one un-quenchable protest against the possible annihilation of our national-ities. But I should be deceiving my own fellow-countrymen and running counter to the very end which I pursue if, in order to flatter the prevailing way of thinking and excuse our faults, I were to be surprised at manœuvres which are to be found at every turn in the history of the world. All nations have faults. But those of the Anglo-Saxons are against others; whereas ours are against ourselves. And it is more sensible to try to correct the latter than the former. It is naïve to cry out against injustice, for we have already seen that every group extends its ambitions as far as its arms can reach. It would be madness to desire the ruin of the United States, since at the stage which we have reached, this ruin would be the signal of our own downfall. Matters are not made better by lamentations or hatred. We have to face the truth in its twofold aspect.

First, in that aspect which leads us to grasp the true volume of this great entity, and obtain a clear idea of what it stands for in the world. Since the war it possesses the greatest fleet (the one which incites us at Pan-American Congresses to disarm),* handles the greatest known wealth, and exerts a preponderant influence over weaker nations. If we place them by its side, some republics of our Latin America virtually disappear. A single company, the United Fruit Co.—which has not the importance of the Standard Oil Co., nor of other similar monster companies—divides among its shareholders an annual dividend amounting to more than the united budgets of the five governments of Central America.[8] The most powerful empires of Europe and Asia, before making a political move, watch what way the wind is blowing at Washington; for even within their own exclusive sphere of influence, they are all dependent upon the movements of the White House. Thanks to its economic power and the prestige of its decisions, it is its word alone which prevails. As to the ultimate philosophy of things, it may be said that the chief result of the war has been the shifting of the political centre of the world. Cities are extending from east to west, and it looks as if universal empire is emigrating in the same direction. After the hegemonies of Asia came the pre-eminence of Greece and later the sway of Rome. To-day the Mediterranean, and even the English Channel, are balanced by new centres of attraction, and we are faced with another prodigious advance, which may leave Europe to-morrow in a less brilliant position. Even the parent people is threatened. The disintegration started by Canada and Australia

* The disarmament question came up at the Pan-American Congress which met at Santiago in March, 1923.
8 *New York Commercial*, February 24, 1923.

may even prejudice the British power, and perhaps we shall see—no new thing in the course of the ages—the former colony treating with the metropolis of yesterday on terms of superiority, by a natural substitution of new civilisations for those which, having reached their apogee, have not continued to accelerate their evolution.

The second aspect of this truth is that in which we ought to seek an idea of our exact position, the measure of our capacities, the right angle for estimating future possibilities. An ideal gives people an energy which is like an accent on a letter, and this is what Latin America requires, in order to emerge from that scattered condition in which she is wasting her best energies. The spread of public instruction in the Argentine [9] and in Uruguay, and democratic electoral laws are a point of departure for the renovation of our community of nations. The mobilisation of wealth, the exploitation of our natural resources, mark a vital reaction of transcendent importance. But the former must be placed at the service of a high aim and the latter managed by our own hands. The secret of our future development will lie in the utilisation of the advantages we have acquired.

We have faith in the youth of Latin America. We are confident that the younger generations will endeavour to create an effective new life, by hastening the purification and progress of each republic and preparing to unify their aims and their common course. There are many who are intent upon dragging down the future to the level of their disillusionment; but in spite of the painful struggle which we have passed in review, we by no means subscribe to those pessimistic views which lead to renunciation. Fortune lasts while we have the energy to keep adversity in check. The graver our difficulties, the greater the fortitude with which we must face them. Moral force ends in overcoming all material forces. But optimism is only powerful when it takes the form of a banner beneath which we may fight. And it is only by the aid of an intensive and sustained activity, which shall turn thought into action and will into muscular effort, that our young men will succeed in surmounting circumstances and taking command of events.

From our far south, triumphant and prosperous, might arise a

[9] In 1921 there were 9,648 primary schools in the Argentine, with 39,-352 teachers and 1,195,382 pupils.

formula which should be progressively applied to the whole continent.   Among the clearest lessons of the war one new axiom stands out in peculiar relief: the importance of economic factors in any offensive action, the efficacy in war-time of the peaceful activities of peoples, the warlike preparation which takes the form of an abundant production of articles of the first necessity.   The position of Europe has always been paradoxical.   Those countries which provide the world with everything imaginable, from fuel and iron to textiles and ideas, cannot produce in sufficient quantities from their own soil the elements required for feeding themselves.   The last struggle was a duel of resistance to hunger, and a combat of money and stratagems for procuring food stuffs.   This circumstance may be turned to an international use.   In an age when governments which grant loans stipulate how the money is to be employed, and where purchases are to be made; at a time when what was called international capital is disappearing, and wealth is used as a national weapon, carrying on an implacable war in times of peace, we, who possess something of more value than riches, must learn to utilise it in the form most profitable to our cause.   Just as others know the price of what they lack, so we must know the price of what we possess in superfluity, setting up a scale of equivalent values, and a sort of pact between the continents.   Europe is sick and tormented; but she constitutes a formidable mass, capable of counterbalancing for a long time, if only in part, the influences which decide our fate.   It is to her that the fervent longing of our southern democracies must go forth, gradually substituting for one-sided adherence, arising from inexperience, a formula of mutual benefits and guaranties, an attitude of reciprocity based on harmonious interest.   Our Latin America ought never to let herself be separated from Europe, either in the economic order or from the cultural point of view; for in Europe lies her only support in the conflicts which await her.

The breakdown of Pan-Americanism in its present form is so obvious that even its most faithful adherents are vacillating.   It was many years ago that the writer of this book denounced this political conception as a skilful move in the expansionist policy of the North, and a suicidal tendency of the simple-minded South. The danger which then seemed to be based on theoretical arguments is now supported by actual conditions.   The facts are there, pro-

claiming that it is no use preparing for a purely continental development, in a New World dominated by the pre-eminence of a nation.
Pan-Americanism and the Monroe Doctrine are two aspects of the
same policy, exclusively favourable to one of the contracting parties.
But the time has come when the signs are so clear, that even those who
used to taunt us with being visionaries have had a sudden revelation
of the truth. It is not the time to formulate reproaches. Mistakes should not be recalled in order to apportion blame, but in
order to learn their lesson, for beyond the misleading clamour of
names and activities, we have to look for lasting principles of action.
The Pan-American Congress in Chile, over which hung an atmosphere of mistrust, and at which violent scenes even took place,[10]
only succeeded in drawing attention to its incapacity for dealing with
problems such as the occupation of Santo Domingo, the situation
in Central America, or intervention in the internal affairs of Mexico. The countries of the South, instead of bringing to the assembly
a point of view applicable to all the republics, instead of constituting
themselves a solid centre of attraction for the kindred peoples, stood
aside before the sufferings of others, became involved in secondary
quarrels, and only prolonged their traditional confusion. The future

[10] "Santiago de Chile, May 4. At the last Plenary Session but one of the
Pan-American Conference, Morillo, of Santo Domingo, and Hudicurt, of
Haiti, handed to the delegates, the chairman of the Conference, the diplomatists, and correspondents of the foreign Press, copies of certain pamphlets
in which they protest against the occupation of their countries and beg the
Conference to pass a measure to prevent the violation of the sovereignty of
the small peoples of Latin America. The visible annoyance of the North
American delegation was remarked. The Press of this city has given no
information about this incident. The President of the Conference said that
the matter would be laid before a commission, though it is feared that
complete silence will be observed about it. The words which Manual
Morillo used in speaking to the delegates were vigorous, and in an atmosphere of general suspense he formulated the following accusation: 'In
the name of the republics of Haiti and Santo Domingo, we claim the restoration of our sovereignty, mutilated by the United States, and we beg for
justice.' At this moment the President of the Conference imposed silence
upon Morillo, and the Police tried to eject him from the hall, but did not
succeed, owing to the energy and sang-froid of the Domingan."
                         El Universal, of Mexico, May 5, 1923.*
   *It must be remembered that Mexico was not represented at the Congress,
that Mexicans looked upon the assembly in no friendly mood.

must react against all this. "If Cuba is not to conclude with other powers treaties by which our sovereignty is stifled, why did the United States impose upon us, as the minimum price of our liberation, the grievous interventionist clause?" says Don Luís Machado y Ortega in his book *La Enmienda Platt*,* summing up in the case of this local question an argument which applies to the position of many republics, to the Pan-American theory, to the Monroe Doctrine, and to the commercial pressure which warns us all of the constantly intensified influence of the exports, trusts, and loans of the North.

If we rise superior to our errors, the destiny of our Latin America is bound to be a great one. It is a new humanity that is arising in the Argentine and some of our lands. And there are few who can feel, as much as the writer, that patriotic pride which has made his pen tremble in certain passages of this book. Its appeal is all the more moving by reason of the distance which separates us from our native land. It is in absence that we best appreciate the sacred emotion of patriotism. And it is by speaking our whole thought that we best serve it. These reflections have been inspired by the anxious question, "What is to be the destiny of our republics?" But a word of warning must not be interpreted as a sign of discouragement, nor should any doubt be read into our desire that the will of the young men who have an influence upon the governments should be strengthened. The future belongs to those who know whither it is going. Those who are irresolute, bewildered, and capricious may obtain a fleeting victory, but not a triumph which grows stronger with time. And the future will take on the colour which is given to it by our foresight and patriotism. The fatherland will be a reflection of our love for her. Latin America will occupy that place in the world which the will of her sons is able to win for her.

Our diplomatists, pretending to have found the solution of a struggle which they did not dare to face, have given their consent to a policy of indefinite capitulations, which has no end or limits, because a series of successive abdications ends in a darkness in which renunciation can hardly be distinguished from servility. And the most astonishing thing is the trifling advantage which they have succeeded in obtaining by this attitude. Once they were prepared

* Habana, Imp. "El Siglo XX," 1922.

to treat with imperialism, it would have been better to face the
difficulty and lay down some definite limits to the exactions of one
side and the sacrifices of the other. Even after the disaster Germany has been able to preserve the roots of her national life and
her future. We have been conquered, without a war, by the mere
attraction of cultural and commercial forces; when we might have
obtained other conditions. For this reason we have got to fight
irresponsibility, inexperience, and subservience within our own gates.
Imperialism is born of others' cowardice. And it is urgently necessary for us to put an end to the fog in which they are driving us to
ship-wreck.

"Improvisation is everything in diplomacy," I once heard a politician say. There can be no greater absurdity. We have to
manœuvre among changing contingencies with our eyes fixed on a
distant and higher end. It is meet that we should frame a joint
Latin-American policy, to which local interests should be subordinated or adapted. It is urgently necessary to intertwine this policy
with the commercial tendencies of Europe which are striving for
development within our territories.

With regard to internal matters, every region must consult its
peculiar conditions and possibilities, in order to develop its personality on autonomous lines. The strength of peoples does not lie in
repeating movements dictated by outsiders, but in mobilising their
resources and discovering the centre of their future sphere of influence. England drew from her coal-mines her industrial prosperity and her dominion of the seas. It is no chance whim which
has made thousands of factories spring up in the United States
round Kansas City, Springfield, Charleston, or Pittsburg, but the
existence in these regions of the elements which are required to
support them. There is a logic of progress, which gives problems
a national character, and the development of our republics has to
be adapted to it. So it must be the aspiration of all those who desire
our true prosperity, to consider the possibilities offered by each
region and develop them by means of national enterprise.

If these principles are firmly based upon peace within and without our boundaries, and uplifted by a breath of enthusiastic optimism, they may bring about a triumphant progress. We are
looking on at an irruption of new forces into world politics, and

Latin America will perhaps to-morrow play an important *rôle*, if she keeps her eyes fixed on reality, and co-ordinates the resources offered by her size and vitality.

No people preserve for ever, throughout the ages, an inferior or superior position. The Greeks, Romans, and Spaniards of to-day by no means retain the influence and splendour to which they attained in other periods. There are many communities which have raised themselves from an inferior condition and become ruling powers. We have seen nations which had been conquered and reduced to subjection, come to the surface once more; just as we have seen once triumphant peoples fall into decay. When Cæsar subdued the Gauls, he was far from imagining that Napoleon would one day march his armies into Italy. It was a slave revolt which finished the Roman Empire. The instability of national and racial values allows us to regard our present situation as a stage admitting of change, whether by the influence of general circumstances, or in consequence of the efforts of the community to transform their negative forces into positive ones. The destiny of Latin America depends in the last resort on Latin Americans themselves.

And we must end with a question addressed particularly to the young: "Will the Latin-Americans be capable of this effort, supported by patriotism, the interests of Europe, and the Latin spirit?"

BIBLIOGRAPHY

Álvarez, Alejandro. *The Monroe Doctrine.* New York, Oxford University Press, 1924. (Views of twenty-four Latin Americans are presented in this volume.)

Becerra, Don Ricardo. *Cuestión palpitante.* Caracas, Tip. Moderna, 1898.

Berenguer, Fernando. *El Hispano-Americanismo.* Habana, "El Siglo XX," 1918.

Bermúdez, Alejandro. *Lucha de razas.* San José, Costa Rica, Tip. económica, 1912.

Bingham, Hiram. *The Monroe Doctrine, An Obsolete Shibboleth.* New Haven, Yale University Press, 1916.
"Should We Abandon The Monroe Doctrine?" in *Journal of Race Development,* IV (January, 1914), p. 344 ff.

Bonilla, Policarpo. *The Wilson Doctrine.* New York, n. p., 1914.

Caraballo y Sotolongo, F. *El imperialismo norteamericano.* Habana, "El Siglo XX," 1914.

Cárdenas y Echarte, Raúl de. *La política de los Estados Unidos en el continente americano.* Habana, Sociedad Editorial Cuba Contemporanea, 1921.

Carranza, José Sienra. *Cuestiones americanas.* Montevideo, Imp. "El Siglo Illustrado," 1907.

Cox, I. J. "The Colombian Treaty—Retrospect and Prospect," in *The Journal of International Relations,* XI (April, 1921), p. 549 ff.

Domenech, Roberto. *Méjico y el imperialismo norteamericano.* Buenos Aires, Tip. "Leones," 1914.

Fabela, Isidro. *Los Estados Unidos contra la libertad.* Barcelona, Talleres Gráficos "Lux," [1920.]

Ganderilla, J. C. *Contra el Yanqui.* Habana, Rambla, Banza y Companía, 1913.

294 THE DESTINY OF A CONTINENT

García, D. R. *Cuadros Yankees (escenas hipócritas)*. Caracas, "Imprenta Caraqueña," 1898.

García Calderón, Francisco. *La creación de un continente*. Paris, P. Ollendorff, 1913.

Latin America, Its Rise and Progress, London, Unwin, 1913. "The Monroe Doctrine and Latin America," in *The Atlantic Monthly*, March, 1916.

Gaxiola, José. *La Frontera de la raza*. Madrid, Tip. Artiste, 1917.

Goldberg, Isaac. *Studies in Spanish-American Literature*. New York, Brentano's, 1920. (Many of the literary men fear and distrust the United States.)

Gutiérrez, Alberto. *Notas e impresiones de los Estados Unidos*. Santiago, Imp. Cervantes, 1904.

Ingeneiros, José. *Por la unión latinoamericana*. Buenos Aires, L. J. Rossa y Companía, 1922.

Inman, Samuel Guy. "Imperialistic America," in *The Atlantic Monthly*, July, 1924. (See also the answer of Sumner Welles in *ibid.*, September, 1924.)

Leets, Juan. *The United States and Latin America. Dollar Diplomacy*. New Orleans, L. Graham and Company, Ltd., 1912.

Liga de la Defensa Nacional Centro-americana. *Labor Hondureña por la autonomía de Centro-America*. Honduras, Imp. "El Sol," 1914.

López, Jacinto. "Política norteamericana," "La Doctrina Monroe y el congreso de Panamá," "Colombia y Belgica," etc., in *La Reforma Social*, June, 1915 ff.

Madueño, Mariano José. *Problemas americanos*. Madrid, Mundo latino, 1906.

Manero, Antonio. *México y la solidaridad americana*. Madrid, Editorial-America, 1918.

Márquez Sterling, M. *El Panamericanismo*. Habana, "El Magazine de la Raza," 1924.

Martínez, Marcial. *Obras completas*. Santiago, "La Ilustración," 1919. 3 vols.

Merlos, Salvador R. *América latina ante el peligro*. San José, Costa Rica, Gerardo Matamoras, 1914.

Nieto Caballero, L. E. *El dolor de Colombia*. Bogotá, Tip. Moderna, 1922.

Pereyra, Carlos. *El Mito de Monroe*. Madrid, Editorial-America, 1914.

Pinochet, Tancredo. *The Gulf of Misunderstanding*. New York, Boni & Liveright, [1920.]

Quesada, Ernesto. "La doctrina de Monroe, su evolución histórico, in *Anales de la Facultad de Derecho y Ciencias Sociales*, XX (1920), p. 65 ff. Buenos Aires.

"La evolución del Panamericanismo," in *Revista de la Universidad de Buenos Aires*, XLI (1919), p. 289 ff.

Reyes, Rafael. *The Two Americas*. New York, F. A. Stokes, 1914. *Escritos varios*. Bogotá. Tip. Arconvar, 1920.

Rippy, J. Fred. "Literary Yankeephobia in Hispanic America," in *The Journal of International Relations*, XII (January and April, 1922), p. 350 ff., 524 ff.

"Pan-Hispanic Propaganda in Hispanic America," in *Political Science Quarterly*, XXXVII (September, 1922), p. 389 ff.

"Some Contemporary Mexican Reactions to Cleveland's Venezuelan Message," in *ibid.*, XXXIX (June, 1924), p. 280 ff.

Robledo, Alfonso. *Una lengua y una raza*, Bogotá, Arboleda y Valencia, 1916.

Rodó, José Enrique. *Ariel* (F. J. Stimson, tr.). Boston, Houghton, Mifflin, 1922.

Sáenz Peña, Roque. *Escritos y discursos*. Buenos Aires, Peuser, 1914–1915. 2 vols.

Silva, J. Francisco V. *Reparto de América española y Panhispanismo*. Madrid, F. Beltrán, 1918.

Soraci, J. *Concepto del Panamericanismo*. Buenos Aires, Agencia general de Librería y Publicaciones, 1917.

Torres Caicedo, J. M. *Unión latino-americana*. Paris, Rosa et Bouret, 1865.

Travesí, Gonzalo G. *La revolución de México y el imperialismo yanqui*. Barcelona, Casa Editorial Maucci, 1914.

Trelles, Carlos M. *Estudio de la Bibliografía cubana sobre la doctrina de Monroe*. Habana, "El Siglo XX," 1922.

Turcios R., Salvador. *Al margen del imperialismo yanqui*. San Salvador, Tip. La Unión, 1915.

Ugarte, Manuel. *Mi campaña hispano-americana*. Barcelona, Editorial Cervantes, 1922.

El porvenir de la America latina. Valencia, Sempere y Companía, 1910.

Vargas Vila, José María. *Ante los barbaros.* Barcelona, Casa Editorial Maucci, 1917.

THE END

A NOTE ON THE TYPE IN
WHICH THIS BOOK IS SET

This book is set (on the Linotype) in Elzevir No. 3, a French Old Style. For the modern revival of this excellent face we are indebted to Gustave Mayeur of Paris, who reproduced it in 1878, basing his designs, he says, on types used in a book which was printed by the Elzevirs at Leyden in 1634. The Elzevir family held a distinguished position as printers and publishers for more than a century, their best work appearing between about 1590 and 1680. Although the Elzevirs were not themselves type founders, they utilized the services of the best type designers of their time, notably Van Dijk, Garamond, and Sanlecque. They developed a type face which is open and readable but relatively narrow in body, permitting a large amount of copy to be set in limited space without impairing legibility.